# The Forest Book of the *Rāmāyaṇa* of Kampaṉ

*Translated, with Annotation, and Introduction, by*

George L. Hart

and

Hank Heifetz



UNIVERSITY OF CALIFORNIA PRESS
Berkeley • Los Angeles • London

The preparation of this volume was made possible by a grant from the Translations Program of the National Endowment for the Humanities, an independent Federal agency.



University of California Press
Berkeley and Los Angeles, California

University of California Press, Ltd.
London, England



**Library of Congress Cataloging-in-Publication Data**

Kampar, 9th cent.
The forest book of the Rāmāyaṇa of Kampan.

Translation of: Āraṇiya kāṇṭam.
1. Rāma (Hindu deity)—Poetry. I. Hart, George L. II. Heifetz, Hank. III. Title.
PL4758.9.K27R35213 1989 894'.81111 88-334
ISBN 0-520-06088-1 (alk. paper)

Printed in the United States of America

1 2 3 4 5 6 7 8 9

**Library of Congress Cataloging in Publication Data**

Hank Heifetz dedicates his work on this book
for Mira, kochana

George Hart dedicates his work on this book
to Rama Subramanian,
profound teacher and lover of Tamil

# Contents

# Preface

This translation of the third book of Kampaṉ's Tamil version of the *Rāmāyaṇa* is the result of a series of steps. First, George Hart prepared an accurate literal translation in prose, with different readings and difficult sections annotated, and with key portions of the commentaries translated. Hank Heifetz then composed these stanzas, basing himself on Hart's translation and on his own reading of the text. The results were then discussed, compared with the literal version and with the original, and emended when necessary for accuracy or aesthetic effect. George Hart is mostly responsible for the Glossary and Notes (with the exception primarily of some of the notes to Paṭalam 5), while the Introduction is a joint effort.

Our purpose is introduce Kampaṉ, who is perhaps India's greatest poet, to a non-Tamil audience. To this end, we have changed all of the names from Tamil to their Sanskrit equivalents—not many non-Tamils, after all, would equate Ilakkumaṇaṉ with Lakṣmaṇa. We have depended almost entirely on two editions—the critical edition published by Annamalai University (referred to as Crit.) and the Gōpālakiruṣṇamācāriyar edition (referred to as G.). The numbering follows the critical edition, the first number referring to the stanza's position in the current Paṭalam and the second to its position in the work as a whole.

We are grateful to the National Endowment for the Humanities, which funded this project, and M. G. Srinivasan, who went over parts of this manuscript and provided valuable comments.

# Introduction

The Tamil poet Kampan̲ lived during one of the great flowerings of culture, comparable to the Renaissance of Europe or the golden age of Greece or Rome. During his lifetime in the twelfth century A.D., the political power of South India under the Cholas reached a high point, as did the artistry of its temples, its sculpture, and, largely in the person of Kampan̲ himself, its literature. So influential was the work he wrote, so wide in its scope and perfect in its execution, that he came to be called the Universal Monarch of Poets. As Dante summarized medieval Christianity, so Kampan̲ summarized the extraordinarily rich medieval Hinduism that was flowering in South India. And like Dante—and probably more than any other Indian poet—Kampan̲'s work was characterized by a breadth of sensitivity and understanding that makes him a great intellectual thinker as well as a great poet.

His work is the Tamil *Rāmāyaṇa*—or, as Kampan̲ called it, the *Irāmāvatāram,* "The Descent of Rāma"—in something over twelve thousand difficult stanzas. For the main elements of his story, Kampan̲ followed the Sanskrit *Rāmāyaṇa* of Vālmīki, which was written over a millennium earlier. Yet it would be difficult to find a work that contrasts more strongly with Vālmīki's. Where Vālmīki is secular, Kampan̲ is religious; where Vālmīki uses simple language, Kampan̲ is complex; where Vālmīki often uses imagery with little care to make it fit context, each image of Kampan̲'s is carefully crafted; and where the flow of Vālmīki tends to be a bit monotonous, Kampan̲ endows his story with the dynamic movement and change that are characteristic of the Tamil tradition. He utterly changed the literature of Tamil, which has one of the richest literatures in the world: after his time, no writer could ignore him or escape his influence, and too many attempted to imitate him slavishly.

This is a translation of a central and perhaps the most dramatic part of his huge work into modern American English. We have preserved accuracy carefully, while trying to carry the flow of Kampan̲'s complex rhythms and passages into felicitous English. Above all, we have striven to convey the breadth and quality of Kampan̲'s vision of the world, its complexity, the resonance that echoes through his work; we have tried to give some idea of why Kampan̲ is considered the greatest spokesmen for one of humanity's richest cultural traditions. In the process of translating this work, which has taken both of us five years, we have been surprised at the result—at how different Kampan̲ has turned out to be from anything we know in English and how unlike other Indian works that are available in translation. It seems to sparkle with a radically different sensibility based on a very vibrant culture seen through the eyes of one of the world's great poets.

There is an old verse that gives the date of the official presentation of the *Rāmāyaṇa* of Kampaṉ. Unfortunately, the verse has two different interpretations, yielding a date of either 855 or 1185 A.D. There is abundant other evidence that the latter of these two dates is correct. First, Kampaṉ apparently knew the *Cīvakacintāmaṇi,* a Tamil poem that was probably written in the tenth century. Second, he apparently refers to the third Kulottuṅkaṉ, a Chola king who ruled from 1178 to 1202, in a verse in the *Yuttakāṇṭam* (8893). Finally, there is a story that after a dispute with the Chola king, he went to Andhra and stayed there under Pratāparudra, a king who ruled Aurangal from 1162 to 1197. Besides the *Rāmāyaṇa* several works are attributed to Kampaṉ—*Er Eḻupatu,* a work on farming; *Tirukkaivaḷakkam,* a work praising the Vēḷāḷars; *Caṭakōpar Antāti,* a work in praise of the greatest Āḻvār (Vaiṣṇava saint and Tamil poet); *Caracuvati Antāti,* a work praising the goddess Sarasvatī; and many separate poems. None of these, however, has the grace and felicity of the verses of Kampaṉ's *Rāmāyaṇa,* and it is unlikely that the poet wrote any of them.

Very little is known of Kampaṉ's life. He was born in the village of Tirutaḻuntūr in the Chola country and was a member of the Uvvacaṉ community or caste (see the Glossary under "Varṇa" for the distinction between varṇa and caste), a non-Brahmin group whose hereditary occupation was to perform temple worship of Kālī by ringing hand bells. His patron was one Caṭaiyappa Vaḷḷal, who lived in Veṇṇeynallūr, also in the Chola country. He is supposed to have had a disagreement with the Chola king and to have gone to Andhra for a while. He died in Nāṭṭaracaṉkōṭṭai in Ramanathapuram district in Tamil Nadu, where his memorial is still worshiped by the common people.

The name Kampaṉ has been derived in various ways. Some say that it was given because as a youth, Kampaṉ used to guard millet fields (*kampaṉ kollai*) to keep away birds, others that he was found in a Kālī temple near a column (*kampam*). It is most likely that he was named after the Śiva in Kanchipuram, who is called Kampaṉ in the *Dēvāram.*[1]

The story of the *Rāmāyaṇa* is perhaps the best-known story in the world. The earliest well-known version is that of Vālmīki, whose story Kampaṉ followed. In medieval South India, it became so popular that the medieval Kannada poet Kumāravyāsa felt that he had to justify

[1]This, however, is disputed by Emeneau in a recent article, who says we have no satisfactory derivation for Kampaṉ's name. *Journal of the American Oriental Society* 105, no. 3 (1985): 401-404.

his undertaking a version of the *Mahābhārata* by saying that the earth was sinking under the weight of the various *Rāmāyaṇas* that had been composed. Even today, the *Rāmāyaṇa* and stories from it are extremely popular in all levels and languages of Indian literature, from the oral tales of folk singers to the polished creations of poets. Probably the three most famous versions—each quite different from the others—are those of Vālmīki in Sanskrit, Kampaṉ in Tamil, and Tulsi Das in Hindi. Of these, the Tamil *Rāmāyaṇa* is by far the most sophisticated and poetically complex.

## The Story

Rāma is the eldest son of Daśaratha, king of Ayodhyā. His mother, Kausalyā, is the king's favorite wife. Daśaratha's two other queens have borne him three more sons: Bharata, whose mother is Kaikeyī, and Lakṣmaṇa and Śatrughna, the sons of Sumitrā.

In Book 1, the Book of His Youth (*Bālakāṇḍa*), Rāma shows extraordinary qualities and virtues. His younger brother, Lakṣmaṇa, becomes his inseparable, faithful companion. When Rāma reaches early manhood, the holy man Viśvāmitra appears at Daśaratha's court and requests the aid of Rāma, skilled at weapons but as yet untried in war, to combat Rākṣasas (demons—see the Glossary) who have been harassing holy men in the forest. Reluctantly, Daśaratha permits Rāma, accompanied by the loyal Lakṣmaṇa, to go with the sage. In the first battle of his career, Rāma cuts down the demoness Tāḍakā, his reluctance as a warrior at killing a woman overcome by Viśvāmitra's urgings. Later, he slays other Rākṣasas but not Mārīca, the son of Tāḍakā, who flees across the ocean.

In the city of Mithilā, Rāma bends and breaks a giant bow that once belonged to Śiva and that no man before has been able to bend, thereby winning the beautiful Sītā, daughter of King Janaka, for his wife.

In Book 2, the Book of Ayodhyā (*Ayodhyākāṇḍa*), Daśaratha decides to retire from the throne and to crown Rāma as king. Kaikeyī, mother of Bharata, demands the fulfillment of an old vow, by which Daśaratha had bound himself to grant any two wishes she might have. She requests that Rāma be banished to the forest for fourteen years and that her son be appointed heir to the throne. Daśaratha is horrified, but his honor is at stake. Rāma insists that his father must keep his word. Sītā, though Rāma tries to dissuade her, determines to accompany him into the dangerous forest. Together with Lakṣmaṇa, the couple sets out.

A few days later, Daśaratha dies of grief. Bharata repudiates the machinations of his mother and, accompanied by his army, marches off to bring Rāma back from the forest and crown him king. Rāma refuses, since he considers the word of his father sacred. Bharata picks up Rāma's sandals, sets them on his head, and says that he will rule only as Rāma's regent, while the sandals will rest on the throne. The decision is final. Rāma and Sītā, together with Lakṣmaṇa, will live in the forest for fourteen years.

Book 3 is the Forest Book (*Araṇyakāṇḍa*), which is translated here. As it begins, Rāma, Sītā, and Lakṣmaṇa are walking through the forest and encounter a great demon, Virādha, whom they kill. Then they come to the hermitage of the sage Śarabhaṅga, who attains release from the cycle of birth and death upon seeing Rāma. They have an encounter with the sage Agastya and then with Jaṭāyus, a gigantic bird who was a friend of Daśaratha. After that, a demoness named Śūrpaṇakhā, who is the sister of Rāvaṇa, the great demon king of Laṅkā, sees Rāma and falls in love with him. She changes herself into a beautiful woman and attempts to seduce him, but with no success. Finally, frustrated with her failure, she decides that Rāma is uninterested in her because of the presence of Sītā, whom she attempts to abduct. She is caught, however, by Lakṣmaṇa, who proceeds to disfigure her, cutting off her nose, ears, and nipples. The army of her brother Khara then fights with Rāma, but is totally destroyed, leaving only Śūrpaṇakhā alive. She returns to Laṅkā and encounters her brother, who is horrified when he sees her condition. Śūrpaṇakhā, however, is still interested in Rāma—and jealous of Sītā—and she turns her brother's desire for revenge into the wish to possess Sītā by describing her to him and making him fall hopelessly in love with her. Rāvaṇa decides to possess her by magic and persuades the Rākṣasa Mārīca, the son of Tāḍakā, to assume the form of a golden deer to lure Rāma away from Sītā, so that he can abduct her.

In the forest, Sītā sees a lovely golden deer—actually Mārīca—and, despite Rāma's misgivings, persuades him to chase and capture it. Rāma pursues the deer and kills it with an arrow, whereupon the deer imitates Rāma's voice and calls out, "Ah Sītā, ah Lakṣmaṇa." Sītā hears the cry, thinks Rāma is in trouble, and forces the reluctant Lakṣmaṇa (who suspects a trick) to investigate. While Lakṣmaṇa is gone and Sītā is unguarded, Rāvaṇa appears disguised as an ascetic. After some preliminaries, he reveals his true form and abducts Sītā in his chariot. On the way he is opposed by Jaṭāyus, whom he fights and defeats, after which he takes Sītā to his kingdom in Laṅkā.

Rāma and Lakṣmaṇa return, are distressed upon not seeing Sītā, and then encounter the dying Jaṭāyus, who describes what has happened. At the end of the Forest Book, they meet and kill two more demons and then help a female ascetic named Śabarī escape the cycle of transmigration.

In Book 4, the Book of Kiṣkindhā (*Kiṣkindhākāṇḍa*), Rāma and Lakṣmaṇa meet the monkey king Sugrīva. Rāma kills Sugrīva's brother Vāli, who has usurped Sugrīva's throne and queen. In exchange for killing Vāli, Rāma gains the support of Sugrīva and his army of monkeys as well as Sugrīva's most important supporter, Hanumān, son of the wind god, who then becomes an important figure in the epic. Hanumān leads a troop of monkeys off to locate Sītā. When he comes to the shore of the ocean, Hanumān leaves his followers and performs a prodigious leap across the ocean to the island of Laṅkā.

Book 5 is the *Sundarakāṇḍa,* which may mean "The Beautiful Book"—perhaps because of its many descriptive passages—or "The Book of the Beautiful One," as the epithet *sundara,* "beautiful," is often used for Hanumān. The book opens with a famous description of Laṅkā, after which Hanumān spies out Sītā, who is confined in the Aśoka Grove. He reveals himself to her and assures her that Rāma is coming to rescue her. But Rāvaṇa then captures Hanumān, whom he punishes for defiance by tying burning rags to his tail. The monkey, however, proceeds to use his burning tail to set fire to the city of Laṅkā before dousing it in the ocean with no injury to himself.

In the sixth and by the far the longest book, the Book of Battle (*Yuddhakāṇḍa*), Rāma and Lakṣmaṇa and their army of monkeys and bears fight Rāvaṇa's army of Rākṣasas before the gates of Laṅkā. After many individual and mass battles, Rāma kills Rāvaṇa in single combat. Sītā proves that she has been faithful to Rāma by entering a fire which does not harm her, and Rāma returns in triumph to Ayodhyā and is crowned king, an event that marks the beginning of *rāmarājya,* "Rāma's rule," the mythical golden age of Indian polity. Kampaṉ does not include the *Uttarakāṇḍa,* a later appendix to the *Rāmāyaṇa* of Vālmīki in which Rāma sends Sītā away to permanent exile because the people of his kingdom murmur that she has lived in the house of another man and so is not a fitting wife for Rāma.[2]

[2]The names of the books of the *Rāmāyaṇa* given here are the Sanskrit ones. The Forest Book is called the *Āraṇiyakāṇṭam* in Tamil. The summary here follows the plot of Kampaṉ's version.

## A Comparison of Kampaṉ and Vālmīki

The divine status of the hero Rāma varies considerably in the three most important *Rāmāyaṇas*—the Sanskrit original attributed to Vālmīki, the Tamil version by Kampaṉ, and Tulsi Dās's Hindi *Rāmāyaṇ*. In Vālmīki, Rāma is not a god (except in later, interpolated sections) but a human hero of superhuman abilities. In the sixteenth-century Hindi work, the cult of Rāma as an avatar of Viṣṇu pervades the text completely. Rāma is fully aware of himself as the ultimate divinity, and the other characters are generally conscious of it as well. In Kampaṉ, his status is more complex. Again and again, he is recognized as an incarnation of Viṣṇu by those who meet or confront him, but Rāma rarely shows a direct awareness of himself as the supreme god. He is capable even of despair, and the psychological depth of Kampaṉ's *Rāmāyaṇa* is greatly enhanced by Rāma's paradoxical conception of himself as an ordinary human being.

Kampaṉ's work differs not only in style and tone from its Sanskrit model; it also differs in many narrative details. Frequently, these differences reflect a greater degree of psychological sophistication in Kampaṉ's handling of character, provide more acceptable motivation for those of Rāma's actions that appear morally unacceptable, or incorporate elements from the South-Indian tradition. In the Forest Book, the major narrative differences are the following:

1) The association of the sage Agastya with the propagation of the Tamil language is found only in Kampaṉ.

2) In the Tamil version, the demoness Śūrpaṇakhā turns herself into a beautiful woman when she approaches Rāma. Her lovesickness is presented elaborately, with some measure of sympathy and understanding. The action is extended over two days. In Vālmīki, everything happens during a single encounter, the lovesickness is not presented at any length, and Śūrpaṇakhā does not change her hideous form when she encounters Rāma. She is not presented as a sympathetic figure but is simply a demoness consumed with lust. In Kampaṉ, her breasts are also mutilated, while in Vālmīki, she loses only her nose and ears.

3) The impressive scene in Paṭalam 6 ("The Killing of Khara") in which the Rākṣasa Akampana reads evil omens is not found in Vālmīki's version.

4) The long description of Rāvaṇa's lovesickness, with its rich imagery and extravagant emotional changes, is not in Vālmīki.

5) Vālmīki has Rāvaṇa abduct Sītā by seizing her with his own hands, while in Kampaṉ Rāvaṇa raises a portion of the earth and carries

her away upon it, since he had been cursed to die should he ever lay hands on an unwilling woman.

6) Kampaṉ alters and expands Lakṣmaṇa's encounter with the demoness Ayomukhī to demonstrate Rāma's great love for his brother. In Vālmīki, the entire incident consists of Lakṣmaṇa accompanied by Rāma mutilating the Rākṣasī, while in Kampaṉ, the brothers are separated and Rāma, deeply worried, searches for Lakṣmaṇa.

7) The ode that Kabandha sings to Rāma after being killed by him is not found in Vālmīki.

## Kampaṉ's Aesthetics

The Tamil language sonically runs like a river.[3] Because of its limited use of conjunct consonants, it is highly vocalic and its lengthy word formations are spoken rapidly with a stress accent on the first syllable of each word or word element. As rhythmic and sonic material for poetry, it is a very different language from Sanskrit, even when, as in Kampaṉ, rhythms and imagery do reflect some measure of Sanskrit influence. The medieval Tamil of Kampaṉ has great literary predecessors in the poems of the Caṅkam age, the *Cilappatikāram* and other early Tamil epics, and the hymns of the Śaiva and Vaiṣṇava saints. Such works embodied and passed on an aesthetic with strong realistic elements, great visual delicacy combined with naturalistic precision, and a tropical density of imagery and emotional oscillation.

Very characteristic of Tamil literature is the rapid alternation of emotions—sometimes swinging from one extreme to another—in the brief space of a short Caṅkam poem or a few stanzas of Kampaṉ or even within a single stanza. It is a quality of intense, rapidly rising and sometimes rapidly quenched emotion, sliding and shifting very rapidly in contrast with the Sanskrit *rasa* aesthetic, which values the creation of a stanza or fairly long sequences bound together by a steadier, more consistent emotional tone. Stanza 5:119 (2947) provides a clear example of such movement within a single stanza, as Rāma responds with wonder to the spectacle of the mutilated Śūrpaṇakhā identifying herself as the beautiful woman who had visited him only yesterday:

---

[3]Most of the material in this and the following two sections on meter and sound may be found (in expanded form) in "Issues of Literary Translation from Sanskrit and Tamil," an unpublished Ph.D. dissertation by Hank Heifetz (University of California, Berkeley, 1985).

"Was it you walking here yesterday, like the goddess Śrī on her
[lotus
full of honey, with your long dark eyes like lovely fishes?"
"When a woman has lost her nipples, her ears with their earrings,
[her nose
like a vine, O king with handsome eyes! isn't her beauty
[destroyed?"

The stanza moves through three different colorings of emotion, from Rāma's lush image of wonder and memory to Śūrpaṇakhā's grim realism (also, on Kampaṉ's part, grim humor) which encloses within it a vocative glittering with lust and admiration.

Another important aspect of Tamil sensibility is indicated by this stanza—the presence, often in union, of an aesthetic combining savagery and delicacy. The most lurid images of slaughter may be linked with refined imagery of cultivated human behavior or of nature in its tropical intensity, as in 6:119 (3090):

Headless they tossed and quivered in their golden armor,
seeming like mountains with shields in their powerful hands,
and they looked as if they were dancing many different dances,
amazing the women of heaven in their sounding anklets.

The cultures of Japan and of the Aztecs show a rather similar (though expressively quite different) affection for "blood and flowers." This feature of Tamil can be traced back to the Caṅkam works and to the magical idea that fertility and war are essentially different facets of the same need for survival.[4]

As in Sanskrit ornate poetry, each of Kampaṉ's stanzas is crafted like an individual lyric but also participates in a specific sequence, marked by subject matter, meter, and emotional tone. In contrast to the relatively modulated pace of Sanskrit Kāvya, however, Kampaṉ's descriptions of emotions are unrestrained. Rāvaṇa's lovesickness in Paṭalam 7 ("The Killing of Mārīca"), for example, covers some eighty-seven stanzas (7:82-168, 3245-3331), involving seven sequences in different meters, moving from the initial rising of desire into first frenzy:

[4]See George L. Hart, III, *The Poems of Ancient Tamil: Their Milieu and Their Sanskrit Counterparts* (Berkeley, Los Angeles, London: University of California Press, 1975), pp. 32-37.

It couldn't be calmed. His love was growing
by hundreds and hundreds of leaps.
The flowers on his soft bed though moistened
by the cooling drops of water
from the fragrant north wind turned black.
His arms that had defeated the eight
Elephants of Space and his body grew thin.
His heart weakened. His life caught on fire.
(7:90, 3253)

The description continues through a number of elegant changes on the sufferings of unsatisfied desire until the Rākṣasa king makes his decision:

"Death will come to me right now
if I cannot win what I wish
to be mine—mercy, the true kind,
from Sītā who has black eyes like spears.
Bring my ministers," he said, "with their capacity
for judging what is to be done next!" (7:168, 3331)

In this section with its many variations on the theme of obsessive sexual desire, Kampa<u>n</u> shows another quality that pervades his work and that further articulates and fleshes out the rush of his words: his psychological perceptiveness. For example, in 7:161 (3324), he masterfully shows the confusion of the senses, the total one-pointed immersion that sexual frenzy can create:

The way his mind was, he could not
tell touch or sound
or any of his senses, one from another.
Not knowing what to do,
just as desire might bind and
draw him into entering
another body in another birth, he came
and entered the pavilion.

But Kampa<u>n</u> can also show his psychological acumen in smaller ways. When Rāma, at the last moment, hesitates to pursue the golden deer, Kampa<u>n</u> has Sītā speak as an angry lover who feels slighted, shaming Rāma with tears:

Then she who was like a wild goose,
    in a sweet soft voice slipping
from her red mouth as if it were pouring out
    amṛta, with the sweetness of a parrot,
sadly said, "Husband, so it seems
    you won't catch it and give it to me!"
and she went off angry, weeping as if pearls
    were falling from red-streaked water lilies. (7:238, 3401)

And Rāma goes off after the deer. When he later returns and finds Sītā gone, Kampaṉ shows his distress not only by his lamentations but also by his inability for the first time to take command or even make decisions:

They came to a place where the trail
    of his passing chariot
vanished as if risen into the sky.
    His heart pierced with pain
like a spear into the raw burn on a body,
    Rāma said, "What
do you think that we should do now,
    my younger brother?" (8:165, 3581)

Another striking example of Kampaṉ's psychological realism occurs in 5:94 (2922), when Lakṣmaṇa mutilates Śūrpaṇakhā:

In anger, she tried to get up, thinking
    to hold him back by strength
and escape into the sky, but easily Lakṣmaṇa
    pulled her down and saying these words,
"Don't make people suffer!" he cut off first
    her nose, then her ears, then the nipples
of her hard burning breasts and his own anger then
    cut off, he released her hair.

Here, Kampaṉ uses repetition ("cut off") to suggest the aroused state of Lakṣmaṇa, whose assault on Śūrpaṇakhā is not merely one of anger but has a strong sexual component. Lakṣmaṇa is, after all, the loyal younger brother, living in the forest devoid of the love of women, but in the constant company of Sītā, the most beautiful of all women, toward whom his role is one of service and respect. It is as if in Kampaṉ's handling of this action, all of Lakṣmaṇa's frustration and loyalty come boiling out toward another beautiful woman, Śūrpaṇakhā, whom he mutilates for attempting to abduct Sītā.

## Kampaṉ's Meters

It would be nearly impossible to stress too strongly the importance of rhythm in Kampaṉ. His poetry works in passages of stanzas bound together by the same meter and subject matter or narrative episode. He shows enormous sensitivity in the fitting of meter to emotional tone and content; there are usually very clear reasons for rhythmic choices, and the points at which rhythms change serve important dramatic and mood-shifting purposes. Rhythm in Kampaṉ is both story and music.

The fundamental units of Tamil poetic rhythm are the *nēr* and the *nirai*—the first, a single syllable long or short, and the second, two syllables the first of which must be short. (In this discussion, a nēr is represented by a long mark ¯ and a nirai is represented by two short marks ˘ ˘.) Poetic feet—*cīrs*—are made by combining nērs and nirais in various ways. The most common cīr consists of two in any combination: ˘ ˘ ˘ ˘, ¯ ˘ ˘, ˘ ˘ ¯, ¯ ¯. These basic cīrs may optionally be augmented by one long syllable (a nēr) to make a new longer cīr: ˘ ˘ ˘ ˘ ¯, etc. Various combinations of these units (which may be extended with an extra nēr or not) constitute the various poetic feet (*cīr*). The classic Tamil line of the oldest Caṅkam anthologies, the *āciriyappā,* is made up of four cīrs interspersed with some lines of three cīrs.

Unlike the meters used in the Caṅkam works, Kampaṉ's meters are *viruttam,* "fixed" (Sanskrit *vṛttam*): under the influence of Sanskrit meters, each stanza contains four lines that use the same rhythm. These rhythms are generally relatively fixed patterns of cīrs. Another characteristic of Kampaṉ's verses not found in Caṅkam literature is beginning rhyme. This means that the consonant beginning the second syllable of each line is the same throughout the stanza. Sometimes, there is more rhyme than just this consonant, but at least this consonant must be rhymed.

Like Sanskrit, Greek, and Latin meters, then, these Tamil meters—whether Caṅkam meters or viruttam meter—are determined by length rather than stress. Yet when one reads a Tamil stanza, stress is also an important element. This is because the first syllable of each cīr tends to receive a stress because of the nature of the language (which is to stress the first syllable of each word). Perhaps this is why the rules regarding long and short syllables are less fixed than in the Indo-

European classical languages—a nirai can end with a long syllable, while a nēr may be short if it is the second element of a cīr. This importance of stress makes Tamil meter closer to English counterparts than Sanskrit, or than classical Greek or Latin, with the result that the rhythms can sometimes be rendered more directly into English.

Examples will serve to illustrate various points and problems. Let us first look at two different kinds of four-cīr lines. The first is 5:73 (2901), part of the sequence (stanzas 72-89) describing the lovesickness of Śūrpaṇakhā. Its rhythmic pattern consists of a *mā* (a foot of two components ending in a nēr) and three *viḷams* (a foot of two components ending in a nirai). In this section, the original in each case will be given first as metrical feet, then by word divisions, and then in Tamil script by word divisions.

¯ ¯|¯ ˘ ˘|¯ ˘ ˘ | ¯ ˘ ˘|  
*tāṭa kaikkoṭi yāṭaṭa mārpiṭai*  
¯ ¯ | ¯ ˘ ˘ | ¯ ˘ ˘ | ¯ ˘ ˘ |  
*yāṭa varkkara caṉṉayi lampupōl*  
¯ ¯ | ¯ ˘ ˘ | ¯ ˘ ˘ | ¯ ˘ ˘ |  
*pāṭa vattoḻiṉ maṉmataṉ pāykaṇai*  
¯ ¯ | ¯ ¯| ˘ ˘ ˘ ˘ | ¯ ˘ ˘ |  
*yōṭa vuṭki yuyiruḷain tāḷarō.*

*tāṭakaik koṭiyāḷ taṭa mārpiṭai,*  
*āṭavarkku aracaṉ ayil ampupōl,*  
*pāṭavat toḻil maṉmataṉ pāy kaṇai*  
*ōṭa, uṭki, uyir uḷaintāḷ arō!*

தாடகைக் கொடியாள் தட மார்பிடை,  
ஆடவர்க்கு அரசன் அயில் அம்புபோல்,  
பாடவத் தொழில் மன்மதன் பாய் கணை  
ஓட, உட்கி, உயிர் உளைந்தாள் அரோ!

While the arrows of the Love God who is practiced at his work  
flew at her like the sharp arrows of Rāma, king of men,  
when they pierced the great chest of Tāḍakā the cruel,  
ah! she was in pain and frightened for her very life.

The meter is not totally inflexible, and in the second cīr of the last line, Kampaṉ has introduced a foot of two nērs, so that the meter slows down at the word *uṭki*, "became frightened," thus breaking the flow at a critical juncture.

The second example is 5:113 (2941), part of the sequence (101-132) that immediately follows the mutilation. The metrical pattern is one of four *kāys* (a long foot of three components ending in a nēr):

– – – | ˘ ˘ ˘ ˘ – | ˘ ˘ ˘ ˘ – | ˘ ˘ ˘ ˘ – |
*kallīrum paṭaittaṭakkai yaṭaṟkaratū ṭaṇarmutalā*
– – – | ˘ ˘ ˘ ˘ – | ˘ ˘ ˘ ˘ – | ˘ ˘ ˘ ˘ – |
*vallīruñ cutarmaṇippū ṇarakkarkulat tavatarattīr*
– – – | ˘ ˘ – – | ˘ ˘ ˘ ˘ – | ˘ ˘ ˘ ˘ – |
*kollīrum paṭaikkumpa karuṇaṉaippōṟ kuvalayattu*
– – – | ˘ ˘ ˘ ˘ – | – ˘ ˘ – | – – – |
*ḷellīru muṟaṅkutirō yāṉaḻaittal kēḷīrō*

*"kal īrum paṭait taṭakkai aṭal, kara tūṭaṇar mutalā,*
*al īrum cuṭar maṇip pūṇ, arakkar kulattu avatarittīr!*
*kol īrum paṭaik kumpakaruṇaṉaip pōl, kuvalayattuḷ*
*ellīrum uṟaṅkutirō? yāṉ aḻaittal kēḷīrō?"*

"கல் ஈரும் படைத் தடக்கை அடல், கர தூடணர் முதலா,
அல் ஈரும் சுடர் மணிப் பூண், அரக்கர் குலத்து அவதரித்தீர்!
கொல் ஈரும் படைக் கும்பகருணனைப் போல், குவலயத்துள்
எல்லீரும் உறங்குதிரோ? யான் அழைத்தல் கேளீரோ?"

"You whose murderous force can split rocks with the weapons in
[your giant
hands! Khara! Dūṣaṇa! You others born as Rākṣasas and
[ornamented
with jewels that flash apart the darkness! Do you sleep on the
[earth
like Kumbhakarṇa with his sharply honed weapons? Can't you
[hear me calling?"

Here, Kampaṉ breaks the pattern in the fourth line, in the two last cīrs, which consist of more long syllables than the corresponding cīrs in the preceding lines. This effectively finishes the stanza, providing a concluding rhythm.

Lines such as these of four cīrs, called *kali viruttam,* constitute the classic middle rhythm of Tamil poetry. In Kampaṉ, these lines are usually composed of mās and viḷams, as in the first example; the heavy use of kāys exemplified in the second stanza is far less common. In a survey of Kampaṉ's meters K. V. Dakshayani shows that kali viruttams are used for more than 50 percent of the epic stanzas.[5]

In translating the common kali viruttam, we have chosen a five-stress line, loose enough to accommodate a variety of rhythms. The translation of stanza 73 is an example of this standard but supple five-stress treatment for the normal four-cīr line of mās and viḷams. The kali viruttam of stanza 113, in contrast, with its four long feet and its content of rage and anguish, obviously calls for a very different treatment from stanza 75. The translation therefore uses many small words that must be spoken quickly, creating long rapid rhythmic units; the diction is broken up to mirror the bursts of speech natural to the emotion of anger, the nature of human breathing in this specific emotional state, a quality beautifully drummed by Kampaṉ into the Tamil.

Transition points between meters are vital turns in Kampaṉ's art. In the translation, these are always marked by metrical changes in English. An example will enable us to focus on some further points to be considered in the translation of Tamil poetic rhythm. In 5:71-72 a meter of six feet (*aṟucīr āciriya viruttam*) with the pattern of one viḷam plus two mās plus one viḷam plus two mās changes to a type of kali viruttam we have already met above, consisting of one mā plus three viḷams:

– ˘ ˘ | ˘ ˘ – | – – |<br>
*niṉṟila ḷavaṉaic cēru*<br>
˘ ˘ ˘ ˘ | ˘ ˘ – | – – |<br>
*neṟiyiṉai niṉaintu pōṉā*<br>
– ˘ ˘ | – – | – – |<br>
*ḷiṉṟiva ṉākam pullē*<br>
˘ ˘ ˘ ˘ | ˘ ˘ – | – – |<br>
*ṉeṉiṉuyi riḻappe ṉeṉṉāp*<br>
– ˘ ˘ | ˘ ˘ – | – – |<br>
*poṉṟiṇi caraḷac cōlaip*<br>
˘ ˘ ˘ ˘ | ˘ ˘ – | – – |<br>
*paḷikkaṟaip potumpar pukkāḷ;*<br>
– ˘ ˘ | ˘ ˘ – | – – |<br>
*ceṉṟatu, pariti mēlpāṟ*<br>
– ˘ ˘ | ˘ ˘ – | – – |<br>
*cekkarvan tiṟutta taṉṟē.*

---

[5] K. V. Dakshayani, *The Metres in Kamparāmāyaṇam* (Annamalainagar: Annamalai University, 1979), pp. 19, 126.

*niṉṟilaḷ; avaṉaic cērum neṟiyiṉai niṉaintu pōṉāḷ;*
*“iṉṟu ivaṉ ākam pullēṉ eṉiṉ, uyir iḻappeṉ” eṉṉāp*
*poṉ tiṇi caraḷac cōlaip paḷikkaṟaip potumpar pukkāḷ;*
*ceṉṟatu, pariti mēlpāl; cekkar vantu iṟuttatu aṉṟē.*

நின்றிலள்; அவனைச் சேரும் நெறியினை நினைந்து போனாள்;
"இன்று இவன் ஆகம் புல்லேன் எனின், உயிர் இழப்பென்" என்னாப்
பொன் திணி சரளச் சோலைப் பளிக்கறைப் பொதும்பர் புக்காள்;
சென்றது, பரிதி மேல்பால்; செக்கர் வந்து இறுத்தது அன்றே.

She left. She went away trying to think
  of some means by which she might have him
and she felt that if she did not embrace
  his chest this very day she would die.
She entered her grove lined with trees,
  the air full of golden pollen,
and then her palace of crystal where she remained
  through the evening, as the sky turned red. (71)

˘ ˘ – | – ˘ ˘ | – ˘ ˘ | – ˘ ˘ |
*aḻinta cintaiya ḷāyayar vāḷvayiṉ*
˘ ˘ – | – – | ˘ ˘ ˘ ˘ | – ˘ ˘ |
*moḻinta kāmak kaṭuṅkaṉaṉ mūṇṭatāl*
˘ ˘ – | – ˘ ˘ | – ˘ ˘ | – ˘ ˘ |
*vaḻinta nākattiṉ vaṉṟoḷai vāḷeyiṟ*
˘ ˘ – | – ˘ ˘ | – ˘ ˘ | – ˘ ˘ |
*ṟiḻinta kārviṭa mēṟuva teṉṉavē*

*aḻinta cintaiyaḷ āy ayarvāḷ vayiṉ,*
*moḻinta kāmak kaṭuṅkaṉal mūṇṭatāl,*
*vaḻinta nākattiṉ vaṉ toḷai vāḷ eyiṟṟu*
*iḻinta kār viṭam ēṟuvatu eṉṉavē.*

அழிந்த சிந்தையள் ஆய் அயர்வாள் வயின்,
மொழிந்த காமக் கடுங்கனல் மூண்டதால்,
வழிந்த நாகத்தின் வன் தொளை வாள் எயிற்று
இழிந்த கார் விடம் ஏறுவது என்னவே.

Blazing up in her despair, the desires she had told to Rāma
ravaged her heart like cruel fire. It seemed as if
the black poison that descends through the hollow sharp fang
of a strong snake, newly molted, were rising through her. (72)

The rhythm of 71 is a very common meter in the *Kamparāmāyaṇam,* accounting for upwards of a quarter of the entire work;[6] and it is a meter handled in a very regular manner: "the pattern is uniformly followed except in a few instances where *kāyccīr* interchanges with viḷam."[7] This smooth and regular meter breaks up naturally into two equal halves. Kampaṉ tends to use it for lengthy, emotionally restrained (at least by classical Tamil standards) description and dialogue. It is an alternate middle rhythm, more elaborate than the various kali viruttams. It has a stately, processional quality, very evident in this stanza and therefore in the translation, which responds to the structure of the Tamil. The shift to the kali viruttam then requires a burst of speed, matching the onrush of the night and the surging of Śūrpaṇakhā's desire. The transition is underscored by the stressed first syllables of lines 1 and 2 in the translation, which help to alter the rhythm from the previous even procession to a line with an initial stress involving few syllables followed by a series of rolling, multiple-syllabled rhythms, modeled after, but not narrowly copying, the meter of one mā plus three viḷams. In order to give the reader a better idea of how metrical changes occur in Kampaṉ, we have discussed all the changes that occur in Paṭalam 5 in the notes.

Tamil meter is an extremely complex subject—considerably more so than Sanskrit, Greek, or Latin meter. This is because it concerns not only the bare metrical pattern but the link between feet.[8] In our estimation, however, there are three basic points that the translator of Kampaṉ's meters must keep in mind: that Tamil rhythms are essentially created by stress and hence that similar effects can be created in English; that meter is absolutely essential to the articulation of Kampaṉ's art even at the level of narrative and hence requires translation; and that the English rhythms must in some measure imitate the speed of Tamil speech and verse (insofar as our much more consonant-clustered language permits) so that the emotional flavors and density of imagery may be carried along with enough rapidity to accommodate their riverlike profusion.

---

[6]Dakshayani, *Metres,* p. 138.

[7]Ibid., p. 138.

[8]The link between cīrs is called *taḷai.* See Hart, op. cit., pp. 197-200.

## Sound

It has already been remarked how Kampan̲ uses initial rhyme in all of his verses. Beyond this, he uses alliteration in an extremely skillful manner. An example is a famous verse from the fifth Paṭalam, stanza 31 (2859):

*pañci oḷir viñcu kuḷir pallavam an̲uṅkac*
*ceñceviya kañcam nimir cir̲atiyaḷ āki,*
*am col iḷa maññai en̲a, an̲n̲am en̲a, min̲n̲um*
*vañci en̲a, nañcam en̲a vañca makaḷ vantāḷ.*

பஞ்சி ஒளிர் விஞ்சு குளிர் பல்லவம் அனுங்கச்
செஞ்செவிய கஞ்சம் நிமிர் சீறடியள் ஆகி,
அம் சொல் இள மஞ்ஞை என, அன்னம் என, மின்னும்
வஞ்சி என நஞ்சம் என வஞ்ச மகள் வந்தாள்.

All the loveliness of bright red cotton
 and cool shoots
were shamed by her as she moved
 on her small feet
like graceful red lotuses. With words that were sweet
 like a young peacock,
a wild goose, a swaying Vañci vine, like poison,
 the wily woman came.

In his chapter on Kampan̲ in *The Smile of Murugan,* Kamil Zvelebil analyzes the sound symbolism of this stanza, which depicts the swaying walk of Śūrpaṇakhā as seductress. He comments on "the extremely skillful use of high and front vowels and palatal consonants" and on the fact that "for the Tamil reader, there is—apart from the direct acoustic effect of the sounds—a subconscious association between the palatal cluster *-ñc-* and things which are bizarre, uncouth, dangerous, deadly, e.g. *añcal* 'fear,' *kañcam* 'trick,' *kiñci* 'crocodile,' *nañcam* 'poison,' *pañcam* 'famine,' *piñcam* 'killing,' *muñcal* 'dying,' *vañcan̲am* 'trick,' *vañcalam* 'serpent,' etc. The sound symbolism is found, in a different layout, in many parts of the poem."[9] We have

[9]K. Zvelebil, *The Smile of Murugan: On Tamil Literature of South India* (Leiden: E. J. Brill, 1973), pp. 214-215.

attempted to reproduce something of this effect by filling the verse with liquid sounds—*l*'s and (to a lesser extent) *r*'s.

Two more stanzas—5:77-78 (2905-2906)—will help clarify the use of alliteration :

*"aṇaivu il tiṅkaḷai nuṅka arāviṉaik*
*koṇarveṉ, ōṭi" eṉak kotittu uṉṉuvāḷ,*
*paṇai iṉ meṉ mulai mēl paṉi māṟutam*
*puṇara, ār ūyir ventu puḻuṅkuvāḷ.* (77)

*kaikaḷāl, taṉ katir iḷaṅ koṅkai mēl*
*aiya taṇ paṉi aḷḷiṉaḷ appiṉāḷ;*
*moy koḷ tīyiṭai ventu muruṅkiya*
*veyya pāṟaiyil veṇṇey nikarkkum āl.* (78)

"அணைவு இல் திங்களை நுங்க அராவினைக்
கொணர்வென், ஓடி" எனக் கொதித்து உன்னுவாள்,
பணை இன் மென் முலை மேல் பனி மாருதம்
புணர, ஆர் உயிர் வெந்து புழுங்குவாள்.

கைகளால், தன் கதிர் இளங் கொங்கை மேல்
ஐய தண் பனி அள்ளினள் அப்பினாள்;
மொய் கொள் தீயிடை வெந்து முருங்கிய
வெய்ய பாறையில் வெண்ணெய் நிகர்க்கும் ஆல்.

Angrily she thought, "I will run and bring the snake able
to swallow down that moon which is beyond my reach,"
and her precious life was burning at the touch of a cool wind
to her large, soft, sweet breasts and she was seething.

She scooped up handfuls of ice, miraculously cool
and placed them down on her young, radiant breasts
but they were no better than butter that would melt away
laid out on a hot ledge, with fire blazing around it.

In stanza 77, we have attempted to bring across the harsh effect of the *k*'s with the first syllable of "angrily" plus the words "bring" and "snake." The translation also aims at a more generalized harshness of sound with the inclusion of the word "down" as part of the verb "to swallow," its echo in the second syllable of "beyond," and the phrase "beyond my reach" that concludes the line. The third and fourth lines in the Tamil are a masterly example of a murmuring sound pattern culminating in a final harshness. Literally, the lines mean:

> large sweet soft breast upon/to cool wind
> as (it) joined-with/came dear life burning she suffered/seethed.

The music of the third line in the Tamil consists of softly moving labials and liquids that are echoed, with a lesser frequency, in the last line, where the final *r* of *mārutam* (wind) is picked up and repeated, until the repetition harshens into the "American *r*" sound of *ḻ* which occurs in the same syllable with the hard cluster *ṅk*. It is not possible to reproduce the Tamil sounds in English, but we have given a sense of the Tamil sound pattern. The caressing murmur of the third line is suggested by the softness of "at the touch of the cool wind / to her large, soft, sweet breasts," while the harshness of the final Tamil verb affects the final "and she was seething."

For stanza 78, the translation reacts somewhat more directly to the Tamil sound effects. The first line corresponds semantically, for the most part, to the second line of the Tamil, but it has been possible to reproduce the pattern of *k* sounds with which the Tamil stanza begins—"She scooped up handfuls of ice, miraculously cool"—translating the brisk, jagged movement of Kampaṉ's line. In the final two lines of 78, Kampaṉ uses a mixture of labials (including *v*), harsher velars, and the sound of hard Tamil *ṟ* in a key position (in *paṟaiyil,* "on a . . . ledge"). In our translation, we have used the labial *b*—"better," "butter," "blazing"—and the *m* of "melt away" to contrast with the clear, clipped sound of the first two lines.

## Kampaṉ and the Western Epic

Kampaṉ lived as a contemporary of the European High Middle Ages, about a century and a half before Dante Alighieri, who, as the third figure among the great epic writers of Western literature, would sum up the religious weight and strains of the Middle Ages in the *Divine Comedy,* echoing in a new key the voices of Virgil and of Homer. Some three hundred years after Dante, John Milton would write *Paradise Lost* and *Paradise Regained,* the last great Western epics. A few comments comparing Kampaṉ's work with these four Western authors may help the reader understand Kampaṉ's aesthetic and the nature of his great work.

Kampaṉ's elaborate metrics and complex sound patterns stem from a much more sophisticated climate of literary composition than the Homeric epics, but the savagery of the battle scenes in Kampan̲ brings the *Iliad* easily to mind. Even though Kampan̲'s battles are between superhuman antagonists, magical weapons are used, and impossible feats of slaughter and endurance are accomplished, the Tamil tradition of realism fills these battle sequences with tangible blood and hewing of limbs, in forms considerably less aestheticized than similar sequences in Sanskrit Kāvya:

> The rutting elephants fell quivering and the horses and chariots.
> Crowned heads lay quivering and right braceleted arms,
> small intestines, skin and flesh quivering, pairs
> of quivering legs, left arms falling, quivering. (4:165; 3136)

In the *Iliad* also, there is a sense of realism in the battles that renders them stark and convincing. As in many of Kampan̲'s scenes of battle, there is often little sympathy with the victims:

> Then Thoas the Aitolian lunged at Peiros,
> hitting him with a spear above the nipple,
> so the bronze point stuck to his lung; and Thoas
> at close quarters, wrenching the heavy spear,
> pulled it out of his chest, then drew his sword
> and killed him with a stroke square in the belly.[10]

For Virgil, in contrast, sympathy with the dying is generally interwoven with the texture of battle:

> Aeneas
> Drove his tough sword through the young man's body
> Up to the hilt—for it pierced the half-shield, light
> Defense for one so menacing—and the shirt
> His mother had woven him, soft cloth of gold,
> So blood filled up the folds of it. His life
> Now left his body for the air and went
> In sorrow to the shades. But seeing the look
> On the young man's face in death, a face so pale
> As to be awesome, then Anchises' son
> Groaned in profound pity.[11]

---

[10] *The Iliad of Homer,* translated by Robert Fitzgerald (New York: Doubleday and Co., 1974), 4:530-537.

[11] *The Aeneid of Virgil,* translated by Robert Fitzgerald (New York: Vintage Books, 1984), 10:1141-1151.

In Kampan̲, the suffering of those who die in battle is mitigated by the sense that death is ephemeral, a door of pain leading to other existences. When death comes at the hands of Rāma, death is often a blessing, as it is the transition to a higher sphere of being:

> Through a touch of the lovely hand of the Lord who rules all [beings,
> the old bad karma that had brought a curse upon him was ended.
> He gave up his flawed body from which the arms had been [severed
> and flew up into the sky, like a bird released from a cage.
> (10:40; 3882)

Interspersed through Kampan̲'s work, and in strong contrast with most of the sections in which Rāma is treated as a human being, are odes of praise to Rāma as an incarnation of Viṣṇu, for Kampan̲ the ultimate and only real God. Sometimes these sections occur when a demon is killed by Rāma—in the Forest Book, when Rāma kills the demons Virādha and Kabandha and they gain a more exalted state. Sometimes also such odes of praise are addressed to Rāma by sages or gods overjoyed with their good fortune at meeting supreme divinity incarnate walking on the earth. It is primarily within these odes that direct statements of philosophical or theological doctrine occur. As a philosophical poet, Kampan̲ does not show Dante's interest in the continuous articulation and justification of a fixed body of dogma; rather, Kampan̲ presents in his baroque, incandescent language—which could hardly differ more from Dante's sweet and verbally simple gravity—a number of pan-Indian ideas about divinity, colored with Vaiṣṇava devotionalism. For example, when the demon Virādha dies at Rāma's hands, he asserts the widely held Indian idea of the unity of all beings, as well as the specifically Vaiṣṇava interpretation of this unity as the subsumption of all into the being of the personal god, Viṣṇu:

> "You whose feet cover the world,
> whose anklets resound like the Vedas,
> how many forms are there for you
> to have, you who are everywhere!
> Between destruction and creation of a universe
> you lie on the cool ocean of milk
> and still you enter into all the disparate
> elements! How can they possibly contain you?"
> (1:47; 2652)

"Never agreeing, the religions
worship gods who, like men
of good and bad karma, endure
arduous tapas to acquire power,
but you are the one on whose precious chest the goddess
Śrī lies. What is there you need do?
Like those with no karma at all, always
in deep yogic sleep, you are awake!" (1:56; 2661)

Virādha also recognizes Viṣṇu-Rāma as savior, awareness or direct experience of whom liberates the individual soul from rebirth through final entrance into the paradise of Viṣṇu:

"God far beyond all that is! Because,
in my lives, I who am your servant
have carried through arduous tapas, you,
leaving your sleep on the waters, came to me
and now I have crossed the ocean of birth.
I will not be reborn! You have wiped away
my karma, the good and the bad,
with your feet that have the glow of coral!" (1:60; 2665)

In the second Paṭalam, the god Indra, who has encountered Rāma by chance, breaks into an ode of six stanzas composed in a very long meter of eight feet (*cīrs*), and offers ideas and images similar to the theologian-philosopher Rāmānuja's Viśiṣṭādvaita position, combining reverence for a personal god with a notion of fundamental monism which includes the responsibility for evil itself within the single absolute:

"At the very root of time, you were one and became
many! You became awareness and lives and bodies!
And when an aeon has reached its end and passes, once more
you are one! and then again you become the varied world!
O incomparable, ever-new sprouting of knowledge! Magnificent
and good! You who take away our sins, you who protect
those whose will is good and burn the others down,
but Lord, aren't even the evanescent acts of evil your own
[creation?" (2:30; 2707)

When we set Kampa<u>n</u>'s work beside John Milton's epics, we find an intriguing similarity in characterization. Kampa<u>n</u>'s Rāvaṇa has often been compared to Milton's Satan: Rāvaṇa has been called the true hero of Kampa<u>n</u>'s work, just as Satan has been considered the hero of

*Paradise Lost.* Some who espouse the modern Tamil Dravidian movement even read Rāvaṇa as a Southern champion unjustly defeated by overwhelming power from the North. It is true that Kampaṉ's Rāvaṇa, like Milton's Satan, is a chaotically powerful figure, whose entanglements in deep feeling and rebellions against conventional morality ring more human and conform far more to Romantic ideas of the heroic than the immaculate (and, to the uncommitted observer, often self-righteous) behavior of Absolute Good. In the Forest Book, not only Rāvaṇa but his sister Śūrpaṇakhā at times draw our sympathies to their superhuman humanity. But there is no question that within the value system of the *Kamparāmāyaṇam*—values that are clearly and constantly presented in example and in direct statement—Rāvaṇa is evil, though magnificent and intricate evil, just as Satan is for Milton.

To conclude these brief comments with perhaps the most telling juxtaposition, it is to the work of Virgil that Kampaṉ's voice can perhaps be most fruitfully compared. Stylistically, the baroque density of Kampaṉ's Tamil resembles the elaborate mosaic arrangements of Virgil's Latin, effects that cannot be reproduced (given our lack of inflections) in even the finest of English translations. In Book 6 of the *Aeneid*, Aeneas is led by the doves of Venus to the tree that holds the golden bough:

> pāscentēs illae tantum prōdīre volandō,
> quantum aciē possent oculī servāre sequentum.
> inde ubi vēnēre ad faucēs grave olentis Avernī,
> tollunt sē celerēs liquidumque per āera lāpsae
> sēdibus optātīs geminā super arbore sīdunt,
> discolor unde aurī per rāmōs aura refulsit.[12]

> And they fed and then flew on,
> Each time as one who came behind
> Could keep in view. Then when they reached the gorge
> Of sulphurous Avernus, first borne upward
> Through the lucent air, they glided down
> To their desired rest, the two-hued tree
> Where glitter of gold filtered between green boughs.[13]

The flight of Jaṭāyus the vulture king has, in the Tamil, some of this same verbal density and visual glow:

---

[12]*The Aeneid* 6:199-204.

[13]*The Aeneid of Vergil,* translated by Fitzgerald, 6:285-291.

*Urukkiya cuvaṇam ottu, utayattu ucci cēr*
*arukkan̲ iv akal iṭattu alaṅku tikku elām*
*terippur̲u cer̲i cuṭarc cikaiyin̲āl ticai*
*virittu iruntan̲an̲ en̲a, viḷaṅkuvān̲ tan̲ai.*

*Muntu oru karumalai mukaṭṭu mun̲r̲ilin̲*
*cantiran̲ oḷiyoṭu tal̲uvac cārttiya,*
*antam il kan̲ai kaṭal amarar nāṭṭiya,*
*mantara kiri en̲a vayaṅkuvān̲ tan̲ai.*

உருக்கிய சுவணம் ஒத்து, உதயத்து உச்சி சேர்
அருக்கன் இவ் அகல் இடத்து அலங்கு திக்கு எலாம்
தெரிப்புறு செறி சுடர்ச் சிகையினால் திசை
விரித்து இருந்தனன் என, விழங்குவான் தனை.

முந்து ஒரு கருமலை முகட்டு முன்றிலின்
சந்திரன் ஒளியொடு தழுவச் சார்த்திய,
அந்தம் இல் கனை கடல் அமரர் நாட்டிய,
மந்திர கிரி என வயங்குவான் தனை.

He shone as if the young sun were rising, all molten
gold over the peak of the Eastern Mountain, where it had spread
out its wings through the shining directions of the air,
its bright mass of rays lighting up this wide earth.

Floating near the dark peak of a mountain, he was gleaming
before them as if the light of the moon had been brought
together with and then fastened to Mount Mandara by the gods
for their churning stick fixed in the endless roaring ocean.
(4:2-3; 2782-2783)

Kampan̲ also resembles Virgil in his note of morality merged with psychological insight, drawing the reader into emotional identification. In Paṭalam 9, for example, when Lakṣmaṇa, against his better judgment, accedes to Sītā's wishes and sets off in search of Rāma, his uncertainty and final reluctant commitment to an ambiguous action for immediate moral reasons resembles much of the frequently tormented soul-searching of Aeneas before he too can plunge into action:

"If I stay here, she will not be, she will die in the fire,
and if I should go to him who is like an immovable mountain,
evil will arrive without fail and unfold. What should I do,
who seem to have some great desire for my dear life?" and he
[wept.

"If the god Dharma is able, he will make it come out well.
Rather than have her die, I will dare to do this, leaving
her here and going. I am an ignorant man, I feel this
suffering because I was born, because of actions in some other
[life!" 9:17-18 (3433-3434)

As with Aeneas, all that Rāma does (some of it, to the modern mind, morally ambiguous) is portrayed as having an ultimate moral purpose: for Aeneas, the reestablishment of the Trojan people through their settlement in Italy; for Rāma, the firm establishment of *dharma* (in Tamil, *aṟam*)—Righteousness, the Order of the World—through defeat of the forces of evil embodied in Rāvaṇa and his Rākṣasas. Though Rāma is ultimate deity, he is also, like pious Aeneas, "pious" Rāma in his human behavior, respecting holy men and his elders and the prescriptions of dharma. The same is true of Sītā and Lakṣmaṇa. Even Lakṣmaṇa's disfigurements of the Rākṣasīs Śūrpaṇakhā and Ayomukhī are moral acts. Their behavior merits punishment, which is "just," but the punishment must stop short of death, because it is wrong for a warrior to kill women.

Yet Kampaṉ's capacity for sympathy with suffering, which also brings Virgil to mind, continually counterpoints the prescriptions of stern justice. With the exception, already discussed, of death in battle, the poet's *mitgefühl,* his sympathetic entrance into the raw emotions of his characters, is wide-ranging and continual. Śūrpaṇakhā, for instance, nothing more than an ogress in the Vālmīki *Rāmāyaṇa,* is treated by Kampaṉ with considerable, if ambiguous, sympathy. She suffers like the lovelorn heroes and heroines of courtly Sanskrit poetry, and her suffering is both genuine and moving:

First thinking to quiet the ocean with her lovely hands
by filling it with mountains, because the sounds of the waves
gave her pain, she grew weak and anguished while the moon,
[high
and firm in the sky, troubled her with its long light. (5:75; 2903)

"Make this suffering vanish," she said, "that enters my heart
and deceives me with cruel, innumerable illusions,
mountain dark as collyrium, show me your grace!"
she said, and she trembled as if she had licked up poison.
(5:86; 2914)

Where Kampaṉ greatly differs from Virgil is in his capacity for suddenly switching gears, a swift turn to comedy for instance in the midst of such scenes of extreme emotion. Śūrpaṇakhā is treated humorously at times in the midst of her lovesickness; and during the slaughter of the Rākṣasas by Rāma in the Khara Paṭalam, a stanza like the following appears:

Some ran hard and cut their way
    into the wound in the belly
of a great rutting elephant and entered
    that giant cave and lifted
their hands over their heads, entreating
    a headless corpse nearby to protect them.
"Friend," they were saying, "If Rāma comes,
    tell him you haven't seen us!" (6:140; 3111)

## Kampaṉ and Tamil Culture

Of course, Kampaṉ's work is an integral part of the development and history of South Asian culture, and especially of Tamil culture. This is true even more for Kampaṉ than it might be for one of the great Western epics, since South Asian culture is essentially syncretistic. Its writers and thinkers tend not to attempt to create a coherent system by discarding earlier cultural elements that do not fit in with their ideas but rather to synthesize everything that has gone before, throwing away nothing but rather subordinating everything to the idea or point of view that they wish to advance. In Kampaṉ, for example, we can see several vastly different sources that he has drawn upon and synthesized. These include the Sanskrit *Rāmāyaṇa* of Vālmīki, which we have discussed above; Northern ideas about yoga and the heterodox tradition, which makes the point of human existence an escape from the cycle of transmigration by renouncing the world (see Paṭalam 2); Sanskrit Kāvya literature, which is the source of some of the elements of the viruttam meter and which clearly served as a model for many of the rhetorical figures used by Kampaṉ; the basic philosophical ideas of orthodox Indian religion that first appear in the *Upaniṣads* and are taken up and developed in the *Bhagavad Gītā* and then by the great theologians like Śaṅkara and Rāmānuja; and the *bhakti* movement of religious devotion, which had come to characterize most of Hinduism by Kampaṉ's time.

On the Tamil side, Kampaṉ appears to have been acutely aware of all that had gone on in the literature. He knows and uses the conventions of Caṅkam literature (at the beginning of Paṭalam 5, for example) and is apparently strongly influenced by the Tamil devotional literature that preceded him, especially by the Vaiṣṇava *Divyaprabandha*. But the Tamil quality of Kampaṉ's work goes even deeper than this, basing itself on a dual view of the world that is inherent in the history of South India and in Tamil culture itself.

In an important article published about 15 years ago, Burton Stein showed that South Indian history can be characterized by two basically different tendencies or patterns.[14] The land is divided into many small self-sufficient food-producing units called in Tamil *nāṭus*. In the first pattern, each of these units tends to have its own chieftains and its own armies and to try to subdue the other nāṭus near it. This sort of society is described in detail in the heroic (*puṟam*) poems of the Caṅkam anthologies (dated from the first to the third centuries A.D.)[15] The second pattern is first manifested during the rule of the Pallavas in about the sixth century A.D. In this model, the upper-caste landowning non-Brahmins (who have generally been the real power in South India) ally themselves with the Brahmins and adopt a Hindu life-style characterized by large kingdoms in which the landowners of each nāṭu support the central king in return for his protection from local chieftains and armies. In this second pattern, the upper castes adopt Hinduism with all its characteristically South Indian attributes: respect for Brahmins and the Northern traditions of Hinduism; devotion to Viṣṇu or Śiva; and temple worship.

In the Tamil psyche, both of these traditions are very much alive, even today.[16] They were present even in the oldest Tamil literature,

---

[14]B. Stein, "Integration of the Agrarian System of South India," in *Land Control and Social Structure in Indian History*, ed. R. E. Frykenberg (Madison: University of Wisconsin Press, 1969), pp. 175-216.

[15]In his thesis, "The *Cīvakacintāmaṇi* in Historical Perspective" (University of California, Berkeley, 1985), James Ryan argues that the Buddhists and Jainas, most of whom disappeared from South India before Kampaṉ's times, came from groups that espoused this form of social order.

[16]When Annadurai, the most important Tamil politician of modern times, died, he was buried rather than cremated—a custom

where the indigenous view was characterized by the word *maṟam* and the Hindu view was called *aṟam* (often an equivalent of the Sanskrit word *dharma*). For example, in poem 362 of the *Puṟanāṉūṟu,* a work of the first or second century A.D., a poet addresses a group of Brahmins, who represent the new order of dharma. He describes the soldiers of a king who are ferocious in battle and who seek death so that they can go to the paradise of fallen warriors rather than continue to live in the world. He says, "Listen to the voice of attack of the army, whose strength cannot be withstood, which is like Death, Brahmins! Since it is not [connected with] kindness [*aruḷ*], it has nothing to do with the four Vedas. And since it has to do with worldly gain [*poruḷ*], it has nothing to do with aṟam." In general, maṟam is connected with battle and the glorification of the king, who must fight often and well. The valorous army is often characterized as being like Death or (in another place in the poem quoted above) like a possessing demon spirit. Aṟam, in contrast to maṟam, is connected with the Brahmins and the upper-class landholders, with the four Vedas, and the nonmilitant life that the Brahmins symbolized. The new order was fostered by the great Tamil kings (especially the Pallavas), who wished to create a stable order in the areas they governed to replace the older order in which warlords arose periodically to challenge their authority.[17]

In Kampaṉ, Rāvaṇa represents the older Tamil king, surrounded by hordes of beings who praise him and are terrified of him, and constantly entertained by his many beautiful women. His army is so powerful that nothing in the world has been able to overcome it, and he himself is enormously strong in battle. His main concern is power and enjoyment, and he is prepared to go to any length to preserve these. When Kampaṉ describes Rāvaṇa, he does so with real admiration and sympathy, for he epitomizes the ideal Tamil king, who has been an important figure throughout Tamil history until even today.

Suddenly a totally new element intrudes on the stability of the old Tamil order symbolized by Rāvaṇa and his court: Rāma, an incarnation of God himself, appears and destroys in one moment the stability and balance of Rāvaṇa's empire and world. This he does through the mutilation of Rāvaṇa's sister, Śūrpaṇakhā, who appears alone and

---

from the militaristic model of Tamil society, with which his Dravidian Advancement Party attempted (idealistically, at least) to identify. This is said to have upset many upper-caste Hindus, who felt he should have been cremated according to orthodox Hindu custom.

[17]We have translated *aṟam* (or *dharma*) as "Righteousness" when used in a general sense and as "Order of the World" when used in a more specific way.

bleeding at the gate of Rāvaṇa's great city, Laṅkā. Kampaṉ paints the scene with his usual flair for the dramatic: Paṭalam 7 ("The Killing of Mārīca") begins with a description of the greatness and splendor of Rāvaṇa's court, suddenly interrupted by the appearance of his sister covered with blood. The old system of values that makes maṟam the highest virtue has suddenly been challenged and will be utterly destroyed by Rāma, after which, at the end of the work, Rāma will be crowned king and the Hindu dharma will be triumphant. It is notable that Kampaṉ makes his idea of dharma totally dependent on Rāma-Viṣṇu. It is through the person of Rāma that dharma is established and maintained, and it has no meaning without the worship of Viṣṇu.[18]

Thus Kampaṉ is able to synthesize all of the cultural traditions that went before him. Those elements of the Tamil tradition that do not fit in with his notions of dharma he assigns to Rāvaṇa. And by making the entire dharma dependent on Rāma, he is able to subordinate to the divinity of Rāma those elements from the orthodox Hindu tradition, such as karma and the belief in release from transmigration through one's own efforts, which would seem to contradict his notion that Rāma-Viṣṇu is the source and meaning of everything. This notion is taken so literally that in Kampaṉ God becomes the source not only of good but of evil as well. Thus Indra cries out in stanza 2:30 (2702), ". . . but Lord, aren't even the evanescent acts of evil your own creation?"

This is why we should not be surprised to see Rāma toying with Śūrpaṇakhā, mocking her and her desire in Paṭalam 5. One of the basic tenets of the bhakti movement is that God and his devotees are not constrained by normal acts and notions of morality.[19] It may be true that Rāma represents the Hindu dharma and social structure as opposed to the militaristic worldview of Rāvaṇa, but he also represents

[18]See stanzas 3059, 3245, and 3343 and the notes on them.

[19]An interesting example of this occurs in the Telugu work *Basava Purāṇa* of Pālkuriki Somanātha, who lived in the twelfth century. In chapter 4, the Tamil devotee, Ciṟuttoṇṭar, who had sacrificed his son to feed Śiva disguised as a wandering ascetic and who then through Śiva's grace, got his son back, is called a poor devotee by the god in comparison with Nimmava. That devotee killed her son when he was hungry and ate some food she had prepared for devotees before they had touched it. When Śiva wanted to bring the son back to life, as he had with Ciṟuttoṇṭar's son, Nimmava refused, calling her son unworthy and reviling Śiva for even thinking of bringing him back to life. This work has recently been translated by V. Narayanarao and Gene Roghair and will soon be published by Princeton University Press.

the intrusion of a new, mysterious dimension into ordinary reality. His acts have as their purpose the establishment of dharma, the Order of the World, and yet they are also beyond understanding, seemingly capricious and even cruel. God may have a purpose for the world that embodies perfect order, yet he is constantly playing a game with the universe that no man can understand and that is sometimes one of darkness and suffering rather than of sweetness and light. It is this paradox that enlivens Kampaṉ's work and makes it reach far beyond the simplistic notion of dharma and aṟam.

## Kampaṉ's Place among the People

Recently, Stuart Blackburn has done some preliminary studies of shadow–puppet performances in Kerala. The performance he studied consisted of nearly two thousand verses from Kampaṉ's *Rāmāyaṇa,* followed by oral commentary. As the two or three performers sing the verses and then narrate the commentary, they sit behind a screen and manipulate leather puppets whose shadows are visible on the other side. Such performances are held as part of the annual festival in over a hundred temples in the central districts of Kerala. They are conducted for the goddess Bhagavati (a local form of Kālī or Pārvatī, Śiva's wife), who watches the play from inside her temple. Among the material collected by Blackburn was a story about Kampaṉ and how he came to write his work. We end this introduction with this story, which is obviously apocryphal (though it contains some elements—such as the name of Kampaṉ's patron and Kampaṉ's association with Kālī—that are probably true), because it shows how deeply Kampaṉ's work has entered into the substance of South Indian society and how great the reverence of the common people for him is to this day. It is as follows (in Blackburn's translation):

> Kumuda threw a mountain into the sea,
> whose roaring, frothy water
> reached to the heavens where the gods danced
> hoping the ambrosia would rise again.[20]

[20] This is verse 6844 in the critical edition (42 of the *Cētupantaṉap Paṭalam* in the *Yuttakāṇṭam*). The story refers to the ambrosia [*amṛta*] that rose from the ocean when it was churned by the demons and the gods. See "Churning of the Ocean" in the Glossary.

(Commentary:) This is a verse that carries many meanings. It's said that it was the very first verse Kampaṉ wrote and that he wrote it to make a point. It also contains the story of how that point was demonstrated to the court poets. So much history lies behind this single verse, but we can begin with what we all know—that the earth was ruled by the Chola, Pandya, and Chera kings. The Chola kings ruled over the region of Tanjore, and each king kept sixty-four learned men, skilled in poetry, who would sit in two rows of thirty-two people each in the courts. At that time in Tanjore there also lived a great man named Caṭaiyappaṉ who had the reputation of helping everyone who brought their troubles to him; he offered them support and so was given the title of *vaḷḷal*, or "Great Benefactor."

This generous Caṭaiyappaṉ was also a close friend of the Chola king and would often visit his court. One day he spoke to his friend: "Oh Raja, you have sixty-four poets and scholars in your court, but we have no Rāma story in the southern language, in Tamil. It's only in the northern language, in the Sanskrit written by Vālmīki, who has put many details in each part. If it were in Tamil, all of us could enjoy that story. Therefore, summon your best poets—Oṭṭakkūttaṉ and Kampaṉ—and order them to compose a *Rāmāyaṇa* in the southern language." The Raja called the poets, made the request, and they agreed.

From that day, Oṭṭakkūttaṉ began to write. He finished the *Bālakāṇḍa*, the *Ayodhyākāṇḍa*, the *Araṇyakāṇḍa*, the *Sundarakāṇḍa*, and came to the beginning of the *Yuddhakāṇḍa*[21] when Śrī Rāma, Lakṣmaṇa, and the monkey army traveled for twelve days and reached the edge of the salt ocean. When Oṭṭakkūttaṉ told the king he had completed this much, Kampaṉ was embarrassed: "I've not yet written a single verse, but if I admit it, the name of Kampaṉ, which is praised everywhere as a great poet, will become inferior to Oṭṭakkūttaṉ. Certainly there are books that admonish us not to lie, but there are other books that say we can lie. How do we know when to lie and when not to? Well, if we do lie, the most important thing is that it should not cause any trouble or evil. Or if you lie to accomplish something good, then it's not wrong. In fact, it ceases to be a lie and becomes the truth. The law book says you can tell not just one lie, but two, three, a hundred, even hundreds of lies, and all at the same time. There is a verse,

[21]The storyteller has inadvertently omitted the *Kiṣkindhākāṇḍa*.

Getting a woman married, or having a spy do his work,
Creating good, or teaching the three essences of philosophy,
Or saving an innocent man from death—
At these times a hundred lies may be told.

This is what philosophy teaches us. In order to get a beautiful woman married and give her a good life, you have to tell a hundred lies at the same time. Those lies become the truth. If you don't tell lies, how can you arrange a marriage? To do something good, to avoid evil, you may tell a hundred lies. And if a cruel person goes to kill an innocent man, it is all right to tell lies to save him. At such times, lies are like truth."

Now Kampa<u>n</u> thought about this and said to himself, "The lie I'm going to tell won't have any evil consequences." So he looked at the king and said, "I have written up to the point when Rāma comes to the ocean, is unable to cross, meditates, fires arrows at Varuṇa the sea god, waits for Varuṇa to appear, and then strings the weapon of Brahmā, after which Varuṇa garlands Rāma, worships him and asks forgiveness, and then tells Rāma that to cross to Laṅkā he may build a bridge by throwing rocks into the ocean. Then

Kumuda threw a mountain into the sea,
 whose roaring, frothy water
reached to the heavens where the gods danced
 hoping the ambrosia would rise again."

When Kampa<u>n</u> told the king he had written up to that verse, he lied and Oṭṭakkūtta<u>n</u> knew it. He had seen him wandering about and knew he hadn't written a single verse. He also saw that some of the wording was ungrammatical and so, hoping to expose Kampa<u>n</u>'s lie, Oṭṭakkūtta<u>n</u> challenged him: "Kampa<u>n</u>, your verse may sound fine, but look at the line about the gods dancing when the water [*tumi*] reached the heavens. I ask you: is the use of *tumi* grammatical? Does it have any basis in common speech?"

Kampa<u>n</u> had to stop and think because at that time the word *tumi* was not used: "Oh," he thought, "even if it were grammatical, that would not be enough. It must be used by the common people." Then Oṭṭakkūtta<u>n</u> continued, "No one uses the word *tumi* in his speech. If it were commonly used, many people would use it, wouldn't they? You must prove to me that they do." Kampa<u>n</u> simply answered, "All right, I'll prove it tomorrow."

Without taking any food, he went straight to the temple of Ampikai [a local form of Pārvatī, wife of Śiva] and called to her, "Goddess, with your blessings I am a poet sitting in the Raja's court.

He ordered us to compose a Tamil *Rāmāyaṇa* and I told him a lie about a verse with the word *tumi* in it. Now the other poets have challenged me to prove it's used in common speech. Of course, if you don't want to help, it's no loss to me." With this plea, he fell into a half sleep. Then Ampikai appeared and spoke: "Kampaṉ, why worry like this? Before the night has gone tomorrow, bring them all to the shepherds' lane and I will prove to their ears that the word is used." Suddenly she vanished and Kampaṉ felt relieved.

Early next morning, he finished his duties and went quickly to the Raja, who greeted him, "Well, Kampaṉ, can you show us the word *tumi* today?" "I can," he replied, "but you must all come tonight before it gets light." That night, the king, Oṭṭakkūttaṉ, Caṭaiyappaṉ, the ministers, and the other poets stayed awake and were ready. Off they went to the shepherds' lane, where they saw two rows of houses. They looked on both sides, but nowhere was there an open door or a burning lamp. Going ahead, they looked carefully and then, at the very end, they saw a single house with a light. Inside was a woman surrounded by four children. She was churning curds and shouted to the children, "Get back, the *tumi* [drops of liquid splashed while I churn] will fall on you. Watch out for the *tumi*!"

The king, poets, and ministers considered the matter. Why, among all these houses with no one awake and no light, does this single house have a lamp? Who is this woman? And who are the children?[22] They ran forward to find out, but when they reached the spot, there was no house, no children, no woman, no lamp—only a wilderness!

Then Oṭṭakkūttaṉ, the ministers, and everyone there tried to understand what had happened. "This is the work of Ampikai," they said. "It can be nothing else. And Kampaṉ has her powers. How can we debate with him about the use of words? What goddess or god can we summon to help prove our arguments?" And so they felt joy and left that place.

Then Kampaṉ began to write. With the help of the best Tamil scholars and Sanskrit pundits, he composed seven hundred verses between sunrise and sunset every day. In the evening, he would go to Ampikai's temple, bow down to the image that received the rituals, and place his manuscript near it. After his rituals, he would look at it again and all the errors would have been corrected. This is how Kampaṉ wrote his *Rāmāyaṇa* in 12,116 stanzas and six books.

---

[22]Blackburn remarks that local tradition identifies the mysterious woman as Sarasvatī, the goddess of learning, and her children as the four Vedas.

# The Forest Book of the *Rāmāyaṇa* of Kampaṉ

# The Invocation

2605

Under every different form he is the same. Though they branch out,
in him they are one. And only through him do men finally understand
words they have recited over and over. He is the primal lord whom no
[Vedas,
no Brahmins or gods have comprehended! O Knowledge for our
[knowing!

# Paṭalam One
# The Killing of Virādha

1. 2606

Walking with the woman whose smile was like smooth lines of pearls,
the two young men with curving beautiful bows arrived at the place
of peace where Atri lived, he who had endured harsh tapas
in the forest thick with groves of fruit trees, leafy and ripe.

2. 2607

The young men who were like the elephants, trunks thick with gold
and small-eyed, the sight of whom makes one realize the great burden
they carry of the world, entered and bowed to the pure holy man
who had conquered all his ignorance and anger and desire,

3. 2608

who said, "Your coming here, your granting me the chance to see you
is no small thing. As if all the gods and all the worlds had come,
isn't it? O young men! No one must have endured more tapas than I
for this blessing!" and joy flooded him as if all his family had arrived.

4. 2609

They stayed that night, there with the great muni, and they left
with Sītā now wearing clothes worthy of her, jewels and sandal paste
commanded for her by Anasūyā, the chaste and precious wife of Atri.
They entered the Daṇḍaka Forest with her, the gold of her father
[Janaka.

5. 2610

Then they saw him coming with his powerful three-bladed trident,
sharp and well-made, over his shoulder while spitted to its prongs,
all in order, were sixteen rutting elephants, thirty-two lions
and sixteen mountainous yāḷis, with their round blazing eyes.

6. 2611

His head was a tangled mass of dense, burning red hair
and he was rushing across the earth, with force enough to make
giant, glowing, cloud-encircled mountains blow away like cotton
in the power of the wind. He was like a walking hill of poison.

7. 2612

Fire came foaming out of his eyes that gleamed like wounds. The sky
[surrounded
by its clouds trembled. The mountains were shaking. As the sun saw
[him,
it slowed down and lost heart. The earth bounded by the great ocean
quivered. And even the mighty god of the dead, Yama, felt weak.

8. 2613

On the ears so large that glowing lions could enter them and roar, the
[peaks
of Mount Meru with their glistening jewels were his earrings. For bright
sandal paste he had smeared his chest with the blood men had spilled
fighting him and he seemed a black cloud arising in a red evening sky.

9. 2614

Soldiers-at-arms, galloping horses, enormous elephants, chariots,
[shining
striding lions, tigers that hunt prey—all of them had been scooped up
and knotted together with snakes into many massive rows of varied
garlands that were swaying as they stood out across his shoulders.

10. 2615

Heaped like hills pressed together between his fingers were roaring
angry elephants in rut which his large hands fed to his gigantic mouth
that went on and on like a cave, while at one end of it he was
biting and chewing without ever being satisfied, as his hunger grew.

11. 2616

He had seized jewels from the hoods of the snake kings and cracking
[them up,
then sorting them out on the flying chariots of the gods, he had strung
[them all
tightly on a snake where they were flanked with planets and with stars
clanking on his victory garland as it glittered across his broad chest.

12. 2617

Decorating his forehead that rose up large as a water jar, he was wearing
the forehead jewel of Indra's elephant pouring out light, while from its
[tusks
he had taken the ornaments for armlets now in place below his
[shoulders
and they shone beside his hair that hung down like a burning evening
[sky.

13. 2618

He was like the coming of the final age of a world, smeared over with
[darkness,
poison and glowing fire, the worst evils rising up in the midst of it
so as to wipe out anything of worth, and bubbling and seething with
[cruelty,
a deep black growth spreading everywhere, dense and fierce and abiding.

14. 2619

Wrapped around his body were the pelts of tigers cut down by his sword
and he had many elephant hides that were circling his waist and thighs,
held on by a belt of mountain-snake skin set with glittering
heaps of jewels from the elephants of the air that he had defeated.

15. 2620

He wore bracelets shaped like snakes with their red cruel eyes
made of rubies beyond compare plucked from long crimson-eyed
[cobras
and on his hands he wore white bangles of the precious calañcalam
[conch—
rarest among the ocean's heaped conches—that makes a roar.

16. 2621

As he moved majestically along on feet that could kick golden Mount
[Meru
and the silver mountain of Kailāsa, one after another, as if they were
[balls,
even though he had come here and taken his place on earth, his power
was enough to fill the eyes and minds of the gods in their heaven.

17. 2622

Why not say he had a body of a form that could contain all
beings, a thing utterly unheard of, with a voice like the thunder?
To appease the fire of his tapas, Brahmā had gladly given him
the strength of one hundred and twenty-five thousand elephants in rut.

18. 2623

His name was Virādha and he blocked their way, his mere presence
rising up with the force to break open mountains and shake trees in the
[earth.
The demon, with savage burning eyes, whose acts had been as cruel as
lightning, faced the heroes with strong bows who had till now gone in
[peace.

19. 2624

"Stop where you are!" he shouted, opening wide the cave of his mouth,
flashing strong teeth and white fangs dripping the fat of meat just eaten,
and as he came, with one hand, before she could make a sound, he
[scooped up
the woman who was like Lakṣmī on her lotus flower, and he moved on
[though the sky.

20. 2625

The young warriors raced after him, as anger came over them at the
[sight,
crying out to the cunning demon, "Where are you going? Halt! Turn
and come back!" Their left hands were at their shoulders on their strong
[bows
and in the other hand each was carrying his bright-tipped arrows.

21. 2626

"I cannot be killed!" said the Rākṣasa, "Brahmā the Creator gave me
[that boon.
Even if all the worlds were to come into battle against me, I could,
without a weapon, defeat them all. Look, fool, I've given you your life!
Go away now, the two of you, quietly, and leave this woman to me."

22. 2627

Then the hero let the white moonlight of his soft smile show
just a little, while he was thinking, "This one, when it comes to battle,
knows nothing. All his glitter and power will crumble and vanish away,"
and to show his mind, he twanged the string of his heavy, terrifying bow.

23. 2628

Rāma the warrior, whose spear had a leaflike blade, who was like a rising
[cloud,
made the noise of his long wrist-guard scraping the bowstring resound,
roaring like thunder through the seven worlds—the earth of high
[mountains circled
by waves of the ocean and the underworlds of the snakes and the
[heavens with their gods.

24. 2629

The demon set down the woman screaming like a parrot shrewdly
[seized
from its cage and writhing in the huge mouth of a cruel cat, and Virādha
stood for a bit, thinking, as if something had shaken his heart to the
[root,
swelling with anger at that hero who was huge and dark as a mountain of
[collyrium.

25. 2630

Whirling his trident, he hurled it, the weapon so heavy that its points
could spill enough enemy blood to quiet the hunger of those ghosts
[who eat the dead,
and it seemed to have on its blades the fire that rises underwater
out of the mouth of a shining horse and then drinks up the northern
[ocean.

26. 2631

As that trident sailed flashing like the poison that rose churned from the
[primal
ocean of milk, making the gods and the worlds and the directions of
[space
and the elephants who stand in space all tremble, Rāma, with his
[victorious
bow that was as strong as the seven tallest mountains, loosed an arrow.

27. 2632

And the trident shedding light all around it was cut in two, the broken
pieces shooting to the ends of space, so that it seemed as if there were
giant comets falling in bright daylight, crossing the empty sky
as a sign that, from this day forward, the race of Rākṣasas was doomed.

28. 2633

Though he saw the trident that had humbled gods split in two and fall,
nothing of the demon's courage lessened. Raging for battle, he seized
mountains in his hands, tearing them up by the roots so that the earth
shrank back from him, and he flung them in quick succession at Rāma.

29. 2634

All around Rāma the mountains flew, but his hard glittering arrows,
strong heads and feathers glowing, split them apart as they came,
sending mountain after mountain in pieces back at the bulk of the
striking him everywhere, all over him so fast that his body flowed with

30. 2635

The demon uprooted a giant marā tree and with it came at Rāma who is
the sacred syllable Om, whose names are known to those of fullest
[knowledge,
who had left his floating bed of the snake and had descended
to maintain the Order of the World and was standing on this earth.

31. 2636

The hero Rāma, with four of his arrows, shivered the tree apart
into many separate pieces that fell instantly from the air,
then shot his sharp burning arrows that beat and beat at Virādha,
six of them sinking at a time into his towering chest and shoulders.

32. 2637

As if an immense porcupine, wounded, in the sudden rise of his anger,
had erected the quills that encase his body and stretched them out taut
and brandished them back and forth, so Virādha seemed, bristling,
throwing off and scattering the arrows that had rapidly covered him.

33. 2638

Though Rāma kept shooting the long arrows that were now running
[without stopping
anywhere, like fire clear through the Rākṣasa, so that many rivers of
[blood
streamed from him like waterfalls down a mountain, making him grow
[weak,
making him lose his power, still the courage never wavered in his mind.

34. 2639

"He has a true miraculous gift," the brothers thought, "he will not die
as we attack with our strong bows. He will always fight on," and they
[drew
their fierce swords and, thinking to cut off his arms, through their
[strength of hand
in archery and wrestling quickly climbed up to the demon's huge
[shoulders.

35. 2640

Coming to his senses, he knew Rāma and Lakṣmaṇa were on him and
[he clasped them,
holding them there with his arms that were like uplifted bludgeons and
[himself
straightened up swiftly, carrying them off with a speed ten times more
rapid than before while the falling blood poured down from him in
[sheets.

36. 2641

Rushing so fast, and so lofty that he seemed to be battering against
the high peak of the sky, he spun around in a whirlwind of flowing
[blood,
the brothers turning on his shoulders as if they were the sun and the
[moon
who come every day to circle Mount Meru, as men circumambulate a
[temple.

37. 2642

They balanced themselves on him while, making a great noise, he rose
high into the sky, and it seemed they were again, as in other lives,
Kṛṣṇa and Balarāma, riding the wings of Garuḍa, giant king of birds,
on their way into battle to maintain the Order of the World.

38. 2643

As her husband, whose deep compassion she knew, was carried off
by the cruel Virādha, that woman of noble family, Sītā,
with her hair in the dust, like a broken vine, numbed and almost
[fainting,
fell to the ground like a wild goose whose mate has been taken from her.

39. 2644

And she found no friend nor any words to help her, but getting up,
with her waist like a quiver of lightning, she quickly ran after him.
"Let them go, they who are the Order of the World, they who are like
a mother to all," and, falling again, she said, "Let me be your food!"

40. 2645

Weeping, babbling words, her precious life in danger, lost in her
[confusion,
she was like a painted picture of grief. Lakṣmaṇa saw and said, bowing
[to Rāma,
"To play at this would be a mistake when your queen suffers! May you
live long!" and then he spoke who was and is before all the aeons of
[time.

41. 2646

"I had thought it would be good for us to climb on him and ride him
in comfort and speed as far as we may want to go but now,
my matchless brother, his death will be nothing at all," and he whose
[smile
is his very nature kicked the demon over instantly and Virādha fell.

42. 2647

Swiftly with their sharp swords they cut off his arms. Then as the strong
warriors leaped from his shoulders, he swung his eyes toward them,
raging red with his anger, and the brows were curving like scorpions.
He looked like the Snake Planet pursuing the sun and moon to
[consume them.

43. 2648

Though the blood of his life came spilling out of his wounds, he would
[not
die and the hero, knowing that the demon would rise to his feet again
as enemy, thought the matter through and made his plan. "Lakṣmaṇa,"
he said, "the right way is to bury him quickly under the earth."

44. 2649

Then Lakṣmaṇa, like a fine rutting elephant, dug a channel in the
[ground
and they turned a river into it over the body of Virādha, thrust there
by him who has no faults, whose feet are lovely, who fulfills the desires
of those who, loving him, drink the ghee and become pure sacrificial
[fires.

45. 2650

And leaving the lowly body in which, because of a powerful curse
once placed on him, he had endured the fierce pain of birth, now
[knowing
his former lives, he rose shining in the sky, like the ancient first cause,
Brahmā the Creator, when the universe began as a single golden egg.

46. 2651

And by means of a thought that set him firmly on the path that cannot
be reached by a mind that wanders away to objects of the senses, and
[also because,
from his former lives, he carried a love that had not abandoned him,
knowledge came to aid him. He recognized and spoke to the Lord.

47. 2652

"You whose feet cover the world,
whose anklets resound like the Vedas,
how many forms are there for you
to have, you who are everywhere!
Between destruction and creation of a universe
you lie on the cool ocean of milk
and still you enter into all the disparate
elements! How can they possibly contain you?

48. 2653

"When the elephant who worshiped you, his foot
seized by an angry crocodile, raised
his trunk in the air, with his body in pain,
crying out in every direction around him,
'O you who are near, great and incomparable god,
cause of all, difficult to know,
highest one! highest one!' didn't you then
answer, 'Why do you need me?'

49. 2654

"The loving glances of your eyes,
like lotuses that never change
in your calm face, see all
we do in our acts and inside ourselves!
How is it that you wander like a kite
blown around across the sky,
since there is no one strong enough to help you
in maintaining the Order of the World?

50. 2655

"When those are born who have been born
    before to a life where they were completely free,
do they forget what they have been?
    How can they be born as others are born?
How difficult could it be for them
    to take on again the state they had?
O you who have willed for your pleasure
    the game called birth-and-death!

51. 2656

"You are the beautiful form
    of the truth which stands alone,
valued by all those who follow
    the many religions but embrace
you so they may cross beyond
    the great, frightening ocean
of birth! What can even the chiefs
    of gods do, compared with you?

52. 2657

"For the gods who do not die,
    of whom Brahmā on his lotus
was the first and is in continuous
    creation, for everything that lives,
you are the father, the ultimate source!
    Then who is the mother who
bore them and raised them well? O
    single body of the World's Order!

53. 2658

"Beyond the highest, you
    are the beginning, yours
the worlds! And every religion
    bows to you, none of them
understanding you! Why do you hide
    like a criminal? Would it be wrong for you
to appear? Why do you need this great
    unceasing game of illusions?

54. 2659

"No calf can ever forget
    its mother, and every mother
knows its calf. Since you, Lord!
    are mother of the world, you
know everything! but nothing
    can know your being. Why
these illusions, you who are
    already here when you come?

55. 2660

"The world finds many,
    many gods to praise
but the highest give their devotion
    to no great god but you,
for those on the path know that Brahmā
    riding his wild goose and all the other
gods that the Brahmins pray to
    are, without you, nothing!

56. 2661

"Never agreeing, the religions
    worship gods who, like men
of good and bad karma, endure
    arduous tapas to acquire power,
but you are the one on whose precious chest the goddess
    Śrī lies. What is there you need do?
Like those with no karma at all, always
    in deep yogic sleep, you are awake!

57. 2662

"You were the primal snake who carried
    the lovely earth. You were the boar
who lifted her on your tusks, the dwarf
    who strode over her with a step
and in a single bite you swallow her
    when universes end! Wouldn't Śrī
be angry if she knew, who rests on your chest
    with its jewel and fragrant tulsi garland?

58. 2663

"O Lord, what harm could come to you
  if you would save those living beings,
your creation, by letting them know
  only a little of the real truth?
Those who had doubts of you on earth
  or in the heavens were answered
when you gave Śiva the alms
  that at long last filled his bowl!

59. 2664

"When you were a boar, you stabbed
  at the ground. As a wild goose,
before creation, you pronounced the difficult
  Vedas. Did someone teach them to you,
then die? You who are single,
  yet multiple, are you separate
or inseparable from all? How strong
  over everything is Māyā!

60. 2665

"God far beyond all that is! Because,
  in my lives, I who am your servant
have carried through arduous tapas, you,
  leaving your sleep on the waters, came to me
and now I have crossed the ocean of birth.
  I will not be reborn! You have wiped away
my karma, the good and the bad,
  with your feet that have the glow of coral!"

61. 2666

He said all this and
when he stopped, the victor
said to him, "How did you come
to your birth in this form?"

62. 2667

"I praise you who give so much!
The knowledge pouring from your feet
destroys evil births! Hear
me out now!" and he told his story.

63. 2668

"O hero with a blazing bow!
Though born in this world, in this body,
my name was Tumbaru in that heaven
of the sky where one can live for ages.

64. 2669

"When Rambhā danced and sang
on the great stage, I felt joy
and because of making love to her then,
I entered this cage of a body.

65. 2670

"Driven by the misery of desire
to the sin that made what I know
disappear, I was cursed mercilessly
to become a Rākṣasa's son.

66. 2671

"Kubera condemned me but gave
the gift that would cut off my suffering,
O first being! when he told me
how it would end at your feet.

67. 2672

"I became son to Kaliñja, that demon
who won flashing victories, circling
heaven as if it were a temple, tormenting
and consuming it with his deadly spear.

68. 2673

"Since then till now, O first
being! in my ignorance, I have not
known the good from the bad
and I have stubbornly followed evil.

69. 2674

"Touched by your feet that in beauty
wear the wisdom of the Vedas desired
by all since ancient times,
my mind today has cleared.

70. 2675

"In my ignorance I have harmed you,
O eternity! you who have cut off
all the flow of evil I amassed!
Forgive me!" he said and was gone.

71. 2676

The two master archers, thinking,
"His life has ended who was famous
for fighting the gods," moved on then
with the woman who wore swaying flowers.

72. 2677

Their deadly spears in hand, they came
to a dense grove where holy men
who embody the truthful Vedas
live, and they stayed there the day.

## Paṭalam Two
## Śarabhaṅga Escapes Saṃsāra

1. 2678

As night was falling, the brothers and the woman like a branch
blossoming with kuṟava flowers and clusters of koṅku
came to the fragrant grove where Śarabhaṅga meditates
on his tapas in the midst of shining koṅku and saffron trees.

2. 2679

And as they drew near with their crimsoned spears, Indra,
king of gods in heaven, came to visit the sage
and every one of his thousand eyes was shining clearly
like glowing lotuses that never close even in the night.

3. 2680

From all over his body, a great rich radiance
shone out like thick sheaves of lightning bursting open,
interweaving and surpassing the light of the ornaments on his golden
women who surrounded him like wild geese walking on the earth.

4. 2681

His ears were bees absorbed in the honey of the music
the holy Nārada, garlanded, was playing on the veena,
and his eyes were drunken bees settling on the forest
of eyes like flowers of his shining women of the sky.

5. 2682

That mighty ruler had performed the hundred sacrifices
at the site of the Vedic fire with every requirement of tradition,
and the gold of his anklets had felt the touch of crowns
worn by all the ancient gods except for the highest three.

6. 2683

With his wife as beautiful as the Goddess of Wealth who sits
on her great red flower, Indra rode his fierce elephant,
striding and white, glowing with the three flows of rut,
and he looked like Śiva, master of the tall silvery mountain.

7. 2684

His white umbrella shone as if the heaven in the sky
had taken on this form and descended to hover above him
so that, next to it, the moon of cool rays shrank away
and found no purpose in remaining while that umbrella shone.

8. 2685

His chowry glittered as if he had lashed together all the fame
that had abandoned the Asuras when they lost their speed and balance
and were entangled on the ripe liquid of rut during their many
pitched battles with the elephants who are stationed in the air.

9. 2686

The gleaming of his crown made it seem that the radiant sun
who roams around without resting had found a city to live in
and his necklace of gems glowed like Śrī at the precious
chest of Viṣṇu, skilled warrior of the discus.

10. 2687

His blazing armor was pouring out clusters of rays
from the rubies that flared in it like embedded suns
while the bracelets shining all around his arms were like
the white cooling laughter of the Goddess of Victory.

11. 2688

As the swarms of brilliance streaming from the ornaments
worn since ancient times sparkled out, in many thousands
of great jewels all flashing at once, he seemed
like a dark cloud glowing with one of his own rainbows.

12. 2689

He had a beautiful garland that was thick with honey
and fragrance sweet enough to fill the disparate worlds
and he wore a sword that, like the eyes of his heavenly women,
had the shape of a fish and wins the highest victories.

13. 2690

He carried a weapon of indestructible lightning, the sharpness
of its blade not blunted, nor the luster lessened, nor chipped
so much as the tip of a rice grain, when, eager for the victory,
he fiercely hurled it at Rāvaṇa whose garland was like the sunlight.

14. 2691

So he stood and, facing him, the sage who had performed
great tapas welcomed him and walked with him in respect
and with grace, and when Śarabhaṅga said, "Why have you come?"
he whose golden anklets never wear away answered:

15. 2692

"The moment Brahmā realized not even he could approach
any description of your powerful and fitting tapas,
he called on you to be with him, O you who have endured
arduous tapas, come, with your matted golden hair!

16. 2693

"He who created all the worlds and every being
gives you a place to live, my father! and he himself
will come out to meet you as you arrive in that land, won
by the greatest tapas, the merit of which does not perish.

17. 2694

"You are of an age to know, without my explaining it,
how much higher that heaven is than all the other worlds,
go there now at once with your pure wife!" and at that,
the sage with his faultless knowledge answered, "I will not.

18. 2695

"O you whose fame foams up in the words of men! shall I
become part of things that perish like paintings when their color
fades? I have no wish at all for something so slight!
Do you see the tapas I have endured, as the aeons passed!

19. 2696

"O god who wears the anklets! This is not worth discussing.
It would be like having gotten something which even
in the having is not mine. But what good are so many words?
I came here and have finished the time I needed for my tapas.

20. 2697

"Ruler of the heavens, I will reach that place which is imperishable
even when every being is swept away in the great wind,
a place that is utter purity, no growth, no lessening,
the unchanging state beyond the smallness of time."

21. 2698

And as the sage was speaking of these things in this way,
the two heroes arrived, carrying their powerful bows,
and they stopped a moment to think because they heard a noise
rising from the place and they wondered what it could be.

22. 2699

"We can see an elephant standing at a diamond-studded post,
glowing and with four tusks that are exactly even,
and so," Rāma knew and said, "this is the king of the higher world
who has come to visit the greatest of ascetics here on earth."

23. 2700

Outside the grove that was filled with flowers, Rāma left
his younger brother and the woman who was like a doe,
and he entered the spacious grove, moving in a way
that seemed like a bull or like the male among lions.

24. 2701

Those thousand eyes of the king of gods like lotuses
turned toward Rāma, who seemed to be a dark sun
come down on this earth, and Indra knew that he was seeing
the fruit of the Four Vedas that is so hard to reach.

25. 2702

He saw who this was and was stunned and his heart was troubled
and he with his noble crown, he with his arms like columns,
he who bows down every day to this ruler of those who are holy
threw himself to the ground before a form of the highest Lord.

26. 2703

As he saw that being who protects him from destruction, like his armor
    or his precious life or his eyes, or tapas truly endured
or limitless knowledge, as he saw the killer of enemies in the ancient
[battles
    where many flags waved, who teaches the words and substance of
[the great
ocean of revelation, who is a guide for every day of living on the path
    of good conduct and the giver of riches in this world and of ultimate
liberation, his power of thought wiped out by that presence,
[unconsciously,
    as if he knew nothing at all, Indra spoke all that he knew.

27. 2704

"Though you pervade everything, nothing can contain you, O
    light! you who become kin to those who break all attachment!
Ocean of great compassion that is so broad no one
    could find a boat to cross it! O knowledge
of what can be known through following the way of the Vedas!
    When we who are your servants, harried by our enemies,
praise your feet, at once, my father! you come with your help.
    Can these be the two lotuses of your feet touching the wide earth?

28. 2705

"There are no enemies for you and there are no friends,
neither light nor darkness, no up and no down,
not youth or old age, no beginning or middle
or end, no before and no after, O God!
If I have described you as you are and have always been
while you come now with your bow, troubling your beautiful feet,
if you were not to protect us, what blame could cling to you
or what recompense for your favor, dark sleeper on the ocean of
[milk!

29. 2706

"If Brahmā himself whom you created with his four faces
seated within his lotus were to use all the faultless worlds
for his measuring rod and to measure for many aeons, he could not
arrive at even one of your perfect virtues! O most high!
On that ancient day when you made the earth a churn
and the giant mountain your stick, giving pain to the lotuses
of your hands, you churned amṛta from the ocean for the gods,
only for us! Were the Asuras you refused it to any less your slaves?

30. 2707

"At the very root of time, you were one and became
many! You became awareness and lives and bodies!
And when an aeon has reached its end and passes, once more
you are one! and then again you become the varied world!
O incomparable, ever-new sprouting of knowledge! Magnificent
and good! You who take away our sins, you who protect
those whose will is good and burn the others down,
but Lord, aren't even the evanescent acts of evil your own creation?

31. 2708

"When the limitless power of Māyā long ago deluded us
into joining with those who are confused and question
whether or not you are the Lord and the first cause of all,
as we struggled with our ignorance in those days, didn't you
dispel the doubt that blocked our way and give us access
to the fruit of our righteous conduct when the ancient
Seven Rishis swore, touching the fire for their witness,
that the worlds as far as they may reach are all yours!"

32. 2709

Speaking out his thoughts in these many ways, Indra,
who wears a great crown of shining gold, praised Rāma
and fully understanding what the incomparable holy man
now had to do, he asked leave to go and departed.

33. 2710

In his wisdom, the sadhu, understanding what Indra had felt,
went out to welcome this coming of the highest god,
bowing to Rāma's feet, weeping at the grace that had reached him
as he was about to enter the state he had earned the right to enter.

34. 2711

"May you live with happiness," he said, "let the woman and the young
[man
come," and Rāma went with them, moved by joy as he approached
the ashram of the sage who, aeons past, had begun his tapas and now
could rejoice, thinking, "This is he who sleeps on the ocean of milk."

35. 2712

And there Rāma, in his beauty, with the woman who had eyes
like a doe, remained and he listened to the wise man's
beneficent and righteous words, until that night
which had richly embraced the darkness came to an end.

36. 2713

The sun with its radiance streaming out, its light
shining and penetrating every direction like the fame of Rāma,
with its numberless masses of hands that are rays,
cut the world's covering of darkness away like a sharp sword.

37. 2714

In front of himself, the sage readied a blazing fire
prepared according to the forms handed down by tradition
and with the pure intent of entering the massive
flames, said to Rāma, "Give me your permission."

38. 2715

And he who was skilled with his well-made bow said to him
who was skilled in the Vedas, "Tell me what you will do," and the sage
said, "Husband of the Goddess of Wealth, so that I may attain
the utmost wealth, I intend to enter the fire. I ask permission."

39. 2716

Rāma said, "Why will you do this, just at the time I have come?
You who wear the matchless deerskin on your chest!" and the warrior
who had put an end to the victories of the God of Desire
spoke out in the great ecstasy that came over his body!

40. 2717

"I have endured the thousand faces of tapas, always
sure you would arrive, here where I am! O conqueror!
My good and my bad karma are no more, now that you have come,
as had to be, and there is nothing more I need to do.

41. 2718

"Indra came to me and he told me the day of my death was here,
and he said, 'Brahmā has offered you his world, come
there to stay!' but I would not go with him. O power!
I strive to reach that high state which is endless.

42. 2719

"Because of my effort, grant I may attain it," he said, who had [understood
the highest truth, hard to know even from the Vedas, and with
the woman he loved he sank himself into the raging fire
and did reach that place which is indescribable unity.

43. 2720

Where the gods and holy men, those who know the future, and Brahmā
who sits on his flower that is good and fragrant and all
the others, where they wish to go, ridding themselves of their karma,
good and bad, through knowledge, that place so hard to reach he [entered.

44. 2721

If they enjoy unthinkable good fortune who know even
a single name of the being who, in some inconceivable way,
consumes the universe and all it holds, can the state
of those who see him at the moment of death even be imagined?

# Paṭalam Three
# Agastya

1. 2722

Those young men, the sight of whom is sweet, saw how that muni
came to his end and, with their strong curving bows
and the woman who was like a branch, they slowly moved on,
sad at his passing, away from the pure sage's grove.

2. 2723

Then they crossed mountains and forests and hills that were dark
as blue sapphires and lapping rivers of water and waterfalls
running down slopes and thick-leaved groves, pleasant land,
and with pleasure they walked past ponds that were full and deep.

3. 2724

And all the saints who endure their tapas in the Daṇḍaka forest,
the Vālakhilyas born long ago from the hair of Brahmā
and those who shave their heads and those who vow silence
rejoiced within their hearts as soon as they saw Rāma.

4. 2725

Where before they were in grief, helpless against the Rākṣasas
who raged after them with fierce and unremitting anger,
now they were like dry leaves in a forest that has caught fire
but returns to life under rain falling like the drink of immortality.

5. 2726

The pain of suffering was lifted from them and they who had been [unable
to do anything but murmur the names of the Rākṣasas whose great [strength
had kept increasing now became like a calf that had been left
behind in a burning forest when it sees that its mother is returning.

6. 2727

For them, who had been wasting away, despondent, without means
to fight against the attacks of the Rākṣasas from whom
they could not hide, it was as if, while sinking in an ocean
of Rākṣasas, a raft had come and they were released from suffering.

7. 2728

They looked at him to grasp who he really was, and since the tapas
they had labored at performing gave them wisdom and insight
hard to attain, they felt as if they were liberated from the great prison
of birth that had surrounded them, binding them in fierce pain.

8. 2729

Even though they had performed the true tapas that gives whatever
is desired, they had rid themselves first of anger that flashes
and spreads and so, because of the strength of their forbearance,
they were tormented by the Rākṣasas living in that forest.

9. 2730

They rose up, they came to him, toward the great hero who was dark
as a cloud that has just drunk water from the ocean.
They came to him with love springing up and overflowing
and as he bowed to each one, all of them blessed him.

10. 2731

They took him to a pleasant hut of leaves and arranged
a fitting place for him where he was asked to rest, and they
whose tapas had been arduous went to their own dwellings.
Then all of them returned to speak with him about their trouble.

11. 2732

Sitting there, the Lord bowed to the sages, happy to see them
and praising them as they came. "What may I do for you?" he said,
and they answered, "Son of the protector of the world! Listen
to what has happened because of fierce, cruel violence!

12. 2733

"There are these creatures called Rākṣasas whose hearts
are without mercy, who shun all righteous action,
and because they torment us, we have had to follow ways
we should not and have abandoned our arduous tapas.

13. 2734

"We are like deer in a forest where many tigers roam,
we grieve, we are sad night and day, we cannot endure it,
we have strayed from the path prescribed as righteous conduct.
You who hold the bow in your arms! Will we see our liberation?

14. 2735

"We cannot perform arduous tapas nor can we recite
all the Vedas or give to those who do recite them.
We do not keep the ancient fires. Because we have strayed
from the right path, we are not any longer even Brahmins!

15. 2736

"As for Indra, in his heart he accepts the acts of the Rākṣasas,
taking their commands upon his head as if he were their servant.
Our father! Who else do we have to liberate us of our pain?
You have come to us because of the great tapas we have endured!

16. 2737

"Son of that opulent king who protected the world, rolling
the wheel of his law, we have remained in darkness
that never lifts and you have appeared like the sun.
Hero with the grace to help us, we turn to you for refuge!"

17. 2738

And he who was descended from the line of the sun said, "Unless
they should come to me for shelter, even if they were
to escape to another universe, they will fall by my arrows.
You must give up this sorrow that does not become you.

18. 2739

"Though the king my father died because of it and my mother
suffered, and my mighty younger brother lamented
and the people of my city deeply felt their great misery,
it must be my good karma that brought me to this forest.

19. 2740

"If I do not overwhelm those low beings who have forgotten
the worth of Brahmins firmly on the path of Righteousness,
I would be better dead. If it were not to accomplish this,
why have I obtained the good fortune of being born?

20. 2741

"When you men of the towering Vedas, with joy,
will see the dancing of the rows of headless bodies,
ah then my arms will be lightened of their painful weight
of the quiver, the deadly arrows, and the well-made bow!

21. 2742

"Those who go to their deaths for cows or for Brahmins
or in behalf of the weak or for the good of anyone,
they turn into gods to whom even the gods, those
living in the greatness of paradise, must bow down.

22. 2743

"Even if Murukaṉ who cut down the Asura Cūr were to protect them
or Viṣṇu of the glittering discus or Śiva who destroyed
the three cities, I will cut off at the root all those who stand
against the Order of the World," he said, "Do not be afraid."

23. 2744

When they heard his words, they were overjoyed. Love
rose up in them so that all their pain was gone and they shouted
to the skies, twirled their tridents, sang the sweetness
of the Vedas, danced dances, and then they stood and they said,

24. 2745

"Hero! Even if there were three hundred million worlds
like this triple world coming against you all
together, they could not be equal to you in your anger.
Our great knowledge, gained from tapas, is witness to it!

25. 2746

"Because you are who you are, stay with us for your pleasure
all the years you must and protect us from suffering!"
And the son of the mighty king of kings bowed to the feet
of those who had endured great tapas and there he remained.

26. 2747

The young men lived there for ten years in peace and
without harm. And those whose tapas was great came to realize,
then told them, "Now you must go to Agastya," and the brothers
went off with her whose lovely forehead was like the moon.

27. 2748

They moved slowly, along narrow paths, through forests
thick with bamboo, over rocks that had cracked open,
till they reached the grove where the holy man Sutīkṣṇa
lives, his body shining and beyond the touch of suffering.

28. 2749

When those who have no pride in their hearts bowed down
to the holy man whose feet were glowing like the sun,
he said to them gently, "You may stay here with me,"
and the young men remained there in the fragrant grove.

29. 2750

Once they were there, the sage who had performed arduous tapas,
having welcomed them in all the ways he could, asked Rāma,
"What tapas have I endured to merit your coming here?
O great wealth!" and the Lord answered him with love.

30. 2751

"Of your ancestors, born in the line of that Brahmā
whom the world praises, are there any who have completed
loftier tapas than you and can there have been anyone born
to a more fortunate family than I who have gained your grace?"

31. 2752

To this speech of the hero for whom all comparisons fail,
he who had been performing the fiercest tapas for aeons
answered, "Receive the merit of all the tapas that I
have endured, as my offering for so worthy a guest."

32. 2753

And that Rāma who gives everything said to the sage
whose skill was the Vedas, "Lord, your kindness is worth
more than any tapas. There is but one thing now I ask.
The only need that I have is the sight of Agastya."

33. 2754

"What you wish to do, O hero! is right and I had
already decided I would give you that advice.
Go there! Go to him! and after you have gone,
there is nothing worth having that will not come to you.

34. 2755

"And what is more, because he desires your coming,
he has been happy to wait for you till now. So go!
Reach him!" he said, "O excellence! Your going there
is a good thing for the gods, a good thing for everyone!"

35. 2756

He told them the way and gave them endless blessings
as they bowed to the feet like closely set flowers of the sage
whose tapas was great. Quickly they went to Agastya's grove
where waterfalls shine with the honey that oozes from the combs.

36. 2757

Agastya knew they had come there,
 the strong young men,
and as he came out to meet them,
 Rāma, granter of wishes,
bowed to the feet of him
 who with the great Tamil language
had measured the world as the god
 of the discus did with three steps.

37. 2758

When, long ago, the gods said,
 "The Asuras hide in the sea
and will not die, help us, you
 whose tapas deserves veneration!"
seeing them begging in need, he,
 scooping up all the ocean in a hand,
swallowed it. And when they said, "Vomit it up!"
 Agastya vomited out the waters.

38. 2759

He made the water his food
 purely and then he gave it back,
and because of it his body shines,
 he who was happy to consume
the strong body of Vātāpi,
 the Asura whose acts were deceitful
as swords, and removed that pain
 so hard to remove from the world.

39. 2760

"How will those great beings
 who practice yoga come
to be without suffering?" he thought
 and climbed up and kicked
the Vindhya mountain with its long
 slowly turning garland of clouds
from its place in the sky down
 to hell and stood on it like an elephant.

40. 2761

When long ago the north
    sank low under the weight
of gods, the high god who wears
    thick snakes, addressing him as "You
of ageless flawless tapas!" ordered
    him to the Malaya higher than the sky
and he stood there, as Śiva's equal,
    balancing the world again.

41. 2762

Rising to great heights
    by study of the four Vedas
and by examining poetic and ordinary
    speech as they should be considered,
like the radiant god whose axe
    glitters, whose red eye burns
from his lovely forehead, who gave the sage
    the language, Agastya gave men Tamil.

42. 2763

And Agastya's heart was overjoyed
    as he thought, "What is for everyone
only a conception in the mind,
    though present somewhere
in the sky, on the earth, in the disparate
    worlds or within great wisdom,
I will now come to experience
    ah! in front of my eyes!

43. 2764

"That entity unknown even
    to Brahmā, were he to grind
the four loudly chanted Vedas
    and all their attendant *śāstras*
for many days on the high
    grinding stone of great knowledge,
stands before me now, will speak,
    will help me!" he felt and was happy.

44. 2765

Utterly certain, he thought, "They,
the gods, whose eyes do not
blink, are saved! They who endure
tapas have returned to life.
Brahmins again stand on the path
of Righteous Action. A healer
has come to cut down the poison
of the Rākṣasas' cruel strength."

45. 2766

His heart swelled up as he realized,
"A cloud has appeared in the sky
that will protect the world by putting out
at once the forest fire of the Rākṣasas
with their anger that can burn up
even thunder, eating the flesh
of beings, swallowing into itself
all the trees that are others' lives!"

46. 2767

As he saw Rāma coming,
the love in him grew strong.
He stood there as tears fell
from his eyes bright as lotuses,
he who had carried the faultless
Kāverī River in his pitcher
so that the eight directions, the seven worlds
and all beings would be saved.

47. 2768

The greatness that had come bowed down
to the feet of him who stood there,
and Agastya embraced him then with love
as the tears flowed from his eyes,
and said, "It is good that you
have come" and many more
gracious words, he who is famed
for speaking the sweet, eternal Tamil.

48. 2769

As the Brahmins chanted many other
    blessings from the Vedas and, filled
with love, sprinkled the good water
    from their pitchers that were beautiful,
as those who had endured great tapas
    strewed large, fine flowers,
Agastya led him into the grove,
    cool and fragrant with blossoms.

49. 2770

That Rāma without fault gladly
    entered the grove as his heart
wished him to, and the muni gave him
    the food of hospitality and said,
"King full of compassion! That you
    have come to my home
is reward for the arduous tapas
    that I began so long ago."

50. 2771

To the muni who had said this,
    Rāma bowing answered, "Even the gods,
even the greatest among the great,
    who have done tapas that endures,
have not received the grace of your presence.
    Yet I have received that grace.
I have conquered the whole world now.
    What—beyond this—can there be for me?"

51. 2772

And the holy man who resembled
    that god who on his towering head
wears the moon said to him,
    "When the news arrived that you
must live in the Daṇḍaka forest, I was
    very happy when I thought
that you, whose virtues are to be honored,
    would be coming to this place!

52. 2773

"Stay with me here, Lord,
    if you stay here now,
you will allow us to finish
    the great acts of tapas that we need,
for if the cruel Rākṣasas whose anger
    continually grows should appear,
you will fight till they die, you will clear
    the suffering hearts of our people!

53. 2774

"The Vedas will live on, Manu's Code
    and Righteousness itself will live on.
The gods who have sunk down will rise
    and the Rākṣasas will sink. Be certain
of this truth, O son of him who plowed
    the world with his wheel!
The seven worlds will live on!
    For now, stay here with me."

54. 2775

"I am ready," said Rāma, "to kill them
    quickly, destroying their arrogance
and sending the evil they have done
    in their pride to nothingness.
It is good that I am standing
    in the south now from where
they come! Master of the Vedas,
    what is it you will have me do?"

55. 2776

"You have spoken beautifully.
    Here is this bow that once
belonged to Viṣṇu, who is source
    of the universe. It is a thing
I and the three worlds worship,
    and take this bundle of sharp
arrows, this quiver that cannot be emptied,"
    Agastya said and gave them to Rāma.

56. 2777

And he gave him a sword that,
    were it set on a scale
against this whole universe,
    might outweigh it, and the strong
incomparable arrow with which Śiva,
    when he took on his form as fire
and used Mount Meru for his bow,
    burned away the three cities.

57. 2778

"Near a region of towering
    dunes and mountains and trees
and cool dense groves
    bright with masses of flowers,
there is a place called Pañcavaṭi,
    near a hill, surrounded by the flow
of a river rippling with waves,
    young man, a place where you should stay.

58. 2779

"Plantain trees that are like young girls
    give fruit, and a fine rice
grows there with sharp-tipped seeds.
    Flowers flow with honey
and the holy river Kāverī
    is always filled with water and cranes
and wild geese for this golden
    woman to play with and love.

59. 2780

"Go there now and stay
    for a time," said the sage,
and he who is the color of a rain cloud
    bowed down and took his leave.
While his younger brother and she
    with her voice sweet as sugarcane
followed him devotedly as the muni did
    in thought, Rāma moved rapidly on.

# Paṭalam Four
# The Sight of Jaṭāyus

1. 2781

They walked for a distance of many *kāvatams*, across
flowing rivers and mountains close by each other
as if in friendship, and they passed through regions where the growth
was dense. Then they saw Jaṭāyus, king of the vultures.

2. 2782

He shone as if the young sun were rising, all molten
gold over the peak of the Eastern Mountain, where it had spread
out its wings through the shining directions of the air,
its bright mass of rays lighting up this wide earth.

3. 2783

Floating near the dark peak of a mountain, he was gleaming
before them as if the light of the moon had been brought
together with and then fastened to Mount Mandara by the gods
for their churning stick fixed in the endless roaring ocean.

4. 2784

He made the loveliness of the dark vanish from the air
and instead, like a long vine that was the color of coral
against a giant blue mountain, the sky had come to glitter
with the ruby radiance of his feet as he hung there shining.

5. 2785

He was pure and a knower of the Vedas, skilled in the great arts,
always truthful, with no faults, of penetrating intelligence,
a being who could consider and investigate and then know,
whose small eyes saw into the distances of space and time.

6. 2786

Because he kept on killing cruel Asuras, a feast that he offered
to Death and he himself then eating the bodies that were left,
his beak glistened, worn down and sharpened every day like the goad
that must be used on the small-eyed elephant of supreme Indra.

7. 2787

He wore a necklace that was like that wheel on which
all the nine planets go whirling around together
and he had a diadem sparkling with a radiance like the sun
when it comes to rest on the summit of high Mount Meru.

8. 2788

He was a mass of glory expanding past the range of words.
He was the son of the Dawn whose coming destroys the night
and he had seen innumerable aeons flowing by and being spent
so quickly they had seemed no more to him than passing days.

9. 2789

Sītā and the brothers, with their minds in doubt, approached him,
the hero who had settled high on a towering mountain
not able to bear him so that, under the weight of his great
strength, it was sinking down into the vast earth.

10. 2790

Those heroes with heavy anklets looked at him in anger
and they thought, "This is a Rākṣasa who knows nothing whatever,
who has dared to come and try to kill us all by himself or else,
if not that, he is the divine and powerful Garuḍa."

11. 2791

And Jaṭāyus himself felt doubt as he looked at the strong
young men with their well-strung bows and finely made anklets
and he thought, "These are not men who do tapas to end their karma.
They carry bows and yet wear their hair matted. Can they be gods?

12. 2792

"Whenever I want to, I can see Indra or any other of the gods.
Not Viṣṇu who carries the discus nor Śiva with the axe
for his weapon or Brahmā, the giver of boons, would withhold
their presence from me! I can see them any time I want!

13. 2793

"And having seen the God of Love with my own eyes, I do not feel
he is equal to the dust on the anklets of those feet
lovely as flowers of these heroes with their great hands
and their eyes tawny as lotuses. Who are these beings?

14. 2794

"On their bodies, the immeasurable signs are seen of those
who could make all the three worlds their own possession.
I do not recognize these strong heroes with their bows
who have come with a woman like the goddess Śrī upon her flower.

15. 2795

"The warriors with their burning eyes seem like a black
and a red mountain! Against their chests, the Goddess
of Victory lies in joy. Ah! They resemble my friend
the universal ruler who has power to overcome everything."

16. 2796

With many such thoughts in his heart and with love he flew
toward the heroes with their fierce weapons and he called out,
"Young men! You who are carrying large and well-strung bows!
Who are you? Tell me in words that my mind will understand."

17. 2797

When he asked this, they who had garlands made of flowers
and could speak nothing but the truth answered, "We are the sons
of the universal ruler Daśaratha who, wearing his war anklets,
has protected the broad earth circled by the roaring ocean."

18. 2798

As soon as they had spoken, he was like a surging sea of joy
and, descending to the earth, lovingly embracing them, he said,
"O you with rich fragrant garlands, are the arms of the king
of kings still strong that were as mighty as two mountains?"

19. 2799

Rāma said, "He has gone to paradise and with him he retains
the honor of his word that will never be forgotten." At once
Jaṭāyus, plunged into sorrow at the thought that Daśaratha had known
death, lost consciousness as if he had fallen off to sleep.

20. 2800

They embraced him and lifted him up in their powerful arms
and the two of them washed his face with the water of their tears
and that king, returning to sweet life that had slipped away from him,
wailed out a lament in the desolation of his heart.

21. 2801

"The Wish-Granting Trees that can withhold nothing and the moon,
lord of stars, and this earth circled by ocean
may live at ease now, no longer surpassed by your great virtues—
your indescribable generosity, your cooling umbrella
of royalty and your patience, O king of kings! Enemy of the lie!
Ornament of truth! Living body of glory!
Are you gone? What have you left us to endure, abandoning me and
[your support
of Righteousness and all those who come to you in their need?

22. 2802

"O you whose umbrella of royalty without equal has ornamented
the world and freed it of death, have you
moved on, leaving the earth bounded by the ocean unprotected
so that you might test the strength of love
in my heart, I who have no firmness, I whose actions are evil?
O lord! I have forsaken our friendship
because I am an animal, because, although now I have heard
of your death, I have still not given up my life.

23. 2803

"On that day when you cut down Jambara who was harassing the world
like a spinning churn breaking up curds,
you told all living beings encircled by the sea with its shores
of fine sand that we were so close it was as if
you were a body and I the life within it, O faultless heart
that must be worshiped! Your words still hold!
Unfeeling Death has made the body rise into the sky while I,
the life, have been left here behind."

24. 2804

But he thought, "Instead of at once plunging into the fierce blaze
of the fire so that I may create for myself
incomparable fame, shall I fall to the ground and lie here
weeping as women do, who are foolish
and delicate of feeling?" and he rose as if his resolution was
now clear and, looking toward them, he said,
as should be said, "O you who are sons of him who was the master
of all the seven worlds, listen to me now!

25. 2805

"From the womb of the wife of Dakṣa, fifty women
were born and their breasts were large,
and Kaśyapa then took thirteen of those daughters
together to bed and made love with them.
The finest of those women whose name was Aditi gave birth
to the three hundred and thirty million gods
while the one whose name was Diti, her eyes black with collyrium,
bore the Asuras who are twice that number.

26. 2806

"And Danu bore the Dānavas as well as other creatures
and from the woman Mati, ah! the four classes
of humanity were born that came from their due places
in the diverse parts of the body and the woman
named Surabhi bore the Gandharvas and the cows and more,
while let it be known that Krodhavaśā
who felt a sense of shame gave birth to the donkey, the antelope,
and the camel and others from her womb.

27. 2807

"Vinatā whose hair is like a dark cloud produced the thunder and
[lightning
of clouds and the Dawn and the great birds—
Vaināta the owl, who has wings that are like young leaves,
and the hawk and the rest of the birds of prey—
and Tāmrā who was like a jewel among women bore the sparrow,
the partridge, the quail and the other small birds.
Kaḻai beautiful as a vine gave birth to the plants—these vines
and bushes and all the growth we see.

28. 2808

"Kadrū who was like the lightning gave birth to the many-headed
[snakes
whose massed hoods rise up and terrify
while the woman named Śvetā bore all the snakes who have only
a single head that rises up and frightens men
and the woman named Aruṭṭai gave birth to the large lizards and the
[small
lizards and the squirrels and all their kind,
and you should know that the goddess Iḍā who calms the mind
bore all those many creatures that move through the water.

29. 2809

"Aditi, Diti, Danu, Aruṭṭai, Śvetā, Kaḻai, Surabhi
and the lovely Vinatā and the serene
Mati and Iḍā and Kadrū, Krodhavaśā and Tāmrā,
those delicate women gave birth
to all these in their proper order and when the Dawn
who is the son of Vinatā made love
to Rambhā whose forehead is like the new moon and whose arms
are soft, *we* were then born on the earth.

30. 2810

"I am the son of the Dawn and wherever he may go, through all
the worlds, I go, and I was a friend
of Daśaratha, close as sweet life to him who rolled the wheel
of his law so that the power of the darkness
perished. I came into being with the gods when they created
the four classes of humanity, I am the king
of the vultures. O young men who are glowing with great light!
Sampāti is my elder brother and I am Jaṭāyus."

31. 2811

When he spoke these words, they folded the flowers of their hands
together in respect and the tears more and more
filled the lotuses of their eyes because of the great sorrow
that was growing in them along with love,
and those two with shoulders like mountains felt as if they were seeing
their father come back to them again
who, for the sake of his sons, had entered paradise and established
the great fame that now was his ornament.

32. 2812

With his two wings, he closely embraced them whose virtues
are a sweet thing to know. "My sons," he said,
"You must help me carry out the final rites that befit my karma,
for if I do not die, entering the fire this day,
not even thinking of the pain, I will never forget my grief,
since my body would be only a weight
upon me if it remained here at ease, while he who is the single
life of our two bodies has gone away."

33. 2813

They who wore garlands thick with flowers looked at the king
of vultures who had spoken these words and they bowed to him,
and as the tears that were like pearls in their eyes fell one
after another, they stood there and then they said to him with love,

34. 2814

"He whose duty it was to help us whenever we were in need
has risen to heaven with never a thought of being false
to his word and if you, you who are our lord, abandon us,
then who would be left here for us now as our support?

35. 2815

"O you who never turn away from what is right! will you also
leave us who, because of meeting you, have lost the pain
that came to us when we entered the forest and left our mother
and our father so hard to leave and the gates of our cool city?"

36. 2816

They said these things begging him, with their hearts troubled.
Thoughtfully looking at the heroes who were standing there, he said,
"If you feel that I should not die, then what I will do is wait
and go to him only after you have returned to Ayodhyā.

37. 2817

"But if the king, as you say, has gone to heaven, why are you,
heroes! not at your ease ruling that world which is yours
to support? Why have you come here? What has happened?
Tell me! As I try to imagine why, I feel my mind burning!

38. 2818

"Whether they are gods or Asuras or Nāgas with great power,
whoever they may be, if they have caused you pain,
you whose sharpened gleaming spears are beautiful!
I will first kill them, then give you back your kingdom!"

39. 2819

As soon as he who was like their father had said this,
the husband of Sītā glanced toward his younger brother
who then, without hesitating, told how their stepmother
had brought a great measureless ocean of karma upon them.

40. 2820

"How generous you have been," Jaṭāyus said, "to give a younger [brother
the earth, though he was born after you, and to accept
your stepmother's words on your own head, making your father a man
of his word! Who else could do what my lord has been able to do?"

41. 2821

Lovingly he embraced Rāma whose eyes were like inner lotuses
and kissed his hair, while the tears streamed from his own eyes.
"O power! O my son!" Jaṭāyus said, "you have made me
and that king come into a glory that is beyond measure!"

42. 2822

And then the great being looked at the woman who wore bangles,
who was as beautiful as a wild goose, and he said,
"O son of the king of kings! O my own son!
Tell me who is this woman with her shining forehead?"

43. 2823

His brother Lakṣmaṇa, who was born after the hero, completed
the description in his words of all that had happened since the meeting
with the Rākṣasī Tāḍakā who was like darkness embodied
and the breaking of the bow and now their time for sleeping in the [forest.

44. 2824

He who was wearing a diadem glistening with light was happy
as he listened to those words and then he said, "You who have left
your wealthy land behind you and this woman whose forehead
is lovely should stay here in the forest. I will protect you!"

45. 2825

But Rāma, who is alive in men's hearts, answered, "O lord!
On the broad shore of a clear and beautiful river
murmuring along, there is a bathing place which Agastya,
after long thought, directed me to. We will go there and live."

46. 2826

"A fine thing! You should live at that great bathing place
where you may perform your perfect tapas! Come now!
I will lead you there!" Jaṭāyus said and, rising in the sky, he spread
the shadow of his strong wings over them as they set out.

47. 2827

He whose virtues were without fault, whose heart was pure,
told them how to find the place, so that they understood,
and after he had gone on, the heroes, carrying bows of war,
traveling at their ease, reached the grove where they were to stay.

48. 2828

And Jaṭāyus who knew without any doubt the strength of the Rākṣasas
looked after them who were like his sons and like his daughter-in-law,
that woman who had her lovely breasts bound up, and he took
great care, like a bird looking after its babies in the nest.

# Paṭalam Five
# Śūrpaṇakhā

1. 2829

And the heroes saw the river Godāvarī
which was like the poems of the great poets,
a sublime ornament for the earth
with fields of profound wealth
and its episodes that are watering places
for rescue from the heat, with its flow
through the five landscapes of poetry,
clear and lovely and sweetly running.

2. 2830

With her bright face glittering, gracious
as a lotus where the bees gather
and the glowing eyes of her water lilies
that absorb and hold sweet fragrance
while her hands, the clear waves,
one after another, were picking up and scattering
beautiful flowers, the holy river shone
as if bowing at the noble sight of them.

3. 2831

And O the river seemed to cry out,
cry out and grieve and grieve
with risen love, as if the moving water
were shedding cool drops of tears
spreading from her lovely eyes
of newly open water lilies that had to see
this sadness, those young men who were honest
and faultless living in the forest.

4. 2832

The bowman of the long bow saw
    the cakravāka birds peacefully
closing their eyes on their beds
    of lotuses and looked at the breasts
of his woman, while she whose ornaments
    were lovely looked at the hills
glittering with their jewels and her mind
    turned to her great lord's arms.

5. 2833

And that highest being when he saw
    the swaying walk of a wild goose
smiled a little and looked
    at Sītā walking near him
and she saw how a male elephant
    coming back from drinking at the water
moved and a sudden smile
    showed across her face.

6. 2834

The hero in whose strong hand
    the bow was held saw the vines
dancing by the high river and he looked
    at the waist of his woman while she,
looking at the red lotuses
    flowering amid the expanse
of dark blue water lilies lovely
    as night, saw the body of her lord.

7. 2835

In this way Rāma approached
    the beautiful Pañcavaṭi Grove
where the trees were young and yielded
    coolness near the river fed
by waterfalls and, when he came there,
    his younger brother built a hut
pleasant for them to stay in
    and they lived in that solitary place.

8. 2836

Then she appeared, she who had the power to utterly destroy
the Rākṣasa king whose skin was the color of fine sapphires.
She was a fatal disease that, born long ago, had been waiting
alongside Rāvaṇa's life, until her time would come.

9. 2837

With thick hair deep red as copper and with a body
that was swollen full of burning lust past measuring,
she had the will to accomplish destruction of the gods,
of sadhus, of all who live in this world circled by the ocean.

10. 2838

She had been spending her days alone in that forest,
inflamed with desire, the instrument of a cruel fate,
and, though strong enough to easily go anywhere in the world,
she came to where the descendant of Raghu was living.

11. 2839

She who was the sign of the end of her own clan saw
the Lord who long ago had risen from his precious sleep
on the snake, when the gods who merit worship had said to him,
"The Rākṣasas are now our enemies and you must kill them."

12. 2840

"The God of Love," she thought, "who lives in the heart
had his body destroyed and Indra has a thousand eyes.
Śiva has three eyes like lotus flowers and Brahmā
who created the world from his navel has four arms.

13. 2841

"I think this is the God of Love who was destroyed by flames
from the third eye of Śiva whose massed and matted hair
is lovely and, bodiless, the god has done arduous tapas
since then to gain a form more beautiful than before.

14. 2842

"His arms are handsome and long, as the canons of good looks
prescribe, and even the trees are not their equals, even the mountains
compared to them are tame. They seem trunks of those elephants
who with their strength support the high directions of the air.

15. 2843

"Mountains merely of stone do not match the shoulders of this hero
who is skilled at fighting with the bow. Even famous Meru
cannot compare with them, unless it were not of gold
but a great mountain of dark and ancient sapphires.

16. 2844

"He seems himself a mountain with his noble eyes
that are like the petals of lotuses high on their stems.
If I tried, in one glance, to cross his broad chest
from shoulder to shoulder, my eyes would be too small.

17. 2845

"Does the bright face of this beautiful man shining
with unwavering intensity resemble the bud of a lotus
that has opened into a flower? Not the moon whose rays wane
can equal it, nor the full moon streaked by a flaw.

18. 2846

"To what purpose does he who has gained such sweet beauty
punish himself so that his lovely body uselessly suffers?
That this lotus-eyed man, the sight of whom is continual joy,
should do tapas, what tapas did tapas itself perform?

19. 2847

"Fortunate is the Goddess of the Earth to have been born a woman,
she who wears the ocean for a robe, whose swaying walk is graceful
as an elephant. Because the soles of his feet have touched the grass,
it seems as if the earth's hair is standing up on end!

20. 2848

"Has the sun who is lord of light not seen this radiance,
this glow of a being whose smile is like glistening moonlight,
that he goes on his way without shame in his heart, spreading
his lesser light on high through all the distances?

21. 2849

"This man with his huge shoulders like towering mountains
has a lower lip for which no comparison possible
on this earth is adequate. What could I ever find
to say that marks a redness even greater than coral?

22. 2850

"For the happiness of encircling this lovely waist that dispels
the darkness, I think that not even a golden robe
could have done the tapas of that bark garment
for this noble being who shines as brightly as the moon.

23. 2851

"Ah! if instead of matted hair, he was wearing
the black tuft of a young man with its curls
all through it like long clouds hanging down,
surely he would put an end to every woman's life.

24. 2852

"If the best of ornaments, radiating light, were to embrace
this body, could they make its loveliness grow any more?
Does the beauty of the faultless ruby, king of gems,
shine any brighter by the presence of some other jewel?

25. 2853

"When Brahmā created this body, collecting and displaying
every virtue possible, keeping nothing back, then blame
came to him since Indra, ruler of all the worlds, though he beg
for more, in beauty is not worth the dust on those feet!"

26. 2854

As the love in her heart swelled higher than a flooding river
or even the ocean, as her wisdom disappeared, her purity
waned like the fame of a man who hoards up wealth
and gives nothing with love as his reward for praise!

27. 2855

Like a picture of a woman sketched against the sky, she stood there
with her heart on fire, her sight fastened to the shining
handsome shoulders of the hero and she could not manage
the strength to pull her eyes free from that vision.

28. 2856

So she stood. And she thought, "I will make love with that man
or else I will die, even if I were to swallow the drink that
gives immortality. I feel that now nothing else is possible."
She moved closer and tried to think of some means to approach him.

29. 2857

"He will refuse me," she thought, "if he sees me as a Rākṣasī with
[fangs
and a belly that eats any and all life. Therefore better
to go to him with lips red as a kōvai fruit, with speech
as soft as a kokila bird and all the beauty of a peacock."

30. 2858

She visualized the goddess Śrī seated on the lotus,
uttered a mantra she had in her power and appeared
as a beautiful woman, her face shining brighter than the moon
and the radiance of her rose, glowing, into the sky.

31. 2859

All the loveliness of bright red cotton
and cool shoots
were shamed by her as she moved
on her small feet
like graceful red lotuses. With words that were sweet
like a young peacock,
a wild goose, a swaying vañci vine, like poison,
the wily woman came.

32. 2860

Beautiful as Śrī on her flower flowing gold,
like a streak of lightning
fallen, never to vanish, out of the sky,
with her jeweled chariot,
fresh as that of a young girl and
softly clothed,
and her shining face, the swords of her eyes,
like a lovely myna bird,

33. 2861

she came as if a peacock were coming,
with eyes like a deer,
of a sweet, abundant beauty, with a perfumed
honey of words
that would draw out desire for her who had taken
a body just like the vaḻḻi,
glowing vine of heaven, given its life by the tall
and fragrant Wish-Granting Tree.

34. 2862

"The sounds of anklets and of jeweled
belt-strings
and of the bees buzzing around the flowers
in the black sand
of her hair, tell me that a woman
is coming now,"
thought the Lord and he looked over
in that direction.

35. 2863

Like sweet amṛta coming as a gift
from those in the sky,
she came to him with her lovely breasts,
her waist swaying,
and Rāma, who grants the eye of true knowledge
that rises and wipes away
all ignorance once he has entered the mind, looked
toward her with his two eyes.

36. 2864

As he saw a body so softly gentle
it could never be found
in the immense world of the Nāgas, in heaven
or on this earth,
he thought, "Who is she and who could equal this woman
wearing ornaments
that are lovely and is there any limit
to the beauty within her?"

37. 2865

With that desire she had in her mind, staring
at his handsome face,
she bowed down to his feet and she touched them
with her red-painted hands
and throwing the spears of her eyes at him
that were long and cruel,
she looked away like a doe, a little ashamed, withdrawing,
and stood nearby him.

38. 2866

"May your coming be without evil,
lovely as Śrī!
with all your excellence! We must have acted well
for you to have come.
What is your city and your name? Who are your relatives?"
said the Source of the Vedas,
and then the young woman described to him
who she was.

39. 2867

"I am granddaughter of Brahmā, the god
 in the flower, younger sister of Kubera,
his hands filled with wealth, who is the ally
 of Śiva, destroyer of the three cities,
and I am sister to the overlord of the three worlds
 who has defeated all the elephants of the air,
who has lifted up the silver mountain of Kailāsa.
 I am a virgin and my name is Kāmavaḷḷi."

40. 2868

As the hero listened to those words
 with doubt in his heart, feeling
something wrong in the way she acted
 that soon he would come to understand,
he said to her, "If you are the younger sister
 to him who is so fierce a sight,
whose eyes blaze, then truthfully
 tell me why you have this form?"

41. 2869

Before the pure being had even
 finished his words, she spoke out
forcefully and said, "Not willing
 to live with the Rākṣasas who are vicious
and deceiving, I have searched through my heart
 and chosen Righteousness. Because I performed
tapas, the gods have granted
 that my evil actions be burned away."

42. 2870

"If you are the younger sister of him
 who so rules the three worlds
that even the king of the gods
 obeys his orders at once,
then, woman, for what reason
 do you come all alone now
without a companion, without
 any show of your enormous wealth?"

43. 2871

As soon as the hero had spoken,
    the lying woman said, "O perfect man!
I do not mingle with those beings
    who are without virtue. I seek
the presence of the gods or of sages
    who are noble. Lord! Because
there is something I am in need of,
    I have come to see you here."

44. 2872

When she had spoken, the Lord thought,
    "The ideas of women with foreheads
so lovely are not easily understood
    nor do they follow the path of virtues.
Later this will come clear," and he said,
    "You who wear bangles on your arms,
tell me what it is you want of me.
    I will do it for you if I can."

45. 2873

"For women of noble family," she answered,
    "themselves to express their desires
honestly is said to be wrong! Ah!
    I am in grief for my troubled life
without anyone to be my messenger.
    What is there that I
can do? Protect me from the cruelty
    of Kāma, the god of love!"

46. 2874

The dark swords of her eyes spread
    with red lines were darting,
turning, shining out her varying feelings,
    looking into the distances and returning,
and her ornamented breasts were heaving
    as she spoke these words. The Lord thought,
"She is not a good woman, she is not
    virtuous, she has no shame."

47. 2875

The woman created of illusion,
as in her hair the bees were loudly
buzzing, moved here and there
in her doubt, not knowing what
was in the heart of the Lord who gives
everything and who stood there silent.
"He has seen my desires. Will he agree
or not?" she thought and spoke to him again.

48. 2876

"You with your body no one
could ever picture! I have been doing
my work, carrying out the orders,
as they should be done, of the holy men
who know everything, before I knew
you had come here and it seems as if
I was passing my youth as a faultless woman
vainly in useless hours and days!"

49. 2877

And he who gives everything thought
in his heart, "This Rākṣasī has no honor.
She cannot mean well. Her coming has
some selfish purpose to it." And he said,
"Beautiful woman, this would go against
the ancient rules of ancestry.
You are a woman of Brahmin descent
and I was born to the class of kings."

50. 2878

"My father," she said, "is a Brahmin
learned in the Vedas but
my mother, pure as Arundhatī,
is descended from the royal line
of Sukeśa that protected the world.
You whose handsome spear is ornamented
by battle, if this is the reason you reject
being with me, then I am alive again!"

51. 2879

Full of desire, she said these things
    and he, who was like a dark cloud
streaked by the silver light
    of his smile, decided to play with her.
"Woman!" he said, "the wise always
    have said it is not fitting
for human men to marry a woman
    from the Rākṣasas who live at their ease."

52. 2880

She thought, "It seems truly foolish
    for him to call me the sister
of Rāvaṇa and not consider this body
    born of love and indescribable devotion."
"I told you before," she said, "you
    who are like the pure being whose bed
is the snake! By worshiping the gods,
    I have abandoned that flawed birth."

53. 2881

"Well, one of your brothers is the exalted
    ruler of all the three worlds
and the younger of your brothers is Kubera.
    I will take you only if they
give you to me. But if not, woman,
    go off somewhere else by yourself,
for I'm afraid to stay here with you," he said,
    who is beyond the wisdom of the Vedas.

54. 2882

"There is a rite called the Gandharva,
    a marriage prescribed by the Vedas
for men and women whose hearts
    have mingled in love. You
with your large, handsome shoulders!
    After it has taken place, the king
my elder brother will approve it,
    and let me say one thing more.

55. 2883

"For long now, the Rākṣasas who know
 nothing of what is right have shown
intense anger toward all who do tapas.
 And you live alone. It is right
for you to form a friendship with them
 in this way. They will give you command
of the heavens and with pleasure they will come
 to stand by you waiting for your orders."

56. 2884

"Ah! I have received the grace of the Rākṣasas
 and you with all your power of delight!
I have received wealth I will never lose!
 and not only that but the tapas I have done
since leaving my lovely city has
 here borne fruit!" he said whose arms
held a cocked bow and he laughed at her
 with his bright, flashing teeth.

57. 2885

And then, to stand near that radiance
 who shines in the eyes of Brahmā
and all the others in heaven and the men
 in this world and the Nāgas below it,
from their hut fragrant with the odor
 of the trees, she came, that queen
among women, like a jeweled vine rising
 from the earth, for the salvation of the gods.

58. 2886

The Rākṣasī's mouth fell open, suffering,
 as if burned by hot meat, stunned
to see with her own eyes the shining
 that came there like a flood of light
from the sun in the heavens, her, the fire
 of purity grown to burn the forest
of warring Rākṣasas spread over the earth
 and the sky glittering with its stars.

59. 2887

Confused at heart, the Rākṣasī
    thought to herself, "He would not bring
his wife with her fragrant hair
    to the forest nor is there anyone here
with a form like hers. Could she
    be the goddess Śrī who has left
her lotus flower and come
    to touch this earth with her two feet?"

60. 2888

For a long time, she stood looking
    and absorbing the perfection of that form
and she thought, "Beauty that remains
    with us in our hearts has no flaw
beyond the limitations of its creators.
    My eyes cannot leave her
nor my thoughts. If I, born a woman,
    feel this, what must she be for others?"

61. 2889

She stood there looking at the warrior
    and the woman lovely as a myna bird
and she thought, "Those two must be
    the ultimate in beauty of form
created by the god in the lotus
    for the two sexes in the three worlds
through his reasoned and incomparable skill!
    What else can I possibly imagine?

62. 2890

"He who is dark as a kāyā flower,
    whose incomparable body is like gold,
does not accord with her whose waist
    is thin as lightning, whose feet
are tender shoots, more beautiful even
    than others who, like her, are beautiful.
She must have come upon him just
    as I have and I will make him hate her!"

63. 2891

And she said, "This woman coming now
 is a deceiving Rākṣasī. She is skilled
at illusion. We know nothing
 of what is in her heart. O splendor!
you do wrong to trust her. This body
 is false. I am afraid of the woman
who lives by eating flesh. Hero!
 Avoid her! Do not go near her!"

64. 2892

"O woman like lightning! Your insight
 is impressive! Who has the strength
to deceive you? Your obvious virtue
 has made this clear to your mind.
Even she, it seems, is a Rākṣasī
 skilled at illusion, but look now
closely at her!" the hero said, laughing,
 showing his teeth like white pearls.

65. 2893

Then as Sītā arriving there like amṛta,
 her arms more rounded than bamboo,
pure as Arundhatī, her voice
 lovely, moved toward the hero,
the other woman like a burning fire,
 her heart full of lies, spoke,
threatening her, "Rākṣasī woman!
 Why are you intruding here?"

66. 2894

And Sītā was afraid. Like a wild goose,
 she was shocked and ran in her fright,
with her waist thin as lightning and her feet
 as soft as cotton pained
by the running, and as if a bolt like a vine
 of coral were to flash across a cloud
in the rainy season, she embraced the huge
 shoulders of that hero who was like an elephant.

67. 2895

Rāma, as he realized that even though
this was just a game one plays
with demons who have curving fangs,
something evil could happen, said,
"Woman! Don't cause pain to anyone
or my younger brother quickly
will notice you and he will turn
fiercely angry. Go away at once!"

68. 2896

"With love in their hearts, Brahmā
who sits on the flower, Viṣṇu
whose bed is the waters and Śiva
living on his mountain and Kāma
and the rest of the gods do tapas
to have me. Why do you despise me
and desire this woman without patience who is
all deception!" the beautiful Rākṣasī said.

69. 2897

And he thought, "Even when I say we want
nothing at all to do with her, she won't go.
This woman with her swollen desires,
stubborn as a rock, keeps telling lies,"
and like a cloud moving along with its lightning,
he who is pure and she, the gold
of the king of Mithilā, entered
their hut within the flowering grove.

70. 2898

When they had gone, she felt her life
falling away, leaving her body.
With her senses stunned, shrunken into herself,
she stood there and could hardly breathe.
"He has no affection for me at all,"
she thought, "no room in his heart for me.
He has turned angry, unyielding in his love
for her with hair black as collyrium."

71. 2899

She left. She went away trying to think
of some means by which she might have him
and she felt that if she did not embrace
his chest this very day she would die.
She entered her grove lined with trees,
the air full of golden pollen,
and then her palace of crystal where she remained
through the evening, as the sky turned red.

72. 2900

Blazing up in her despair, the desires she had told to Rāma
ravaged her heart like cruel fire. It seemed as if
the black poison that descends through the hollow sharp fang
of a strong snake, newly molted, were rising through her.

73. 2901

While the arrows of the Love God who is practiced at his work
flew at her like the sharp arrows of Rāma, king of men,
when they pierced the great chest of Tāḍakā the cruel,
ah! she was in pain and frightened for her very life.

74. 2902

Now as the warm wind from the Malayas entered her chest
like Death's long spear, she who had thought herself
able to consume the God of Love and the full moon
for a curry along with him was suffering and losing her strength.

75. 2903

First thinking to quiet the ocean with her lovely hands
by filling it with mountains, because the sounds of the waves
gave her pain, she grew weak and anguished while the moon, high
and firm in the sky, troubled her with its long light.

76. 2904

"So that every flower on this earth may become dust,
I will shatter all the gardens," she thought, burning with anger
while she trembled and her strength faded as she listened to the song
of the red-headed an͟ril bird who is never away from her mate.

77. 2905

Angrily she thought, "I will run and bring the snake able
to swallow down that moon which is beyond my reach,"
and her precious life was burning at the touch of a cool wind
to her large, soft, sweet breasts and she was seething.

78. 2906

She scooped up handfuls of ice, miraculously cool
and placed them down on her young, radiant breasts
but they were no better than butter that would melt away
laid out on a hot ledge, with fire blazing around it.

79. 2907

When the water she bathed in began boiling, she was terrified
in fear of the flames burning away her life and the body
that she so cherished and she thought, "Where can I hide
from the roaring ocean or the cruel arrows of love?"

80. 2908

Whenever a dark cloud appeared or she happened to look at a column
of blue sapphires, she would join her palms in praise, with her body
so on fire that even a giant moonstone that is moistened
by the moon's touch would catch fire from her and burn.

81. 2909

So that the huge lovely moon would never find her
nor the cool north wind nor the God of Love, she almost went
to the safety of a deep mountain cave where there lives
an angry snake, with sharp, terrifying fangs.

82. 2910

Then, as the flame grew higher and higher, not knowing
what to do next, with her breasts burning and pouring out
three times more fire than before, she began to roll
around on a bed of long, fresh, golden shoots.

83. 2911

The form of the hero took shape before her burning eyes
and thinking she was seeing him, huge and dark as a monsoon cloud,
she was pained and ashamed and stunned as that body
vanished away and she fell to the ground, in great suffering.

84. 2912

As a black cloud passed, she tried to press it to her breasts,
imagining it was her lord and when she saw those clouds
warming up and dissolving, she would weep! Was there
any end at all to that unholy woman's delusion?

85. 2913

Though it seemed as if she were caught in the blazing fire that
[consumes
a universe, that mindless woman did not lose her life
saved by the drug of her desire to have that man
with his body the color of the dark ocean and then to live!

86. 2914

"Make this suffering vanish," she said, "that enters my heart
and deceives me with cruel, innumerable illusions,
mountain dark as collyrium, show me your grace!"
she said, and she trembled as if she had licked up poison.

87. 2915

"And he has that wife with eyes like blue water lilies
or a pair of darting fish! She is lovelier than Lakṣmī!
Would he look at me as well, I who am so impure?"
she thought, with her desire that even death could never end.

88. 2916

"That woman is all purity, she is beautiful, and she
is the mistress of his broad chest!" Śūrpaṇakhā thought,
"Ah how the Love God destroys us with his touch
setting fire to the bodies of those who feel desire!"

89. 2917

She was enduring this overflowing pain of love
when the sun rose as if it were the coming of Rāma
to free the sky of its utter darkness that seemed
like the Rākṣasas clouding over all the three worlds.

90. 2918

As soon as she saw the dawn, she knew she had lived
through the night though her body was burning,
and she thought, "He will never look at me while she
who has no equal is near him.
Best for me to run there fast, take her
and hide her away somewhere quickly
and then I will assume that form that
he loves and I will live with him."

91. 2919

She came there and looked. She saw that he
who gives everything had gone to perform
his morning rites on the shore of a clear lake,
but she did not see his younger brother,
he who was there to protect the woman
with her forehead lovely as the moon
who was standing nearby in the dark grove
from which fragrance was spreading.

92. 2920

"She has been left alone. What I wished for
is happening. No reason to think
now or hold back or delay," she thought,
her cruel heart filling with jealousy
and she moved after that woman who was as beautiful
as a peacock, while in the grove
that was large and filled with fruit, Lakṣmaṇa,
there to protect, saw her coming.

93. 2921

"You! Stop!" he shouted, hurrying toward her,
deciding not to take his bow
since this was a woman, and with his fine hand,
he seized her strong, thick hair
that was welling out like a glowing fire
and dragging her down by it,
he kicked her and then he drew out his curving
sword that flashed radiance.

94. 2922

In anger, she tried to get up, thinking
to hold him back by strength
and escape into the sky, but easily Lakṣmaṇa
pulled her down and saying these words,
"Don't make people suffer!" he cut off first
her nose, then her ears, then the nipples
of her hard burning breasts and his own anger then
cut off, he released her hair.

95. 2923

Instantly her mouth fell open and a shrieking
sound pierced through all the directions
and went rising up into the ears of the gods!
What can anyone say of this
thing that had happened to her? The flowing
blood as it came pouring down
from the hole that had been her nose seemed
to be melting the earth with its touch.

96. 2924

When Lakṣmaṇa's cruel and radiant sword,
famous for killing his enemies,
had sliced off that fierce woman's fine nose
and the nipples of her breasts, it was as if
that day marked the beginning of the labor
to be ended by cutting off the heads
of Rāvaṇa, each one with its jeweled diadem,
like cutting down so many mountains.

97. 2925

As the Rākṣasī rose up, wailing and stamping
her feet so that the great earth
was shaking, she seemed to be a black cloud
pouring down a rain of blood
as an omen signaling the end for Khara
and those Rākṣasas under his command
who were without equals in fierce, raging war,
whose shining spears were like Death.

98. 2926

She leaped into the air, fell to the earth
and lay there in her suffering.
Throwing her arms around and growing weak,
she fainted away and woke up
screaming, "What sin have I done for this misery
of being born a woman!"
she with her ancient lineage that Sorrow itself
had feared even to approach.

99. 2927

She tried to press her nose back on.
She breathed like fire in a forge.
She hammered her hands on the ground and grasping
her two large breasts,
she looked at them and her body broke out
sweating. She went running
on her great strong legs everywhere
and she weakened as the blood flowed.

100. 2928

She wandered in a flooding swamp of her own blood
that came streaming down like a waterfall
swollen full by many springs and, through calling out
all those names of her family
that can frighten even Death, made
the gods run away in terror.
Unable to bear the pain, she stood there and summoned them,
speaking in a torrent of words.

101. 2929

"You! with your power on this wide earth, are you not offended by these
holy men wandering carrying bows who have made me not able
any more to raise my head before the gods! O incomparable mountain
who lifted Śiva's own mountain! Won't you come look at these things?

102. 2930

"The world encircled by the roaring ocean believes that no one
takes a tiger's cub even when the mother is gone. Is this
a lie? O you who are stronger than Asuras and gods and the three
who are highest! Won't you come to see the pain I feel?

103. 2931

"You saw the back of Indra when you fought him as he was riding
the king of elephants who trumpeted in battle and, fighting for him,
there was a dense army of gods! You defeated him in war. He broke out [sweating
and barely escaped with his life! Won't you come to see the shame I [feel?

104. 2932

"You who are served by wind, fire, and water and Death
who is cruel time, and the sky and the planets! Have you lost
your strength? Do you retreat before two men, you who seized
the sword you carry out of the mighty hand of great Śiva!

105. 2933

"Though in form they resemble the God of Love, why do you not show
your anger at these men not worth the dust under the soles of your
[sandals,
O strength! who, lifting your arms, broke Kailāsa and the tusks of the
[Elephants
of Space who flow with musth, whose feet make the dust sparkle!

106. 2934

"Has his strength abandoned Rāvaṇa who has the power even to
[destroy
the gods who wear fragrant garlands that are filled with nectar?
Has strength left his younger brothers? Has it gone to stay
with men, the meat of whose bodies is meant to be food for our race?

107. 2935

"Did this happen because of the power of two holy men who are hiding
in the great forest thick with trees or because Rākṣasas good at killing
have given up? You! whose hands are so strong your enemies can only
be Śiva or Brahmā or Viṣṇu! Will you look at the pain I feel?

108. 2936

"Where Indra and Brahmā on his flower and the other gods ask for your
[orders
and the women of heaven sing to wish you long life and the seven
[worlds
praise you, sitting in the midst of your court under your umbrella
[unrivaled
like the moon, can I who am your servant, with no shame, show you
[my face?

109. 2937

"Am I to remain here crying out my pain while that man admires
his arms after he kicked and rolled me across the ground so that my
[strength
broke and faded and then he cut off my nose? Should I have to endure
[this
in Khara's forest? O brother who moved Śiva's mountain! O my brother!

110. 2938

"Isn't your good name sullied by this stain, because I acted
without a sense of shame and due to my lust, I have lost my nose?
You whose arms have the great fame of having fought and tired
out the Elephants of Space! You broke their tusks! Rāvaṇa! Rāvaṇa!

111. 2939

"And you my nephew! My nephew! You who made the gods serve you,
who put Indra himself in chains and wiped out clans of Asuras!
Am I to die here, because of this disgrace, I who sinned and had
my nose and my ears cut off by those two in the middle of the forest!

112. 2940

"Once the seven worlds grew angry and came against you and you,
strong in your rage, broke them with a single bow and scattered them
in all the directions. Then, chaining Indra's legs, you put him
in a great prison! My nephew! Won't you come face the strength of
[men?

113. 2941

"You whose murderous force can split rocks with the weapons in your
[giant
hands! Khara! Dūṣaṇa! You others born as Rākṣasas and ornamented
with jewels that flash apart the darkness! Do you sleep on the earth
like Kumbhakarṇa with his sharply honed weapons? Can't you hear me
[calling?"

114. 2942

As the Rākṣasī, she who was the enemy, went on shouting out these
[things,
wailing and lamenting as she rolled on the beautiful earth, he came,
who by that river had finished the full morning rites of his tapas, a
[mountain
of emerald, whose long arms with their strong sturdy hands held a bow.

115. 2943

Looking at his face as he came, she beat her belly and her raining
tears and the torrents of her blood turned the rich soil to mud.
"By the sin of love risen in me for the beauty of your body, ah
my lord! See what I have suffered!" and she fell on the ground before
[him.

116. 2944

Within the beauty of his heart that has no equal, he knew something evil
had been done by this woman whose hair was spreading loose and he
[realized
it must have been his younger brother that same day who had cut off
her long ears and her nose. He said to her, "Woman! Who are you?"

117. 2945

Hearing these words, the strong Rākṣasī said, "Don't you know me?
My brother is Rāvaṇa whose rage silenced even a single word
raised against him in any of the worlds, he who holds heaven
and all other worlds by his cruel spear with its leaflike blade."

118. 2946

"Why have you left those Rākṣasas with all their power and come here
so far away, to where we live and carry on our tapas?" he said,
and she answered him, "O best cure for the cruel sickness of desire
burning me like hot charcoal! Don't you remember my coming
[yesterday?"

119. 2947

"Was it you walking here yesterday, like the goddess Śrī on her lotus
full of honey, with your long dark eyes like lovely fishes?"
"When a woman has lost her nipples, her ears with their earrings, her
[nose
like a vine, O king with handsome eyes! isn't her beauty destroyed?"

120. 2948

The king, looking into the face of his strong younger brother and
[smiling
just a little said to him, "Hero! What evil thing did she intend
to do that you at once cut off her long ears and her nose like a vine?"
and the great hero, bowing to his brother's feet, gave him this answer.

121. 2949

"Whether she meant to use her sharp teeth and consume what she had
[tracked
or whether a crowd of malevolent Rākṣasas somewhere behind her
was urging her on, she came running, evil, with her eyes spitting fire
at your noble woman. She was in a towering rage beyond belief."

122. 2950

Before Lakṣmaṇa with his curving, well-strung bow had finished, the
[Rākṣasī,
their enemy, said, "You are from a rich land bright with rivers where by
[a stream
a pregnant frog, furious at the sight of her husband hovering near a
[conch,
troubles the water! Doesn't a woman's heart burn when she sees her
[rival?"

123. 2951

That being who is past the reach of words said to her, "We came here
searching for the great clan of Rākṣasas to destroy them all who fight
in their strength against the weak. Run now far from this forest where
[truth
is sought, or else you will be killed as you give us these vicious
[answers."

124. 2952

"Since Brahmā whose hair never turns white nor does his skin wrinkle
and all the other gods are subjects and pay tribute to Rāvaṇa,
it would be wrong of you to hurry me away. I have something else,
something different to tell you, if you have any sense of what's best for
[you!

125. 2953

"Rāvaṇa will tear out the tongue of the man who tells him his sister
has had her nose cut off, lost to her forever. He is not
a cultured gentleman. By cutting off my nose, you ended your clan
without escape! You have poured all your beauty out on barren ground.

126. 2954

"The gods in heaven and the kings on the earth and those who rule
where the great Nāgas live will stay where they are now protecting
their own heads! Who is there to protect you? Care for me and I
will protect you, but if you will not, then be aware that Rāvaṇa exists!

127. 2955

"Though women who are firmly modest should not boast of their own [might,
yet I speak out to you because of my love, great with desire.
Won't you tell your younger brother that I am stronger than anyone
in this world, and the honored sister of him who is stronger than the [gods?

128. 2956

"In your mighty battles, I will stand by you and protect you. I can
pick you up and carry you away on the air! I can give you endless fruit
as delicious as meat! Why reject your protector? I will give you [anything
you wish for! Tell me what you gain from this one who is delicate as a [flower!

129. 2957

"Among women who wear their lovely ornaments here on the earth
or in the sky, who are young and beautiful and accomplished, the finest
in their clans, who can summon for themselves whatever they may [want,
will you tell me if there is a single one fit to be compared with me?

130. 2958

"So what if you made me lose my nose, now that it's gone, if you can't
[bear it,
instantly I will create it again! I will be beautiful again! Am I
any less a woman if in this way I gain the fortune of your grace?
Isn't a long nose rising on a woman's face only a frill?

131. 2959

"If I want someone and he doesn't want me, mustn't he be impotent?
Isn't my life yours, because of the love that has risen in me?
Beauty that others may look at and desire, isn't that a poison?
Shouldn't you welcome a body that only a husband will caress?

132. 2960

"You! as if Śiva and Brahmā who on his flower faces the directions
and Viṣṇu and Indra with his devastating thunderbolt had joined in one
to stand here! Is Kāma whose flower arrows take life away from the
[worlds
your younger brother too? He is as merciless as this one has been.

133. 2961

"Is there any reason for you to have cut off my nose and made a hole
show, you with your war anklets
beautifully fashioned of gold! unless you had the thought in your mind,
'She will stay here with us, she will
not go, she who has this form that is delight.' So that no stranger
might ever look at me, you cut it,
didn't you? Did you harm me? Because I understood your wish, don't
[I know
that my love is twice as strong?

134. 2962

"If the Rākṣasas with their spears and their great anger like
[unquenchable fire
should come to know what has happened
and see it in their rage, all the worlds would be destroyed because of
[you
who have wronged me. Born in a lineage
so high, with Righteousness always in your minds, you would not
[cause the worlds
to be destroyed! Consider carefully
and stay here with me, in happiness, clear of blame, saving all life,"
she said and, standing up, bowed down to him.

135. 2963

"I still have the arrow that ended the life of Tāḍakā, the mother
of your mother who was a Rākṣasī guilty
of causing pain such as living beings here had never known
and now I have taken on as my tapas
to live in the forest where I exist to destroy the enemy race
of Rākṣasas who around their shoulders
wear garlands of thick, lovely flowers. Strong Rākṣasī!" said the Lord,
"Stop behaving in a way so low!

136. 2964

"We are the sons of Daśaratha, the wheel of whose law ruled the world
unrivaled! Obeying our mother's command,
we entered the forest where fragrance is everywhere. Brahmins and great
[sadhus
have asked us to destroy the race
of Rākṣasas whose army is an ocean with no shore to be seen.
Only then will we reenter our city
where the mansions of the families rise like ancient mountains. Take
[these things
to heart. Understand them clearly.

137. 2965

"You should not be thinking that these are just any two men,
even though the great gods themselves
were defeated, unable to stand against the Rākṣasas who do not
travel the path of virtues.
Bring, if you can, everyone you think is powerful, all of them,
the Rākṣasas with their sharp spears
smelling of flesh and all the Yakṣas who always win their victories!
Then right in front of you we will kill them."

138. 2966

"Yes, you can kill them," she said, "you can be told what strategies
they will try, you can win
and end their string of victories, you can overcome every one
of their tricks if only you see me
not as a woman with a gaping mouth, with all of my teeth showing
because my upper lip has been cut away!
Listen to me! You who come from a land where water nourishes
all grains and offers them to the people!

139. 2967

"Even if you don't give her up, she whose arms are as graceful as
[bamboo,
would I be nothing at all to you?
If you are determined to go into battle against the Rākṣasas who are
[outlaws,
who are ignorant and murderous, then
since I understand the various magic powers of their intricate weapons,
won't I be able to repel them?
Don't you know what the proverb says, that a snake is the one
to search out the lair of a snake?

140. 2968

"If you feel that you must keep this woman in your heart, still you
[should
realize that if you intend to fight
and prevail on the battlefield against the Rākṣasas, we three here
[together
could make that field a pool
of blood! Should that give you pain? And if then you will marry me
to this young prince who does not realize
what there is to gain, I would never weaken even before him
who has imprisoned the sun and the moon.

141. 2969

"On the day you return to your city, when it will be filled with great joy,
I will skillfully take on whatever form
you wish for, and if your younger brother should say, 'How can I live
with a woman who has had her nose
cut off completely?' even though it was he who became enraged and cut
[at me
in his anger that could not be satisfied,
won't you tell him he has been living for a very long time
with a woman who has no waist at all?"

142. 2970

The younger brother glanced at his spear with its bright blade like a leaf,
thinking to pierce her as she spoke
and he said, "If we don't free ourselves by killing her right now,
she will trouble us for a long time.
O king, what is your will?" The Lord said, "That would be the right
[thing
to do, if she doesn't leave us alone!"
and the Rākṣasī thought, "These men will show me no compassion.
I will lose my life if I stay."

## 143. 2971

She said to them, "Could I ever bear to live with you after I have
lost my nose as lovely
as a long vine and my two ears and the nipples of both my breasts?
What I said was meant to find out
all about you. Now I will bring him who is swifter than the wind,
him who is crueler than fire,
Khara, who will be your Death!" and she set out, feeling herself
full of hatred that had no calming.

# Paṭalam Six
# The Killing of Khara

1. 2972

Ah! with her hair and her blood flowing free,
mouth and nose streaming like sluices as if she were
a black cloud set against the red sky of evening,
she came to where great Khara was and fell at his feet.

2. 2973

As if she were beating a kettledrum to proclaim at the command
of the God of Death, "Today the Rākṣasas are destroyed!"
she screamed there alone and rolled like a cobra agonizing
under the fierce fire flashed from a roaring cloud.

3. 2974

In his fury at her cries, smoke poured out of his mouth
and he looked down at her and he said, "Who did this to you
and then went away without any fear?" his eyes
staring, fixed on the blood streaming from her nose.

4. 2975

"Two of them did it, they are men, they do tapas in the forest.
They carry powerful bows and swords, with bodies
like the God of Love, Righteousness as their nature, the beloved
sons of Daśaratha, searching out Rākṣasas to meet in battle.

5. 2976

"They have no respect whatsoever for your strength. Their intent
is to safeguard the noble Order of the World, to establish it
so that it will endure. Their firm resolve is to kill
and eradicate the Rākṣasas whose spears have always been victorious.

6. 2977

"There is a woman there who is so lovely no woman
can be considered her equal whether on the earth
or in the distant heavens or anywhere. With my own eyes,
I have seen her and that beauty of hers cannot be described.

7. 2978

"When I look at her, she with her loveliness so difficult
ever to find, I thought that I would bring her to the king
of our people in Laṅkā but as I rushed against her,
they grew angry at me and they sliced away my nose."

8. 2979

He heard what she was saying and with his own eyes he saw
her nose like the hole in a scooped-out palmyra fruit.
"Show them to me!" he said, who makes the world tremble,
rising, burning the eyes of those who looked toward him.

9. 2980

He rose and stood, seething, so full of his anger
fire poured out of him that could burn and destroy
the seven worlds. "Even if you were to tell me, 'The men
are dead,'" he said, "would this indelible shame be wiped away?"

10. 2981

When he said, "Bring my chariot!" those who were standing by him,
those fourteen who were like towering mountains with hands,
each of them strong enough to hold up the world
with only a single hand, said, "Give this job to us!"

11. 2982

They were carrying tridents, swords, axes and iron bars,
the nooses of the God of Death, discuses and clubs. They roared
so that it terrified the earth surrounded by its ocean.
Their bodies were like massed, black Hālāhala poison.

12. 2983

Before him they stood, raging fires of anger.
"Lord!" they said, "what good is it to serve you unless
we can do our work? Are you moving in fury today against
gods? Shall we remain shamed here on this earth?"

13. 2984

"What you say is well said! Were I to go into battle
against these puny beings, how the gods would laugh at me!
Kill them, drink their blood, defeat their intentions.
Then," he said, "return to me here with that delicate loveliness."

14. 2985

As soon as he had spoken, they bowed down to him in gratitude
and following her who was like a messenger of death, without shame
for the words she had uttered, they arrived at the place
where they were living who had been beloved by their father the king.

15. 2986

She showed him to those Rākṣasas skilled in clashing battle,
that man with eyes like lotuses within whose thoughts were
the stainless feet of the god with the discus, who has a thousand
pure and ancient names. She pointed him out with her hand.

16. 2987

"We will seize him and, lifting him up, break him against the ground!
We will catch him with a great noose! We will complete
what is to be done according to the words of our king," and they
surrounded him and looked as if they were encircling a mountain.

17. 2988

Rāma, who is to be praised for always speaking the truth,
said, "Protect the woman" to his younger brother and picked up
the fine mountain of his bow, with its string fastened
by his matchless hand red as a flowering kalpaka tree.

18. 2989

He bent his bow, and with the sword and the quiver filled with arrows,
he whose eyes were like red lotuses left that hut of leaves,
and crying out to them, "You! Come on this way!"
the hero, with his broad shoulders, began his battle.

19. 2990

Though they seemed the raging fire at the end of a universe,
their tridents flashing light and their swords and their axes,
Rāma with his arrows leveled those long, powerful
hands that looked like twenty-eight columns to the earth.

20. 2991

Their arms holding swords tall as trees collapsed
as the arrows released by Rāma's strength were streaming,
striking them though they crowded him with their chests. The heads
of those Rākṣasas flowed down as the woman of evil fled.

21. 2992

Like an elephant cow running, trumpeting with her trunk
held high over her head, because a cruel and plundering
lion in roaring fury has killed all her bulls, she recounted
what had taken place to Khara of the glittering spear.

22. 2993

When she said to him, "The Rākṣasas have fallen on that field
and died!" he whose name was cruel Khara grew enraged
and the blood came seething up, surging across the eyes
of that being even Śiva who rides the bull cannot restrain.

23. 2994

"Bring my chariot! Ready my strong weapons of war!
Let those who serve me instantly run and beat
the great war drum that thunders like a cloud on its elephant!"
he roared out, and savage lions trembled in their caves.

24. 2995

The moment the sound of the kettledrum rose up,
a chariot army gathered like the coming of clouds
without end full of great rains, and the world
of the gods and the underworld of the snakes felt anguish.

25. 2996

A great army assembled for battle with the trumpeters blowing
booming conches, long powerful arms rippling
like waves on water, a clamor like the thunder of black clouds
at the end of a universe above the dark wind-whipped water.

26. 2997

Like a forest that had surged up so high that it was hiding
the sky, great battle-flags swelled up everywhere
and swayed like dancing demons rising up full of joy
at the thought that soon their hunger would be swept away.

27. 2998

They were like a herd of rutting elephants who had torn free
from their stakes, each with two strong trunks hanging down,
obeying no one, and fires flared up in the forest
from the sparks of swords against swords in the dense throng.

28. 2999

It was like the darkness gathering together, thrusting
enraged at the sun that is a beneficent mass of grace
as they signaled their attack, beating both eyes of the ***muruṭu*** drum,
the noise melting into the sound of crowding chariot wheels.

29. 3000

Every mountain that towers up in the seven worlds
which endure seemed to have gathered together in one place,
as if they were wrenching the back of the body of the earth,
making it reel on the head of the snake who carries it.

30. 3001

Was it multitudes of tigers
or a swarming of clouds?
massed shining elephants
or mountains towering up?
No, you would answer, but
an army of lions,
tens of thousands of warriors
with weapons in their hands.

31. 3002

They were drawn by yāḷis,
drawn by lions,
drawn by mighty elephants
drawn by tigers,
they were drawn by dogs,
drawn by foxes,
drawn by twisted demons
and drawn by horses.

32. 3003

Harnessed to buffalo herds,
harnessed to pigs,
harnessed to monsters that ride
the winds, harnessed to donkeys,
harnessed to flocks of vultures
who encircled the world as they
appeared in all the directions,
and resounding with conches,

33. 3004

crowds of chariots swarmed out,
and the glowing faces
of tiny-eyed elephants large
as clouds, cavalry advancing
on their legs like the wind when,
great as the ocean,
that assembly moved forward
like irresistible Death,

34. 3005

carrying their axes, their spears
    and their strong swords
and long lances and their staffs,
    their clusters of javelins,
entire boulders, war hammers,
    their clubs, their tridents,
like iron bars, their nooses
    like those of Death himself,

35. 3006

barbed stabbing spears and thunderbolts,
    great poles, missiles
and arrows and discuses and
    bows without end,
shining conches and the deadly
    *valayam* discuses and
balls of fire and throwing
    darts and twisted cords,

36. 3007

while other weapons dripped
    blood and flesh,
shining so that even the sun,
    even the fire were afraid,
weapons adorned with vākai
    garlands of victories
and with the force to wound
    every one of the gods.

37. 3008

There were fourteen generals
    for the Rākṣasa army,
and they had eyes of blazing fire
    and they had mouths large
enough to swallow up
    the great vast world
and they had the strength of thousands
    and thousands of elephants.

38. 3009

For those who would count the multitude
of that army in its enormous
strength, each division was of
six million Rākṣasas
and there were fourteen divisions,
all equal in number,
summing up to a total
of eighty-four million soldiers.

39. 3010

Those fierce soldiers had mouths
that roared like thunder.
In their hands were weapons
ready for hurling. They had
protective powers granted them by Brahmā.
On their heads, the clouds
slept thinking they were mountains.
In their pride, they had arrogant hearts.

40. 3011

Their towering bodies rose
to reach the sky.
Eyes could never cross
the breadth of their chests.
They were mighty enough to measure
the earth with their feet
and were honored through their victories
in innumerable battles of heaven.

41. 3012

Their shoulders were of a hardness
to beat down and break
great weapons hurled by Indra
or any god below him.
Their authority was such that Death
bowed to them and was restrained
and their bodies were like ferocious fire
that had taken on forms.

42. 3013

They had tridents, nooses,
masses of thick red hair
and their bravery and their fangs.
They were so dark that compared to them
the Hālāhala poison is white.
The way they looked, even Death
might well think that they
were Death with his strength.

43. 3014

Wearing leg-rings, garlands,
armor on their chests and
sparkling ornaments, they knit
their brows. Their tufts of hair
were red as fire. Hungry
for battle, their hearts
high, they had assembled together
for their single purpose.

44. 3015

Even if Indra with his rutting elephant
of indestructible tusks
should happen casually to behold
their faces, he would run.
Their mountainous shoulders itched for lack
of battles where all
the three worlds come unhinged,
unable to hold their forms.

45. 3016

They had terrifying, fiery faces
of elephants and of horses,
witches, monkeys, powerful
lions, murderously angry bears,
dogs and tigers and yāḷis.
They had eyes that seemed as if,
drawing the poison from the primal
ocean, they had massed it there.

46. 3017

Some had eight hands, some seven,
some had seven or eight faces,
the eyes streaming fire, some had seven
or eight legs. They were indestructible
and proud that they could encompass
living creatures with their
strong hands and then consume them,
dropping them into their mouths.

47. 3018

Treasures they had acquired from Yakṣas
or that Asuras had given them,
treasures they had gained through their strength
after deceiving the gods
or they had taken after driving off
the Gandharvas who never tire
or had seized after wounding
the Siddhas who are to be loved,

48. 3019

flags and umbrellas and peacock feathers,
lofty chowries and banners
carried on elephants, high
canopies and many different kinds
of regal symbols rose everywhere,
crowding the space of the sky
with a density that stripped the worlds
of the light of the sun.

49. 3020

The fourteen generals of those
armies had won victories
that covered all the fourteen
worlds. With their axes
and swords, their shining tridents,
they showed their rage
so fierce that it could ravage
like a tiger or a lion.

50. 3021

With their bows and scimitars,
teeth hanging over their lips,
with enough strength to tear up
Mount Meru, they came
from every direction, in chariots
that were drawn by horses,
the generals! with hearts firmly resolved
to carry out their vows.

51. 3022

There were Dūṣaṇa and Triśaras
and other heroes with their armies
and all the different great drums
and conches were resounding
and the spearmen with their garlanded weapons
that break off warriors' lives
surrounded the generals, multitudes
full of joyous exultation.

52. 3023

With that dense and outspread ocean
of the combat-ready army
encircling him as if he were Mount Meru
which reaches to the sky,
Khara himself appeared with his towering
shoulders in his chariot,
halting it then, and at his arrival
everyone felt afraid.

53. 3024

The dust stirred up by the Rākṣasas
and the chariots hung with
golden ornaments, by the horses
and the elephants flowing with musth
rose to the sky so that even
the yellow horses of the sun,
even his chariot of the deepest, finest
gold was turned white.

54. 3025

The forest was covered with dust,
 there was dust over the mountains
and the sky above. Many clouds
 of dust choked the oceans.
What more is there to say of them?
 That enraged army as it
began its advance was like
 the great ocean rising.

55. 3026

Since they had filled up all the space
 of the earth and the sky,
they seemed great mountains on top of
 masses of mountains,
and they were springing from mountain
 summit to summit
with their hearts seething like poison
 whose use is to kill.

56. 3027

Toward the munificent being an army flooded,
 and leading them was the Rākṣasī woman,
and how like she was to the destined disease
 that cannot be avoided even by those
who have perfected themselves, who have cut off
 attachment, and their great karma born of illusion
has vanished away, but this, having come with them
 at birth, stays with them and kills them.

57. 3028

Terrifying the clouds gathered together in the sky
 with the voices of their drums, putting fear
into all the thunder so that it trembled
 at the roar of the strings on their long bows
and the ocean frightened by their uproar
 quivering and growing faint, the army
of Rākṣasas then entered the place
 where the heroes were living in the dense forest.

58. 3029

And meanwhile, with dry mouths and nearly fainting,
    their bodies hurting them because they did not
rest anywhere on the way as they ran,
    breathing hard and their eyes dimming,
the birds and the other animals, ah!
    how they rushed then as if they were spies
to let Rāma know what they had discovered—
    that the army of the evil had arrived.

59. 3030

As the cloud of dust came after them
    and the sound of trees and underbrush breaking
under marching feet boomed across the forest,
    the yāḷis and the lions fled in terror
and Lakṣmaṇa heard all the uproar
    and he thought to himself, "An army
of great strength, one very hard
    to oppose, is advancing against us."

60. 3031

Holding his bow where light hovered,
    wearing his strong armor and his sword
and his quiver of arrows edged with gold,
    his heart on fire, eager and ready
to act, he said, "You stay here.
    Stand and watch what I will do!"
and then Rāma looked at the younger brother
    who stood before him, and he began to speak.

61. 3032

"So that the promise may not be broken
    which I made before those men of great tapas
who hold to the path of their liberation
    when I said, 'I will take the lives
of the Rākṣasas,' hero! this is what
    I want of you right now, stay here
and protect the woman whose hair has
    the smell of flowers. I will kill this army."

62. 3033

And as he was thinking, "This army coming
are Khara's troops who make the whole
dense forest of trees into their road,"
the dark being with eyes like lotuses
threw his unbreakable armor over his shoulders
the strength of which never lessens, and he took up
his bow and tied on the quiver
full of arrows and put on his sword.

63. 3034

"If even the sky and the earth were to come
against me in a battle for survival,
their days would wither and vanish away.
What more should I have to say
to you who are as strong as a yāḷi?
You should leave this fight to me,
so that it may clear my shoulders
of this drowsiness that makes them tight."

64. 3035

As soon as he spoke, the young warrior
consented. In his heart, he contemplated
and recognized the strength of Rāma's shoulders
like mountains nor would he refuse
the command of his elder brother. He folded
his beautiful hands and he remained there
in the hut with her who was suffering
now and her tears were falling to the earth.

65. 3036

Then leaving her who was like a flowering branch
with the moon above it wearing earrings
to wait there troubled and losing strength,
he left the hut of leaves, like Mount Meru
with his incomparable bow, so that the Rākṣasas
who have cruel teeth and roar like clouds
saw him coming like an angry lion
that rises up and sets out from its cave.

66. 3037

As he appeared, she who was like blazing
    glowing fire risen in a bamboo grove
and reaching the sky, the Rākṣasī bringing about
    the destruction of the entire race that she
herself belonged to, pointed out the hero
    with a gesture. "The warrior," she said,
"who has come out now to stand against us
    and fight, this is powerful Rāma."

67. 3038

And from where he stood reaching the sky,
    victorious Khara high on his golden chariot
that terrified the sun so that it ran away,
    he with his shoulders like mountains
said to his soldiers, "I, myself,
    fighting him hand to hand, will destroy
the power of this man and then I
    will wear the vākai garland of victories.

68. 3039

"Since everyone, very naturally, would say
    'A man! A single man, coming against
this strong army, and just look how
    they fill the space of the whole forest!'
what honor could come to me from the victory
    I would gain? All of you stay here
and watch. I, by myself, will eat up
    the life of this being who is meat for us."

69. 3040

Hearing those words, a Rākṣasa came
    whose name was Akampana, of great learning
and one among them who had good to him,
    and he said, "Lord! Let me say something.
It is right to be very fierce in battle,
    O you who are most virile among
all heroes! but around this action
    we pursue, there have been evil omens.

70. 3041

"The clouds have been roaring, pouring down
  a very great rain of blood
and the Sun God, look at him,
  he is surrounded by a halo!
Notice how there are flocks of crows
  that hover above your flag
and fight each other, fall, cry out,
  and fallen roll on the earth.

71. 3042

"Flies are all around the blades
  of our swords and the warriors
feel their left eyes and their left arms
  quivering and our horses
who have such strength drop asleep
  and fall, while many packs
of jackals who have mingled with dogs
  are standing here howling.

72. 3043

"Musth is oozing from cow elephants
  while the tusks are breaking
of the great-cheeked bulls and the world
  trembles! Thunderbolts fall
from the high clear sky and fires
  are burning into vast distances.
The garlands we all wear in our hair
  smell of meat and decay.

73. 3044

"Since these things are happening, do not think
  he is a man, he is alone,
about this one because thinking in that way
  makes no sense at all.
Even if you were to do everything right
  in battle, this one cannot
be conquered. You who wear the garland
  of victories! Bear what I say!"

74. 3045

As soon as he heard the words spoken,
    all the worlds trembled
at his laughter and he said, "Our courage
    is a wonderful thing. My arms
are handsome and they move like grinding stones
    that grind and destroy enemies
and they have grown swollen and angry for battle.
    Will a man find them easy?"

75. 3046

At the moment he said this, that horde
    of Rākṣasas in their burning anger,
screaming out, "Grab him! Throw him down!"
    as if they were elephants gone enraged
surrounding a lion with a mane
    that shines like silver,
there in the forest surrounded the son
    of the king of kings.

76. 3047

As they encircled him, Rāma's hand encircled
    his bow where the arrow was ready,
and now I will tell you how that battle
    began and how it came out.
The leaping horses went rolling on the ground,
    pierced by his swift arrows. Elephants
in war paint lay writhing like falling mountains
    lightning has struck and split.

77. 3048

The tridents were broken and the bright
    axes were broken, the swords
in masses were broken off at the hilt,
    the great maces were broken,
the hurling missiles were broken, and the arrows
    with cruel edges that tear
were broken, spears broken, bows
    and *pallam* arrows broken.

78. 3049

Bracelets were cut off, axes were cut off
together with the arms that held them,
the feet were cut off under rutting elephants
and axles and banners
were cut from the high chariots and horses
were cut down, great heads
were cut off in heaps, pestles
and knobbed clubs were cut through.

79. 3050

First passing through saddled horses
and crowds of mountainous elephants,
his burning arrows ran off into all
the directions and blood
flooded to the earth like the long
line of a waterfall. The chests
of those Rākṣasas were stripped of their splendor
and their heads were lost.

80. 3051

When the descendant of Raghu shot his burning arrows
in such dense lines, who could tell
if there were one of them, ten, a hundred,
one thousand or ten million
which traveled and killed and heaped up
great hills of corpses
like so many mountains assembled together
with arrows through their summits?

81. 3052

Like fire igniting among blackened
dead trees in the wilderness
and catching so that the flames break out,
they seemed with the blood
shooting up as the headless bodies danced
and the sharp arrows rushed
out into the sky as if pursuing
the disembodied lives as well.

82. 3053

Making swords in hands fall to the field,
    cutting through armor and throats,
tearing open chests, shearing off legs
    from great giant Rākṣasas,
leveling the red-haired, dark-skinned heads,
    the arrows then went off
into all the directions, as cruel
    as are the long eyes of women.

83. 3054

The sharp arrows that fell in showers
    created giant mountains
of Rākṣasas' bodies rising up everywhere
    like great shores forming
tanks and rivers and then they filled
    them up with blood,
so that now they had altered the old
    wild state of the forest.

84. 3055

On the great ocean of blood, in the surges
    of its waves, Rākṣasa heads
floated, long bludgeons floated,
    mountains with giant trunks
floated, nimble horses floated,
    strong bows of war
floated and tall chariots floated
    still carrying their banners.

85. 3056

Then the strong Rākṣasas looked at him
    fiery-eyed and they cried out
and they rained down upon him their
    fierce and murderous weapons,
the long cruel arrows and all the rest
    as when clouds encircle
a great mountain ready and waiting for their
    pure streams of rain.

86. 3057

He kept breaking the weapons in pieces
as they poured down. He sliced
them and sent them off broken by his arrows
into all the directions
and the Earth Goddess was crushed and twisted
and the whole forest was filled
by the black heads with their billowing red hair
that he had felled like mountains.

87. 3058

Crowds of headless bodies were dancing
and mountainous elephants bathing
in the hot red streams of the blood
of those Rākṣasas whose acts are cruel,
who had towered up in their rage and, exulting, turned
against Rāma. Now great ghouls
glutted themselves on all the fat. Absorbing their lives,
the other world was thrown out of joint.

88. 3059

Those treacherous Rākṣasas with their long fangs
who had been deluded by arrogance
had the pupils of their eyes that had terrified Garuḍa
taken out by mere crows.
Is it easy to describe the destruction of those
ignorant bodies of darkness?
Is anything stronger than the Order of the World
whose nature is to give love?

89. 3060

With their hate of the bowman shining like the sun that has torn apart
many thousands of darknesses, they glared at him with their looks like
[bright spears,
and made war, sending off every one of their weapons at once like a rain
[of boulders
falling from a dense giant cloud on the final day of a universe.

90. 3061

But with his sharp arrows he cut them all down so no one
could distinguish those who had hurled or shot weapons from those
[who had merely
thought of hurling or shooting. The ones in masses, the ones spread
[out, the fierce ones,
those who had blocked his way and opposed him, he killed them with
[the bow in his hand.

91. 3062

Into the sky, out to the edge of the ocean ring around the world,
into the constellations that surround the moon, into the savage
massive forests, the mountains, as far as the regions of the Elephants of
[Space,
the heads dressed in their earrings were sent off by Rāma's arrows.

92. 3063

On the earth, on the mountains, on the clouds, in the sky reaching to
[the moon
above and under the vast ocean, into the wounds of the strong flew
the arrows after piercing the chests of those giants who had disdained
massive Mount Meru. Rivers of blood poured up in crashing waves.

93. 3064

All of them, with their sharp fierce weapons launched to gain victory,
in their garlands of gold, their eyes filled with flaming fire, perished
under the rain of arrows and their bodies in the ocean of blood became
[imperishable
bodies. "How the Rākṣasas suffer!" they shouted out then at one with
[the gods.

94. 3065

Where floating livers were the lotuses, heaped chariots the mounds of
[sand
and virile elephants the packs of floating crocodiles, enormous
intestines the dense green lotus leaves spreading out
in the many giant waves of the oceans of blood, ghouls dove and rose.

95. 3066

Some Rākṣasas called to anyone for help, some of them fainted,
some of them lost control and ran away, some were in agony, some
rolled on the ground, some were bathed in the waves of the ocean of
[blood
and fat, some died broken on the earth as the killing rain fell.

96. 3067

Moving up in their chariots, the fourteen generals were coming, all of
[them together,
and they whose armies were great oceans thick with swords and spears
were laughing at those who had been shattered, they with their powerful
[bows,
virulent as the Hālāhala poison that rose to terrify the churners of the
[milky ocean.

97. 3068

As when, in ancient times, all the warriors living in the three cities
[massed together
and surrounded Śiva towering in the sky, his incomparable bow a
[mountain,
so those generals came on with the fire inside them flowing out through
[their eyes,
angrily attacking, surrounding that cloudlike bowman, and the battle
[began.

98. 3069

Many Rākṣasas with their white fangs like crescent moons shot and
[threw weapons,
attacked with iron rods, struck at him, pressed near to him, many
rained down rocks and whole hills upon him, flung the fires of their
[anger,
many cursed him, many threatened him, many surrounded him as if he
[were a mountain.

99. 3070

In that killing that arose through Rāma's bow, all the animals yoked to
[chariots
fell to the earth, great rutting elephants became sacrifices and swift
[horses
wearing strings of bells lost the heads from their bodies and Rākṣasas
[fled,
the life loosened in them, as halos vanish from around the burning sun.

100. 3071

From the bodies of those warriors full of delusion, the blood dense as
[rain
came flowing like rivers of red milk in flood covering the earth,
and the crowds of gods filling the broad sky covered their eyes
and Death's messengers, swift as a strong cruel wind, came and seized
[the lives.

101. 3072

Dogs were climbing into the mouths like caves of the Rākṣasas who had
[gone mad
with their rising hunger for this battle now crowded with flesh-eating
[ghouls.
As the sharp, fire-tipped arrows sent them to heaven, giant jackals
[climbed up on their heads
but still more of them, like dark clouds, like strong fierce male lions,
[kept coming on.

102. 3073

The Rākṣasas lost their heads as their eyes shot out sparks of fire
and the elephants were destroyed as they came, like so many shattered
[mountains.
The arrows radiating from Rāma's bow split all the directions apart
into which the bodies, as if they were forges, shot sparks as they were
[losing their lives.

103. 3074

Other than the mighty leaders of that army, all the raging
soldiers with their chariots and their powerful weapons, who had [opposed
the hero and encircled him closely, now because of his arrows
sank down into the great ocean of evil-smelling blood.

104. 3075

The generals looked all around but in the army that had followed them,
they saw not a single body still with its head,
and the generals grew enraged and they ground their teeth.
Swiftly, moving up in their chariots, they surrounded Rāma.

105. 3076

The fourteen chariots came up in an instant, encircling him,
and Rāma shivered them into pieces with his strong arrows.
Losing their wheels and their horses and their drivers, they seemed
mountains attacked by the cruel wind at the end of a universe.

106. 3077

Their chariots were destroyed, so the generals leaped down from them,
taking their cocked bows in hand, cracking the earth they touched.
They did not stop advancing. They showered him with arrows
like rising thunder and their eyes shot flowing fire.

107. 3078

Putting an end with his arrows to all theirs that had always
destroyed their targets, but now, by him, were destroyed,
with fourteen arrows he cut through fourteen bows,
stripping away the ferocity of war, their calling.

108. 3079

All the generals full of anger now that they had lost their bows
quickly picked up mountains embedded with great boulders
and swiftly, as they stood towering into the heights of the sky,
they began to throw them, clashing up sparks of light.

109. 3080

He whose learning transcends the great ocean of all the knowledges
drew out fourteen cruel arrows with tips like leaves
and he curved his eyebrows and his cruel, murderous bow,
and the mountains and the heads fell, all of them to the earth.

110. 3081

As those superb generals of the armies fell, yet more
Rākṣasas clashed their many weapons together and with their burning
eyes crowded in against Rāma, densely below him
and above him, masking the directions and terrifying the gods.

111. 3082

The great kettledrums roared and the huge rutting elephants
roared, there was the roaring of the rapid strings of the bows,
a roaring of conches and horses, all that clamor
of the Rākṣasas was like the roar of a cloud spreading everywhere.

112. 3083

As the Rākṣasas threw their burning weapons
    filling the sky, even the gods ran away
afraid that the weapons would descend on them,
    cut up again and again as they fell
by the hero's arrows, and that the worlds would grow weak
    and would sink down, and that the elephants
who stand, unshakable, in all the directions,
    ah! on that day would close their eyes.

113. 3084

And then the three-headed warrior, whose strength was boundless,
took his place among the army. His crowns were of gold
and he looked like the trident that three-eyed Śiva carries.
He was holding a bow that could send out a rain of sharp-headed
[arrows.

114. 3085

So he was, standing in the midst of his army that roared
like the ocean at the end of a universe, coming from everywhere,
and then that hero appeared, who is like no one else,
alone, like a single lamp against the gathered darkness.

115. 3086

And with his army of arrows Rāma dealt with the forces
arrayed in battle there under Triśaras whose eyes
were burning and his army massive and the noise he made
like thunder and the sword that he held raised high.

116. 3087

Their legs were cut through and their heads cut off,
their arms were cut through the middle and their thighs were cut away,
their swords were cut into halves and so were their axes,
their strength was cut through, their umbrellas of royalty cut down.

117. 3088

Whole armies of wheeled chariots fell to the earth,
their horses' yokes cut through, losing banners and handrests
shaped like lotuses, while tall strong rutting elephants
rolled on the ground like mountain summits broken by thunderbolts.

118. 3089

For the moment not aware that their heads had been cut off,
headless Rākṣasas cocked arrows on their cruel bows
of victory, while those not yet dead surged up
and hurled their weapons like a rain cloud filling the sky.

119. 3090

Headless they tossed and quivered in their golden armor,
seeming like mountains with shields in their powerful hands,
and they looked as if they were dancing many different dances,
amazing the women of heaven in their sounding anklets.

120. 3091

Rivers of blood transformed the ocean with a foam of chowries
and white umbrellas, and elephants were the sharks' fins
sinking down into whirlpools, with saddles looming like ships
that carry dense heaps of gems into the cool harbors.

121. 3092

As the swift and fiercely cruel arrows cut them down,
some of those Rākṣasas with curving teeth and massive strength
became gods and, with the women of heaven around whose ornamented
[hair
bees circle, they saw their own trunks dancing.

122. 3093

And as the pure swift arrows cruelly sliced off arms
for which ghouls fought with dogs who, seizing a side,
held on with locked jaws, some Rākṣasas along with the gods
whose wives wear fine bangles burst out laughing.

123. 3094

And when the chosen arrows sank into and opened wide
their chests, some of them, the great battle past, came
to the other world and thought, "This great army of Rākṣasas is
[immense.
One man alone faced it!" and they felt despair.

124. 3095

He seemed an elephant as his arrows felled the cruel Rākṣasas,
cutting down hordes of bodies at the root as if they were
vicious words spoken in false witness falling back
on a deceiver without virtues, his heart black as collyrium.

125. 3096

Just as a wasp with graceful wings can easily turn
a worm that has come to it into a being of the same nature
as itself, so he who gives everything, with the purity of his red arrows
enveloped the deceiving Rākṣasas and made them into gods.

126. 3097

As if announcing to Rāvaṇa around whose spear garlands hang
that a man had been victorious in war, had prevailed and killed,
those rivers of blood carrying the bodies of the Rākṣasas
who had fought in pitched battle reached as far as Laṅkā.

127. 3098

As great armies that had drawn up in files all around Rāma
rolled on the ground while the piercing arrows drank their lives,
the three-headed general, boiling with his rage, did not hesitate but [drove
his chariot sinking in blood up into the sky and shouted defiance.

128. 3099

Halting his chariot, he showered arrows fierce as thunder,
as if he were a cloud in the sky, and they hid the beautiful
form of the son of that father who had personified the Order
of the World and stood as a paragon of truth for all men.

129. 3100

But with his fierce arrows, Rāma cut to pieces
all those arrows showering down and then using fourteen
arrows engraved with flowers, he destroyed the chariot
of gold and destroyed the life of its fierce driver.

130. 3101

And the next moment, with incomparable arrows edged in bright gold,
he sent two heads of the Rākṣasa rolling on the ground,
leaving one great diademed head on that evil being
whose acts were cruel, and the gods rose shouting their approval.

131. 3102

His chariot destroyed and, as he was, no longer now
fit to be called the three-headed warrior, his courage
did not fail. He stood firmly and bent his bow so far
it had no length and shot arrows like a dark streaming cloud.

132. 3103

He raised his eyebrows in anger and continued to fight
with his bow that seemed a densely black cloud,
and as if the wind in the sky were destroying a cloud, Rāma
used one more arrow to cut through and do away with that bow.

133. 3104

Though he had lost his bow,
        he in no way lost
the burning radiance of his face
        glaring, nor his burning anger
nor his menacing words, nor did he lose
        the strength of his arms nor any
power to unleash a stream of rocks
        or to whirl like a kite.

134. 3105

And then as, alone, in the air,
        as if he were two hundred men,
he carried on his battle, putting
        into practice all his great
skills of illusion, Rāma,
        with two burning arrows,
cut off his two legs, then severed his arms
        with two more burning arrows.

135. 3106

Without his legs and without his arms
        but with glistening sharp teeth,
he came grasping after Rāma
        with his mouth stinking of flesh
and as large as a mountain cave, but Rāma
        looked at him without pity
and then, with his long bow of victories,
        sheared the one head left.

136. 3107

The moment Triśaras, like a mountain summit,
fell all the way to the earth,
the Rākṣasas ran and would not stop even
when Dūṣaṇa tried to block them
as with their shining swords and the shields
in their strong hands, they floundered
through the moist intestines tangling their long legs
in the wide-spread blood.

137. 3108

While the gods in the sky above clapped
and shouted with joy,
they ran so fast that under their feet,
the earth sank down
onto the hoods of Ādiśeṣa. Some fell
sinking deep into the fat.
Some stumbled over the heaped-up corpses,
rolled down and escaped alive.

138. 3109

Some had to stop running because
garlanded swords and spears
lay too thick in the way, some fell
into the rivers of blood
flowing from the dead and could not rise
and were carried off, some
in fear of Rāma tried to swim the great
ocean of blood but sank in it.

139. 3110

As if fear had taken on visible form,
not even noticing how
the waistbands and swords of the dead caught at
and cut off their legs,
they were in anguish as they watched
the burning arrows of the great hero
make deep holes in other Rākṣasas' hearts
and they froze in place.

140. 3111

Some ran hard and cut their way
into the wound in the belly
of a great rutting elephant and entered
that giant cave and lifted
their hands over their heads, entreating
a headless corpse nearby to protect them.
"Friend," they were saying, "If Rāma comes,
tell him you haven't seen us!"

141. 3112

Then Dūṣaṇa, whose chariot had swift horses,
spoke out to the panicking Rākṣasas,
"Do not be afraid of men whose hearts
lack strength for acts of courage!"
and he stopped for a while and he considered,
then he said to them,
"And, having thought this over, I have
something more to tell you.

142. 3113

"If you are so low they can say, 'You live
like children with fear
in your hearts,' women wearing heavy bangles
will not take you to them.
You should know the only lasting
armor is self-confidence.
Do you want fear to be the lovely
companion of your precious life?

143. 3114

"Did any of you Rākṣasas run away
before Indra whose spear
is filed sharp or before the highest three
indestructible gods when in battle
you stood and confronted them? Have you learned
to run from the gods who ran
broken at your hands? Your minds
now are bewildered!

144. 3115

"With so many of you warriors defeated
here by a single man,
when you enter your city again with your swords
and your good names lost,
you who would enjoy your pleasure, will you be able
to make love to your women
with rich eyes, happy to see you as against your chests
their breasts press?

145. 3116

"Your eyes that were bronze with anger
now are white as milk!
Will you show the women of your families
the scratches on your backs
from branches of the burning forest that struck
you again and again
when you ran, or is it scars you will show them
from arrows in the chest?

146. 3117

"Is there a shame worse than what has come to you
here in fierce battle,
fighting against a man, where you have achieved
the disgrace of showing
your backs to add to the infamy of the nose
cut off from your leader's
sister, he whose arms the brave gods
at their best could not match?

147. 3118

"Are you merchants who live by trade
or have you turned your swords
of warriors and your sharp spears into plow blades
and do you furrow the ground?
In your hands you hold the swords of heroes
seized from your enemies
during lives of furious combat, tell me
how are you living now?"

148. 3119

And then he said, “Wait a while” to the other leaders,
“and see what I will do
through the power of my great bow.” With his army
like a throbbing ocean he set out
to attack Rāma, and the gods were amazed
and confused but Rāma,
shouting, “Take good care of your army!”
walked out to confront him.

149. 3120

The dense infantry was cut right through
and the elephant divisions
had their trunks and towering tusks cut through
and the arm supports shaped like lotuses
and forests of banners were cut from the chariots
swift as the wind
and the necks of the horses were cut through
like grain on growing rice.

150. 3121

The burning arrows ran and pierced
the vitals of the Rākṣasas,
and other kinds of arrows which he unleashed
brought down the belts
and the armor, running through bodies
and shield-plates, making
rivers of blood run down
like running waterfalls.

151. 3122

Selected heron-feathered arrows
entered the Rākṣasas’ chests,
burying themselves there and others,
crescent-tipped, did not penetrate
but cut off heads and also blazing hot
arrows pierced the armored chests
of the night-stalkers and the *pallam* arrows penetrated
and split their deceiving hearts.

152. 3123

He cut down all the burning arrows
that Dūṣaṇa released
and all the weapons hurled by those followers
he destroyed as if in play
and he dried up that immense ocean
of Rākṣasas whose strength
had been great, gathered there, standing,
roaring against him.

153. 3124

The gods stood up and shouted
as the great river of blood
rose, uprooting trees and giant mountains,
and the fine arrows that Rāma
poured out followed the Rākṣasas
everywhere, their thinking blurred
by burning rage, in every direction
and rolled them on the earth.

154. 3125

What need is there to picture the demons
whose repulsive stomachs were like
masses of great mountains covered over
with viscous fat? All
who stood and fought there were destroyed.
They quickly died.
And exhausted as he gathered in the sweet lives,
even Death forgot who he was.

155. 3126

But, filled with rage, Dūṣaṇa drove
his rumbling chariot
rapidly over the shining mountains
of elephants and horses
and the tufted heads of those once
furious soldiers and the trunks
and many gleaming weapons and the generals
of his clan and the white fat.

156. 3127

The piled, glittering mountains towered
of those who would not follow
the Order of the World, and they were
beyond counting, and Dūṣaṇa's
chariot, though it was whirled like a kite,
with its great fierce speed
went down and up over the great jungle
of corpses. What it endured!

157. 3128

On his single chariot, the rolling wheels
drawn by twenty-five horses
with well-clipped manes, though the going was hard,
he moved like life facing
death come visible in a long arrow
and reached Rāma who stood
shining like the moon that has emerged
from the darkness of a cloud.

158. 3129

The Lord who gives love looked
straight at Dūṣaṇa riding
in his chariot and holding his bow
like a mountain. Rāma said,
"The firmness you are showing is
very fine, very fine,"
and once he had spoken, the inflamed Rākṣasa
shot three arrows toward him.

159. 3130

The gods were afraid as the arrows
flew at the gold disc shining
on his forehead like the brow ornament of an elephant
adorning him who had allowed
one of those two who, along with the eight
elephants of the distant circling
directions, bear the world's burden to return
home and to rule the earth.

160. 3131

"The way he times his shots is good
and he is strong," thought Rāma,
with his smile that had a red glow to it
as he carefully chose cruel arrows.
He brought the chariot down easily, right there,
smashing it with its swift horses,
cut through the fierce bow in Dūṣaṇa's hand
and destroyed his shining armor.

161. 3132

The gods rose to their feet shouting
and in every direction the blessings
chanted by the holy men surged up
ceaselessly like the roaring of the sea
in the monsoon. "You!" Rāma said, "Save yourself,
if you can, from this!"
then shot an arrow, and Dūṣaṇa lost
his giant head with its fangs.

162. 3133

Victorious Khara, his bow and his cruel weapons in hand,
saw that his younger brother had neither head nor army
cut down by the arrows of Daśaratha's son and he raged
like a murderous elephant with tusks set into his head.

163. 3134

He came on with his ocean of Rākṣasas, terrifying even Death
with his elephants, strong horses, chariots spreading out
through the directions. As a mass of clouds surround the moon,
he surrounded Rāma who was like a rutting elephant with a bow.

164. 3135

The Rākṣasas, cruel, irrestrainable, began their many-sided
attack and drove the great elephants streaming musth, the chariots
and horses over the earth so that the hood of the snake who upholds it
tore, and the great Rāma shot at them with his burning arrows.

165. 3136

The rutting elephants fell quivering and the horses and chariots.
Crowned heads lay quivering and right braceleted arms,
small intestines, skin and flesh quivering, pairs
of quivering legs, left arms falling, quivering.

166. 3137

It was like a forest of swords, of spears, a forest of arms
holding strong bows, all of them bristling up from the standing
forest of Rākṣasa infantry that Rāma cut down with his own powerful
army that was his cruel and lovely forest of arrows.

167. 3138

Those arrows chosen carefully by the Order of the World incarnate
pierced the stars, pierced shining Meru, pierced through
the sky above and pierced through the earth. Does it have to be said
how they pierced the bodies of those coming on with drawn swords!

168. 3139

He showered his chosen arrows down on them that day
to subdue and destroy those surrounding him and their families too.
He killed them quickly just as the wealth that the strong enjoy
after tormenting and killing the weak in secret will destroy them.

169. 3140

As all the Rākṣasas were wiped out, he who wore war anklets,
that hero who was called Khara the cruel became enraged
and, like Mount Mandara in the great ocean, he stood tall
and alone in that unending ocean of blood and fat.

170. 3141

His eyes were scattering fire, his bow scattering arrows.
His heart was ablaze in the seething sea of blood. As if
a boat were racing over the ocean while the crows
and the vultures crowded around it, he advanced on his chariot.

171. 3142

He was coming on, with his courage and his anger, furious as the fire
that blazes up at the end of a universe, and in the face of him, Rāma,
who had, with a hand, broken the bow of the god whose neck
is like a dark jewel, chose a burning arrow and opposed him.

172. 3143

The commander of the Rākṣasas shot a thousand sharp arrows,
shapes of fire, even, swift as wind, cruelly bladed,
and with his thousand arrows, shapes of fire, sharp and even,
swift as wind and cruelly bladed, Rāma cut them down.

173. 3144

The single master of the seven worlds shot nine arrows
that sped along more fiercely than the fire that ends a universe,
and Khara, firing sharp arrows surrounded with radiance,
his bow bent into a wheel, shot and cut them down.

174. 3145

Waging battle with his magic skill at tactics of deception, Khara
hid the form of him who gives everything in a shower of arrows.
With pain in their hearts, the gods ran and hid while the hero
growing angry bit his lower lip with his white teeth.

175. 3146

He thought,
"Now I'll finish him with a single, powerful arrow."
He fit it
and drew the string so it touched his towering shoulder
as he stood there
and suddenly while he was grasping his strong bow
it broke
with a sound like thunder through the great, wide sky.

176. 3147

The gods
who had been shouting out the victory of the hero
now suffered
and trembled at the breaking of the bow and they were thinking,
"There is no
other fierce bow for him!" and they said,
"Our strength
ah! is gone now," and they were fearful.

177. 3148

When they spoke,
without thinking about the bow he had held
being broken,
nor considering that he was alone,
the son
of the king of kings, as was right
for him to do,
stretched out his great hand behind him.

178. 3149

Varuṇa
who was standing in heaven saw this and it was
as if he knew
what was meant, and into the powerful hand
of the leader
of the gods he put the bow Rāma had once taken
in ancient battle
and heroism from him who strikes with the axe.

179. 3150

When he
whose color is that of a thundercloud
received
the bow put into his right hand and grasped it
with his left,
then the left eyes and the left arms
throbbed of all
those who had strayed from the right path.

180. 3151

Before you could blink,
he bent the bow, fixed the shafts to it
while Death itself
was dancing and he released a hundred arrows
against the chariot
with deadly wheels of Khara who opposed him
and he destroyed it,
so that it became nothing but fine powder.

181. 3152

Dropping to earth,
he who had lost his great chariot
that had been built
so well, rose up shouting into the sky,
and against the shoulders
like Mount Mandara of that handsome bowman
without equal,
he showered arrows as if they were rain.

182. 3153

But Rāma
the son of Daśaratha stood there, lasting
out the attack
and with only one of his arrows he severed
the huge
right arm of Khara as it was reaching into his quiver
for fierce
burning arrows that would now remain there.

183. 3154

The moment that
his right hand fell, with his other hand
Khara
launched his iron bar that had won victories.
It fell
like thunder out of the sky but Lakṣmaṇa's elder
brother Rāma
warded it off with a fierce glowing arrow.

184. 3155

In a rage,
like a snake who has lost his white fangs
that enclose
the poison that cannot be withstood, Khara
came on,
who had torn up a marā tree and cradled it
in his hand.
Then Rāma shot a single arrow.

185. 3156

The Rākṣasa Rāvaṇa,
because of the sin of his tormenting all
seven worlds
through the strength of his magic powers
and the boon
that he had received, at that moment had one
of his necks,
Khara who was like his right hand, cut through.

186. 3157

And the gods
rose up shouting, they danced and they sang,
they deluged
Rāma with pure white flowers,
and that immaculate
being shone out like the sun as it
dissolves
a light mist that has obscured the directions.

187. 3158

And as the holy men,
one after another, came and surrounded him,
Rāma, his heart
filled with sweetness, went to his woman,
she who had been
like a body left alone, its precious life
gone from it,
on the cruel field of battle where armies meet.

188. 3159

To wash away dust
and blood fallen from wounds in the bodies
of the cruel Rākṣasas
who had been freed for heaven, the younger brother
of the great hero
and the woman who was like a wild goose
bathed his feet
in the water of the tears that flowed from their eyes.

189. 3160

In an instant,
the blood of wounds from the multitude who had died
went running
in a flood straight to the great ocean
and the gods
sang praises, as if they were the voice
of united oceans
and the hero felt a sweet contentment.

190. 3161

And now
let us tell the rest. The sister
of Rāvaṇa
beat her belly and embraced the body
of Khara
dark as night and she rolled in the warm
blood
welling out of him and spreading into the distance.

191. 3162

"I felt
desire in my heart, a desire that was lost
with my nose
but still I did not die, yet I
am vicious
since it is I who have destroyed your days,
your life,
as the result of my words," she said and she went away.

192. 3163

She, the means
to finish off the Rākṣasas in whose hands were spears
garlanded for victory
and to cut down their families at the root,
went on
like a great wind building to a cyclone
that shakes lives
and quickly arrived at the great city of Laṅkā.

# Paṭalam Seven
# The Killing of Mārīca

1. 3164

Roaring, the demons with their huge army had died
 but Śūrpaṇakhā forgot them as her great hunger
to lie between the arms like high mountains of the warrior
 Rāma tortured her beyond endurance
and she thought, "Running as quickly as I can to the opulent city
 whose moat is the ocean waves, I will tell him
about the beauty of Sītā." And as she was coming toward the city,
 I will describe Rāvaṇa's royal state that has now vanished.

2. 3165

In this world where nothing can last, in that hall built by Takṣan
 surpassing even the power of Brahmā who, sitting on a flower,
created in rhythmic order all that moves or is rooted in place,
 in the hall of a builder able to make whatever
was imagined, beautiful with jewels and reflecting endless knowledge,
 like righteous action done in great care
performed without any fault and showing limitless strength, there
 Rāvaṇa reigned in a shining style that now has vanished.

3. 3166

Not Śiva who wears the tiger skin, not Viṣṇu in his golden robe
 nor Brahmā who is seated in the flower
had the strength left to destroy him. Then where else
 among the gods could he meet with any danger?
And toward his women who were fashioned to win victories
 with their thin waists, their ripe breasts,
the lovely red lines in their eyes, their arms like young bamboo,
 his gleaming row of crowns, vanished now, had never gone begging.

4. 3167

He had once broken off pairs of giant tusks from the
elephants gleaming in the directions of space
with those arms and shoulders covered with gold and shining
like the mountain where the sun rises
and above them his earrings were glittering as if the twelve
great suns that appear at the end of universes
had become twenty rich masses of rays reverently circling Mount Meru
as he sat there in his radiance that now has vanished.

5. 3168

Around the shoulders that were hills of diamonds sending out
the clear unified light of their gems
like so many hoods of the poisonous snake who carries
earth's weight, he wore a necklace resembling
the great prison he had filled up with all the planets
lying there and growing weak,
while nearby all the constellations glittered where the ocean
of his Laṅkā that is gone now terrified the mind.

6. 3169

Unimaginably powerful kings of demigods and demons were trembling
and by touching the jewels of their diadems to his war anklets
were wearing away, wearing away the luster of their fine gold
flashing with rubies as his tapping foot made them jingle.

7. 3170

And the rulers of all three worlds, trying to surpass one another,
ceaselessly offered him piles of tribute while in equal
profusion gods and Asuras and others kept heaping up
fragrant mounds of flowers, laying them out beside him.

8. 3171

Not knowing whether or not he might look at them any moment,
Vidyādhara kings held their palms joined in worship over their heads
and their crowns were flashing jewels like lightning row on row
while, all around him, they approached Rāvaṇa in his palace.

9. 3172

If he so much as said a single word to his women,
Siddha kings, strong as lions, with the spirit shrinking up
in their bodies and their elegant hands folding together,
thinking he meant them, came toward him with heads bent low.

10. 3173

If he happened to look at a minister and speak even
one pleasant word, the Kinnara kings, quivering within,
would say, "What is it? What is your order?"
and bow down as fear lay heavy in their hearts.

11. 3174

Nāga kings, with trembling tongues and anguish in their minds
surrounded him as if they were beings in the hells
whose eyes watch the giant staff of the Lord of the Dead
in his hand rising to beat them in his Southern Kingdom.

12. 3175

Tumburu, musician of heaven, was praising the glory in song
of those arms that, conquering Indra, made all the gods grow faint
and had defeated the eight Elephants of Space and, shaking
the mountain of Kailāsa, had brought even Śiva to shame.

13. 3176

Not falling from the standards passed along through the ages,
playing faultless rāgas while the tālas obeyed his will,
Nārada on the strings of the veena and with his gift of words
poured the Vedas as sweet music into Rāvaṇa's ears.

14. 3177

Mixing fragrant water and the sweet honey
    flowing from the Nāga trees of the Vidyādharas
and from the trees of the gods, using
    what men call a cloud for his sprayer,
shaking with his fear that a drop might fall
    on the clothes of Rāvaṇa's women,
Varuṇa, Lord of the Sharks and the Foam,
    sprinkled him who has now vanished.

15. 3178

All the jewels and the pearls
    falling from millions of trembling
crowns as they were bowing low
    and the streams of honey and pollen
from the fragrant flowers, even before
    they could touch the floor, were each
followed, caught, swept up
    by the Wind God in that time now vanished.

16. 3179

Bṛhaspati, giant planet of gold, in his hand his staff
of shining gold and the silver Evening Star wearing
the long robes that cling to their bodies, tirelessly, pleasantly,
ushered gods and divinities toward their seats according to rank.

17. 3180

Yama, Lord of Death, who had come to Rāvaṇa, and given up
his spear and the rest of his weapons, was covering his mouth
in respect with a fold of his dhoti, and announcing
the passing hours as they were beaten out on a skin drum.

18. 3181

Putting the purest camphor on soft cotton wicks
and adding oil of civet, all of the best, nothing decayed,
the God of Shining Fire, Agni, was kindling lights
that seemed a field of lotuses blossoming on a lake.

19. 3182

Wish-Granting Trees with their wealth freshly blooming,
the Jewels That Answer All Wishes without deception,
Cows That Give Riches, Kubera's Nine Treasures,
seeking his grace, gave so that even Rāvaṇa was amazed.

20. 3183

From his large, fine earrings and his other ornaments,
light spread outward in a great mass so that people
were saying, "Is there any night now in the seven worlds?
There is no darkness in any of the eight directions!"

21. 3184

Gaṅgā and all the other goddesses of the rivers,
balancing their full breasts, swaying at the waist like vines,
were scattering rice and flowers with their lovely red hands
and praising him, one after another, singing him blessings.

22. 3185

As drummers beat out rhythms on drums strapped to them, he [watched
the beautiful dancing of Urvaśī, born from Nārāyaṇa's thigh,
a woman like a painting come to life, and the other women dancing
like peacocks during the monsoon spreading their tails in pride.

23. 3186

He was sitting there without any limit to his strength,
and the three worlds were his through a power he had earned
by long and harsh tapas. In the flood of large dark
eyes under curving eyebrows of his women, Rāvaṇa was bathed.

24. 3187

And his sister, as she now was, holding her red hands
above her head, her breasts joined into a single stream of blood
and her nose bleeding, and no earrings on her ears,
her mouth opening into a howl like a thunder cloud,

25. 3188

blazing with an anger that might have been the sound
of the ocean at the end of a universe, with her mouth
smelling like rotting meat, with her hair as red as the twilight
dying in the west, appeared, moaning, at the northern gate.

26. 3189

As soon as she arrived, the Rākṣasa women of the ancient city
ran out toward her, beating their bellies, in grief and pain.
How could they bear her coming, with her nose cut off,
all alone, and her brother master over the three worlds?

27. 3190

They saw how she was at once and when they had seen her,
they didn't know what to say, and the Rākṣasa men clashed
their hands together as if they were thunderbolts from which
fire rose to their eyes and they stood there, biting their lips.

28. 3191

"Is Indra the guilty one? Is it Brahmā, that being
who created the world? Or was it Viṣṇu who carries
the discus? Is Śiva who wears the moon in his hair
guilty?" some of them asked in their burning anger.

29. 3192

And others said, "Who could even name one of our enemies
able to do this? No one living in the universe
of these three worlds could have wounded her!
Who is there outside the universe to have done it?"

30. 3193

"Instead of thinking, 'This is Rāvaṇa's sister,'
and bowing down at her feet, calling her 'Mother!'
how is it possible anyone ever could have done this?"
some were saying, "She must have slashed herself."

31. 3194

"It can't be Indra because he has given up war now
and follows orders, or Viṣṇu with the sharp discus
who has lost his strength and gone to hide in the sea
or Śiva who is on his mountain. Then who?" some of them said.

32. 3195

And others said, "No one would dare do this to her,
famous for so high a family. It must have been Khara,
her protector, thinking she was unchaste and had soiled
the honor of the family, who took away her beauty."

33. 3196

"Were the minds of the gods confused so that they
acted out this insanity, even though they are weak?
Forces who are carefully plotting the destruction
of the three worlds must have done this!" some were saying.

34. 3197

And some, "Unless a new world era has begun, can there be heroes
with such power and flashing swords and fine anklets?
This must stem from the anger of a holy man disturbed
at his tapas in the forest where men feel afraid."

35. 3198

Their arms like shoots of bangles, the dark-eyed women
of the city rich past all measure, wringing their hands,
suffering changing the sounds of their voices, like milk
already beginning to curdle, were racing to reach her.

36. 3199

Never before in that Laṅkā where the music always
sounded of drums and veenas, of the *yaḻs* with the flutes
and the conches and the trumpets had this sound,
ah! this sound of wailing risen as on that day!

37. 3200

Those women with their swaying waists and their eyes
large enough to shame the ocean ran, leaving behind them
pitchers of toddy with hovering drunken bees and the loves
of their hearts and, embracing Śūrpaṇakhā, they wailed.

38. 3201

Their hearts on fire, those women with means to punish their lovers
whose work is plowing with the sword, the tears
pouring down, inflaming the eyes already burning red
from love quarrels, fell at the feet of their king's sister.

39. 3202

Their slender waists hurting from the running, the women
were wailing as they reached the street, they who had been swinging,
completely happy, on the swings dropping down from jeweled ropes
circling the emerald areca palms with their tops of gold.

40. 3203

Some of them were loosening their arms like tendrils with bangles
from the shoulders of their lovers that rose like columns, like hills,
and with their hearts in pain they wept, and the tears streaming down
the round faces seemed like pearls from the eyes like darting fishes.

41. 3204

Those women with waists so thin they seemed not to exist, rolled
on the ground wailing, the collyrium paint streaming from their eyes,
like skies at the monsoon, while they thought, "When he hears, the [king
without enemies, whose spear is smeared with ghee, how will he take [this?"

42. 3205

Rising from sleep, forgetting the sweet taste of their dreams,
their wide breasts shaking, their clothes slipping down,
the hair on their heads disheveled and dark like clouds
of thunder, the young women, mourning, moved along exhausted.

43. 3206

They cried out, "Can this have happened to the sister of the lord
so powerful that, with his beautiful arms, he took Śiva's Kailāsa?"
Beating their breasts with their red-painted hands, they came,
weak and with their tangled hair, and fell down at her feet.

44. 3207

"Because we have our king with the spear shining in his right hand,
even animals in Laṅkā do not suffer as she has suffered,
but now is our luck slipping away, is it falling out of our hands?"
They felt despair and tears filled dark eyes not used to weeping.

45. 3208

Now you have heard how this fierce suffering entered Laṅkā
and everyone in Rāvaṇa's hall looked for somewhere to run to,
as she fell at the dark anklets dense with gold of the king,
like a cloud striking the foot of a mountain, rolling there in pain.

46. 3209

A covering of darkness covered over the three worlds. Ādiśeṣa,
the snake who carries the earth, shook his many heads
in fear. The mountain ranges trembled. The sun was confused.
The elephants of the sky panicked. The gods looked for hiding places.

47. 3210

His arms coated with shining bangles swelled up.
His eyes burned. The spaces between his teeth burned.
His eyebrows curved in anger across his great forehead
and nothing was stable, the gods forgot their duties.

48. 3211

The whole clan of the gods and even Yama of the south,
of the dead, sat there thinking, "Today is our last
day," and their bodies were shivering, their breaths were sobs,
gods and human beings waited without saying a word.

49. 3212

As he sighed so fiercely that all his mustaches quivering in a row
sent the smell of burning hair from the caves of his mouth,
as his shining teeth were gnashing, burning, glowing with lightning,
he said, "Who did this?" like the menacing thunder out of a cloud.

50. 3213

And she said, "They came to the forest and they protect the earth,
they are beautiful as the God of Love, their bodies have no equal
in this or higher worlds of embodied beings, they who drew
out their swords and cut me this way, they were men."

51. 3214

"Men did this to you!" he said and laughter spilled out of him,
filling every direction of space and all his eyes shed fire.
"Of course! With amazing powers! Now how can that be true?
Don't lie! Don't be afraid! Tell me what really happened!"

52. 3215

"Their bodies glow like the God of Love. By the strength
of their dense and lovely arms, they rise higher than Mount Meru.
Why should I go on praising them now? Throughout the seven worlds,
in the wink of an eye, their bows would break the strongest power.

53. 3216

"They honor great holy men. Their faces are beautiful as the moon
in the sky. They have eyes like the sweet-smelling flowers whose stalks
grow from the waves of the water. And their feet! And their hands!
They can endure tapas without end or limit. Who is their equal?

54. 3217

"They have bark garments and large anklets. They wear the sacred
[thread
as a chest ornament. They are master archers. The Veda is alive
on their tongues. Their bodies are like shoots. For them you are
[nothing,
not even dust. Their quivers, like the art of language, can never be
[exhausted.

55. 3218

"Long ago they took an oath because holy Brahmins came to them
whose minds, in their fear of the Rākṣasas, were no longer
at peace, and they swore they would tear up your family with its will
to conquer all the worlds, killing you down past the root!

56. 3219

"Those two who are like the God of Love, can they really be alive
inside a world? Are there any heroes stronger with the bow?
Is there a single other being anywhere of their stature? O lord!
Each one of them resembles the three supreme gods!

57. 3220

"They are sons of Daśaratha, whose virtues surpass all praise,
he who with his chariot wheels plowed the circle of the earth.
Nothing can be said against them. By their father's order, they live
in the forest so hard to enter. Rāma and Lakṣmaṇa are their names."

58. 3221

"Those who cut with a sharp sword the lovely nose from my younger [sister,
who is like nectar, they are men! and even though they cut her, they [live on
while Rāvaṇa remains here, without a trace of shame, his sword
as if unused, and he looks around and he still holds on to his sweet life!

59. 3222

"Is this truly what I have come to after having taken the kingdoms
by force, after gaining total victory? I have lost fame
which is imperishable! Can you say it will return to me even if
the foremost warriors of the whole world were to lose their heads?

60. 3223

"Those who have caused me this disgrace which has taken root and is [growing
still feel themselves virile, still possess their precious lives!
But the sword is still mine, and the days given me by the god who [drank
the ocean's poison, and these shoulders are mine, and I am still alive!

61. 3224

"Why should you mourn, my heart! now that you have been shamed,
and disgrace, something unheard-of! has come to you? Oh don't grieve!
How can you feel pain? Don't you have all your many arms?
Don't you have a row of ten heads to endure the dishonor?"

62. 3225

So he spoke and he laughed and the fire was blazing out of his eyes
and he said, "Didn't Khara and the other Rākṣasas who have their place
in the forest with its towering hills make use of their swords
and kill those two men who had no powerful support?"

63. 3226

As soon as he had spoken, she beat her belly
    and wept so that her eyes became
like waterfalls descending and she fell
    on the earth and she grieved and she said,
raising her hands, "O my lord!
    All that retinue was destroyed with ease!"
and somehow she began to relate
    what had happened so that he might know.

64. 3227

"After hearing the words from my own mouth,
    Khara and the other warriors like buffalo bulls
went off and the army rose up
    roaring and followed them, and the lord
called Rāma whose beautiful eyes are like lotuses
    that accept the rays of the sun,
with his single bow, in barely a moment,
    made them ascend," she said, "to heaven."

65. 3228

Her account of his younger brother dying
along with his garlanded army
in battle waged by a man alone
had barely grazed his hearing when
all his many long eyes
shot out fire and water
just as showers are born with flame
in a black cloud that encloses the thunder.

66. 3229

Then like ghee poured into the fire
that burns below the ocean, his grief
merging with his rising anger
fed that anger and he said,
"But what offense was it that you
committed against them that made them
act as savagely as they have, cutting
your nose off and the lips from your mouth?"

67. 3230

"The offense that I gave happened
because of her, the one who came
with Rāma whom no one ever
can picture just as he is,
she who left her lotus,
who took her waist from the lightning,
her soft arms from the bamboo,
who took her body from gold!"

68. 3231

"Who is she?" he said and the Rākṣasī
answered at once, "Lord! Listen
with care. Her breasts, round
and heavy, are like containers
of the finest gold filled with vermilion.
The earth is favored by the touch of her feet.
Her name is Sītā," and she began
to describe her, feature after feature.

69. 3232

"Even the goddess who sits on the lotus
and is goddess to the goddesses who sing
the rāgas melodiously with their words
as intensely sweet as honey
and their hair full of fragrant flowers,
even that Śrī is not fit to be
so much as her servant! Though I will, it is
foolishness for me to describe her!

70. 3233

"When bound, her hair is like a cloud.
When loosened, it is like falling rain.
Her feet are like cotton and her toes
seem to be made of coral.
Her words are lovely, like amṛta,
and though, with one lotus, you could
measure the face of that woman,
she has eyes larger than the ocean.

71. 3234

"Those who say that Kāma was burned
by the eye of Śiva know nothing.
Seeing this woman whose hair
has its sweet fragrance and lacking
the strength to carry her off, tortured
by intense illness past describing,
ah! the bodiless god lost his body
and perished through immense desire.

72. 3235

"If you look up, into the world of our enemies,
or down, to the world of the hooded Nāgas,
or look around through this world
surrounded by the waves of the ocean,
from what world does she come
with her eyes that surpass the sword
or the spears forged in a blazing furnace,
she whose features no one could paint?

73. 3236

"Should I describe her arms, should I
    describe her eyes moving like
swords on her shining face, should I praise
    her other features? But I cannot
picture them one by one. Trying
    again and again, I only become confused.
But won't you see her for yourself tomorrow?
    Why should I need to tell you any more?

74. 3237

"You could say that her eyebrows are like bows
    or say that her eyes are like spears.
You could say that her teeth are like pearls.
    You could say that her lips are like coral.
The words are right, the meaning wrong.
    Is there any simile one can use?
If you were to say that rice
    is like grass, would it make real sense?

75. 3238

"Indra has Śaṣi, and Śiva,
    father of the god with six faces,
has Umā. Viṣṇu, his eyes red
    like lotuses, has lovely
Śrī. And you have Sītā.
    If you compare them with each other,
the best of it does not go to them.
    The best, my lord! is yours!

76. 3239

"One of them has found place for his wife
    within himself. Another has drawn to his chest
the golden woman sitting on her lotus.
    Brahmā has placed his on his tongue.
Hero with shoulders towering into the sky!
    if you gain this woman whose tiny waist
surpasses the lightning born in the clouds,
    where will you place her and flourish?

77. 3240

"Once you will have her whose words
    are lovely as a child's, you will not
go wrong. You will give her the plundered
    wealth that is yours. O you
who give everything! I say this for your good
    but aren't I contriving the ruin
of all the wives living in your house,
    who speak as sweetly as parrots!

78. 3241

"Sītā whose yoni is like a chariot
    was not born from the belly of a woman
with bound-up breasts in this world or in the world
    of the gods who in their pride churned
the ocean full of conches and raised
    Śrī who sits on the blossoming lotus.
The earth, to surpass her, brought forth
    Sītā and then surely reached fulfillment.

79. 3242

"So that the world surrounded by the ocean
    in which the fish live and wander
may praise you, take the doe
    who is named Sītā. Unite her to you, she
in whose hair the bees live and wander,
    with her tiny waist! And so the world may see
the power of your sword, so that I may take
    and embrace him, give me Rāma!

80. 3243

"Since all is assigned by fate,
    even for those whose tapas is great,
can what will be come to be theirs
    except on the day that it is to come?
Only today will you gain the treasure
    merited by your ten faces and
your eyes, the beauty of your form,
    your chest and your twenty arms!

81. 3244

"As I was thinking that I would give a woman
like this to you and, as I moved
to seize her, the younger brother of Rāma
stepped into my way, and before I
could act, he cut off my nose
with his shining sword. My life ended
then and I decided I would tell you
what happened," she said, "before I die."

82. 3245

Then his rage and his courage and the surge
of his pride, all of them slipped
away as the force of a righteous act
cannot take hold where sin exists,
and just as you might light a lamp
with another lamp, the disease of his
desire and the burning pain that pierced him,
how they merged with his precious life!

83. 3246

He forgot Khara and he forgot the power
of the man who was still living even though
he had cut off the nose of his sister.
He forgot the shame that he had suffered
and forgot the curse he had once incurred,
but because of the arrows of the God of Love
which have conquered even Śiva, he could not
forget the woman he had heard described.

84. 3247

Once his mind and the name of Sītā
whose waist is slender had met
and the two had become one thing,
was there mind left over for any other
thought? How could he forget her?
How can even learned men,
if they have no true knowledge,
ever cross over beyond desire?

85. 3248

Even before he went and deceived
    that woman lovely as a peacock,
the lord of Laṅkā with the high walls
    had set her in the prison of his heart.
That Rākṣasa who fights with a spear
    had a heart now that was like butter
set out on a day of sun
    and heating and melting bit by bit.

86. 3249

Because of the power of fate, because
    the past was ripening into the present
and the time of destruction was nearing
    for the city, the disease of his desire
burning in his swiftly beating
    heart grew like the evil
an ignorant man who does not value wisdom
    will do while keeping it secret.

87. 3250

It may have been merely his nature
    to welcome a vile urge, it may be
that the Rākṣasa had forgotten just
    who he was so that the Love God
could torment him with arrows released
    when that woman the color of gold
entered his heart. How the power
    of desire destroys men's strength!

88. 3251

He rose from his throne and when he did,
    those who live in the seven worlds
chanted blessings and conches sounded
    everywhere. All who were standing near him
threw showers of flowers and then
    went away, while Rāvaṇa entered
his golden palace, his heart
    gone weak, broken with anguish.

89. 3252

He came to his huge, glittering bed
with the coverlet of flowers, and his beautiful
wives all left the room.
He reached that bed and the eyes,
the breasts, the hair as fragrant
as musk of that woman like a doe
entered his heart and the heat
of his thoughts slowly spread through him.

90. 3253

It couldn't be calmed. His love was growing
by hundreds and hundreds of leaps.
The flowers on his soft bed though moistened
by the cooling drops of water
from the fragrant north wind turned black.
His arms that had defeated the eight
Elephants of Space and his body grew thin.
His heart weakened. His life caught on fire.

91. 3254

When sandal paste to cool him mingled with
sweet-smelling powders and lovely
soft shoots and buds were spread on him,
then as if the skin were burning up
from a caustic salve, his body burned, burned
as he suffered. He sucked his breath and sucked
his breath like a powerful bellows blowing
and blowing up a raging fire.

92. 3255

Without firm virtue, not thinking himself evil,
the sinner had his thoughts never away
from that woman. Desire rising in him to see
her body, she whose eyes were like
a dark lotus, a spear, a blue water lily,
the green flesh of an unripe mango,
he went on in his suffering and his life
was pain for him, was pain for him.

93. 3256

That king who had conquered, who had tamed the giant
elephants who sustain massive space,
had broken their trunks, where the tusks rested,
now as the arrows of Kāma came flowing in to bury
themselves in his chest like wasps that burrow
into wood, it was pain for him,
pain for him, and he kept growing weaker,
ever weaker and he was withering away.

94. 3257

He stayed as he was, wasted, grieving,
and he kept thinking, "I have seen a branch
with hair as lovely as a koṉṟai fruit
enter my heart and lodge there,"
and when the south wind scented with jasmine
came at him, like an arrow of the God
of Love whose own garland is fragrant,
it brought him only growing anger.

95. 3258

It was then that he rose from there
and with his heart suffering had no idea
what he would do next, and in his anguish
as women who were like gold-skinned
Sarasvatī, their mere words more lovely
than rāgas played on the *yāḻ*,
carried innumerable rows of the finest lamps
before him, Rāvaṇa entered his garden.

96. 3259

The jack trees there were rubies and the plantains
of emeralds and the mangoes were diamonds,
the vēṅkai trees were choice gold, the kōṅkam trees
were jacinths and the towering areca palms
*nīlam* rubies, the cālams *kuruvintam* rubies.
The coconut palms were silver. The mastwood trees
were crystal, like cool water. The trumpet-flower
trees were of coral. All of it a wonder!

97. 3260

Where the trees of jewels with their rich colors
towered up thickly into the sky
and their flowers could not be distinguished
from the stars, in that garden flowing honey,
in a pavilion of rich gold, Rāvaṇa,
grown thin, in his grief, oppressed
by his suffering, laid himself down
on a bed that was the color of milk.

98. 3261

The geese who would be drunk from sipping
the juices that fell from the trees
and flowers, the parrots whose sweet speech
was like the soft talk of women, the kokilas
and the bees and every other creature which makes
sounds that are sweet all thought that the king
of Laṅkā might grow angry and they closed
up their mouths, like so many deaf-mutes.

99. 3262

As the cooling mist that comes on the north wind
in season penetrated those hidden wounds
the Love God's arrows had opened and entered,
in his suffering, in his bewilderment, he said
"What time of the year is this?" and, with his words,
the cold season was filled with terror
and ran away, and then the spring
ah! came there and began to unfold.

100. 3263

If the gentle mist that penetrates
burning mountains and trees with thick branches
and cools them had been scorching him, then
how can you describe what the spring did!
For those who have drunk the poison of love,
does a medicine exist that can cure them?
Isn't it true that happiness and suffering
are tied to what happens in the mind?

101. 3264

Since the season of spring was burning him
as well, and made the blazing pain
of his desire heat up to the farthest limits
of the directions of space, he said
"What is happening here? The cold season
was better than this! Let this time
go away! Bring me the fresh autumn
after the rains. Bring it at once!"

102. 3265

When the autumn came to him, his arms
with their strength and thickness began to burn
and he said, "Can autumn scorch? This
must be the cold season that was here before!"
and his servants said, "Our lord! The autumn
would be afraid to scorch without your command,"
and then he said, "Let there be no seasons!
Now send all of them away!"

103. 3266

When he spoke, all the seasons went away.
Like a yogi freed of craving,
everything alive left off doing
the indescribable variety of activity
that suits the range of the seasons.
The whole world seemed through fiercest tapas
to have thrown off the bonds of attachment
and arrived at the state of Freedom.

104. 3267

All the world encircled by the shores
of ocean was without heat, without cold,
but the body like a dark jewel of the Rākṣasa
burned with no oil to feed it.
Was it because of seasons that it burned?
How can the raging fire that rises
from desire be quenched by any action
other than the force of self-control?

105. 3268

Though there lay against his chest
    a cloud risen after drinking water
from the ocean, a woven strip of lotuses,
    cooling sandalwood paste mixed with powder
of musk, and shoots and pearls,
    his heart was worn down and he said
to those near him, "The moon is cooling.
    Run now and bring me the moon!"

106. 3269

Those near him looked at the full moon
    hanging back, unwilling to appear
above the vast city that was ruled
    by the Rākṣasa whose anger was burning
and they said, "You, don't be afraid!
    Come now! The Rākṣasa has summoned
you!" Then the moon abandoned
    all his hesitations and he rose.

107. 3270

Like a wheel the moon was rising
    from all the ocean of water densely
mixed with black sand and he seemed
    the God of Death coming to crush
Rāvaṇa's life as when former enemies
    once defeated rise against a strong man
who has ruled corruptly and do him
    harm and his defenses break down.

108. 3271

Spreading its rays through the sky everywhere,
    beautiful beyond praise by its very nature,
it tormented him for whom no one
    on the earth or in heaven felt love,
as if the Lord who sleeps on the serpent bed,
    realizing that the time was right,
with the intent of destroying the life
    of Rāvaṇa, had hurled his discus.

109. 3272

The moon, gentle and cooling,
sent out its mass of radiance,
spreading all the amṛta it had touched,
drawn up and drunk from the sea of milk,
and it was as if molten silver melted
in the middle of a fire were scooped up
to be hurled at the Rākṣasa with his eyes
reddened and his curving angry eyebrows.

110. 3273

The moonlight falling like lightning
straying across the earth burned
the Rākṣasa who had heard of the beauty
of the lovely daughter to the ruler of fields
beautiful with fine paddy that surround
Mithilā, and all his handsomeness
was lost, as if fame, leaving him,
had gone to an enemy who was undefeated.

111. 3274

The king who was feared even by
the God of Death with his great anklets
gave a black look. "When I said,"
he said, "Bring me the moon,
the rays of whose cool body are sweet
gifts, which one of you
summoned up the sun, with its unbearable rays
spewing endless poison and murderous fire?"

112. 3275

Some of his servants were terrified then.
"Our lord!" they said, "It's wrong
to say we would bring you anyone that
you hadn't ordered us to bring you!
The sun when it travels its glowing way
moves by chariot only, but even if
it is burning you as it goes on its way,
the moon travels by flying car!"

113. 3276

He who had never before this known what it was
to feel unsatisfied desire, as others do who love
women who have yonis more beautiful than the hoods
of cobras and whose speech is submissive, he, because
of the moon, was burning and he himself realized
that this was the very enemy of the cool and lovely
lotus, that this was the moon, not the sun,
and knowing this he asked it for his life again, to be saved.

114. 3277

And he said, "Moon! You are growing thin and your
body is pale. Within you it is black. You have changed
your state and burn. Have you heard about her too?
Have you been told of her by people who have seen her?
I suffer! There is no one here who can withdraw
the flower arrows that have pierced me.
Is there anyone at all who may be able
to protect the life that is within me?

115. 3278

"If you can't win, shouldn't you take hold of yourself
and submit? Your loveliness has been surpassed
by the face like a lotus with eyes like dark water lilies
of Jānakī who comes of a noble family
and is Death to my precious life. Because of this,
it seems that you have grown black, turned thin,
begun to burn! Yet, if you crumble when you see the wealth
of your enemies, will you ever be able to defeat them?"

116. 3279

He said this in his suffering, then said, "Take him away
along with the night! Let the day and let the sun
come that were here before!" The words had not even
been spoken when the moon which is beyond
imagination disappeared and along with it went
the night. Then, in an instant, the sun
appeared, surpassing description, and the day
came with it and they spread across the sky.

117. 3280

When the rays of the sun like molten gold descended
and spread, as when ghee is poured down on the face
of fire by priests who are chanting the mantras
of the Rig Veda and the fire then blazes up,
so the noble lotus opened now and, as the sun came up,
the red water lily closed, resembling people worth little
who live without restraint or unity, gain wealth without
deserving it, which makes them proud, then suddenly lose it.

118. 3281

The moon, ruler of darkness, ashamed as his light
was growing dim and his body was quivering, with his wife
the night following after him, slipped down
from the highest point of the sky, and he went away
like a minor king who loses his rank when another
king of great fame extends his sovereignty,
as did the burning sun who was rising
in the east, like an ornament worn by the day.

119. 3282

There were women who had refused, because they were angry,
to make love with those who had come to them in adoration
on the beds of flowers. When the night left, those women with heavy
[earrings
slept on and their quarrels continued even in their dreams.

120. 3283

Some women whose lives were dwindling away, because their lovers
left them in the middle of the night, could not stop the trembling
they felt and their eyes poured out tears just as dark water lilies
blossoming profusely stream down nectar from their fresh flowers.

121. 3284

Some, after love, were sleeping wrapped around their husbands
sweet as life to them, closely embracing them with hands
like pairs of flowers, and they seemed coral vines enwrapping
giant branches on the flower-covered beds of love.

122. 3285

While swarms of bees buzzed at their cheeks and the beautiful
rays of the sun shone down, proud thoroughbred elephants
slept on without realizing that it was day, like men who are drunk
on beds that help them to their sweet, muddled sleep.

123. 3286

Everywhere, wherever people lived, all the lamps burned on
without running low in oil but they lost their brightness just like
the women of high birth, innocents left behind, who were separated from [lovers
worth their lives and skilled in the difficult branches of knowledge.

124. 3287

Though the sun had risen that ornaments and unfolds their petals,
the lovely flowers that bloom at dawn did not blossom
but took on the look of the long, drowsy eyes
of the women who lay asleep on their spacious beds.

125. 3288

Though dawn had surely come, the eyelids never stirred
on the eyes of all those who were happy in their sleep,
like the doors of great mansions where people are living
who have no thought, in their greed, of ever giving alms.

126. 3289

All the cakravāka birds, freed by the sunrise from their separation
through the night that had been like the pain of poison for them,
rejoiced, the length of day become their refuge, as if they were criminals
who had been released from a cruel prison through an act of mercy.

127. 3290

The singing bees flew to the flowers that were no longer
open now because of Rāvaṇa's order that had warded off
the full moon, and the bees suffered like bards when they come
to the doors of men who have no wealth earned through their skills.

128. 3291

The burning rays of the sun entering through a window
came to wake up women from their sweet sleep
and, though woken, they were so drowsy they seemed like those
who cannot awaken to the clear sight of ultimate truth.

129. 3292

Even though, through restraint and attention, they had learned the
[famous
study of the shifting stars composed by men whose tongues
were skilled but who never imagined the power of Rāvaṇa's command,
the astrologers were still sleeping as were the roosters that crow.

130. 3293

While such things were happening in the world, the Rākṣasa
whose anklets resounded looked up at the sun and he said,
"When the thought of it enters the mind, it burns like fire.
This must be the moon, that was here before, with just this power."

131. 3294

"This isn't the moon," some said to him, "Lord! It's the sun!
He has a chariot with beautiful yellow horses and their manes
swell out! and the sun with its fierce rays truly burns but
coolness rests on the rays of the moon and it should not burn!"

132. 3295

Like a dark blue mountain with all his peaks,
he said, "This sun
is fiercer than poison. Take him away from here
and tell the roaring
voice of the ocean to go away as well.
Quickly summon
the young crescent moon that hovers
in the west in the evening!"

133. 3296

The king of the Rākṣasas spoke and, as soon
as he said those words,
the moon, which on that day was full,
changed right there
instantly into a young crescent moon
of only three days.
Think of it! Is there anything more worth doing
daily than difficult tapas?

134. 3297

When he whose qualities are evil saw the moon
rising in the west,
he said, "It's the fire burning under the ocean
or the cruel poisonous fang
of the snake who holds up the earth
with his neck or else
the evening is angry with me and has
appeared with a drawn sword!

135. 3298

"Śiva who was fit to do it buried
that poison in his throat
which is known to have risen long ago
from the ocean of cool
waves crashing and, when he put this crescent moon
in his matted hair
where pollen rests, he did it thinking
'This is poison too!'

136. 3299

"The moon that was consuming my life
with its strength like thunder
ran off and returned as the lightning
of this crescent moon
which does me no less evil. Is the nature
any the less fierce
of a poisonous snake with a black-marked throat
whether it is large or small?

137. 3300

"Let me see what darkness
fully present is like!
The sun that was here before was better!
Get rid of this moon!
If it burns me, strong as I am,
can someone imagine
that any who live in these seven worlds
could escape from it?"

138. 3301

Then, as that crescent moon went away,
darkness came such that
you could easily touch it or grind with it
better than with any
thing men grind with. You could cut it,
if you wanted, with a sword
and bring it down, like so many handsome columns
all gathered together.

139. 3302

But why compare it to columns you could easily
roll away after trimming
the rough places? That darkness was black as the heart
of a man grown very rich
without mercy or compassion, whom people
point out as blind
to others and never accustomed to entering
the light of the faultless Vedas.

140. 3303

As the darkness came that no one desired
and it grew to cover
the earth and the sky, becoming thick
without a crack and swallowing
the wide world, he said, "Śiva who drank
the poison must have spit it out,
not realizing that all the valued worlds and
everyone in them would perish.

141. 3304

"This darkness would never be gathered in as was
the Hālāhala poison when it came up
from the ocean and was swallowed by the strength of Śiva
who has no equal. I realize,
I know this now—it is the fire of final destruction
with its tongue licking up
all worlds and heavens. It has gone black
drinking black poison!

142. 3305

"In this darkness so thick no fire
or arrow could pierce it,
she appears, with a thundercloud for her hair,
her body an utterly
incomparable branch of fine coral, with her breasts
like a pair of young coconuts
and her face like the moon, a lamp that she raises
before me burning here alone.

143. 3306

"Am I confused because of my delusion
or is there another moon?
What is this that I can't understand? Through
this darkness blacker
than when thick collyrium is mixed, with two
earrings and her deep
black hair, a full moon coming up now
she appears, shining!

144. 3307

"I cannot see a waist between
her hips and the breasts
that rise from their wide base.
Otherwise I have seen
all her form and with her eyes
that have swallowed poison,
this young woman, step by step, has
entered my heart.

145. 3308

"Before this, I have seen all of them
with eyes like swords
throughout the seven worlds but never before
have I seen any woman
formed like this. If she is so different
it can only be she
my sister told me of, this young woman whose hair
swarms with bees!

146. 3309

"She's not been able to bear how much
pain I suffer!
She has come! She has searched me out!
How can I repay her?
Quickly, so that I can ask her if this
form is the same
she saw so sweet to see, summon
my younger sister!" he said.

147. 3310

He spoke and, as soon as he did, they went
and summoned her who would cause
the destruction to the very root of her clan
of Rākṣasas whose energies
are so powerful. Then she came who had lost
her nose and her long
golden earrings when the wrongful fire
of desire burned her heart.

148. 3311

He whose sharp sword is oiled with ghee
looked at her who had entered,
a violent being with a lying heart,
and he said, "Woman!
Look here! She who has come, standing before me
like a peacock with her eyes
like swords dark with collyrium, is this
the Sītā you described?"

149. 3312

"With eyes like red lotuses and a mouth
that is red and sweet,
wide shoulders that are smeared with sandal paste
and strong arms hanging
low, a beautiful garland around his chest,
this man who has come
like a mountain of collyrium is Rāma," she said,
"who carries a strong bow."

150. 3313

"The form I see is of a woman.
Fool! You say
it's a man, which cannot even be thought!
What is this?
Do those whose lot is the earth
work magic on us
who have learned how to trouble them with magic
right in front of their eyes?"

151. 3314

"As your consciousness," she said, "obsessed,
fixes on nothing else
and your great desire, spreading wide,
burns within you,
everywhere that your eyes turn,
they light on her,
and she appears for you! Look!
This is an old story."

152. 3315

When she had spoken, the Rākṣasa said to her,
"Let all this be.
Why is it that you see only that Rāma?
What is the reason?"
and she said, "Since the day that he imposed
incurable suffering on me,
from that day forward I have not been
able to forget him."

153. 3316

"Yes! Yes! That's how it is! My life
and my body are burning
and growing weak. Because my karma is bad,
what hope is there
for my happiness?" and she answered, "Why should you,
sole king of the world,
be reduced? Go seize her whose hair ennobles
the flowers it wears!"

154. 3317

She spoke and went away and the Rākṣasa's
strength vanished.
He had no way to recover. Growing feeble,
he lost consciousness.
His servants trembled beside him and only
because it would seem
there were still some days of life left to him,
he did not die.

155. 3318

Like someone dead who is born again, the king
who had reawakened to his
sweet life became aware of his courage,
and he looked at those
who were standing near him there and he said,
"Have me a jeweled pavilion built
full of beauty and made of moonstones that give
water as if milked."

156. 3319

The carpenter who lives in the great sky
came then and thoughtfully
considered things. Not only with his mind then
but with his own hands,
he made a pavilion of lovely moonstones
with a thousand tall columns
glistening with light so that even Brahmā
was shamed by it.

157. 3320

Above and below he spread out moonstones
that shed drops
of water sweet as amṛta even when
there is no moonlight
from the king of the constellations of time. He made
windows for the south wind
to enter with its smell of flowers and a cool garden
of kalpakas heavy with jewels.

158. 3321

As the women of heaven glowing with ornaments,
the gold on their hands
fit to make the needle that tests gold,
were carrying lamps
beautiful with jewels shining so as to
pierce the wide darkness,
he, great-shouldered, in a flying car set with rubies,
came to see the pavilion.

159. 3322

Even though the darkness was like the massing of
ten thousand million nights,
as the moons appeared of those famous faces
of lovely women sending
out cool, silvery moonlight, they were like
thousands of millions
of moons emitting coolness and the darkness
turned away and ran.

160. 3323

The fresh, bright mass of light
of the kalpaka trees with lovely
gems of nine stones for their flowers
brought the day
through their radiance so that the night's grip
was loosened. Even though
there was no sun, those long rays shone
out in their glory!

161. 3324

The way his mind was, he could not
tell touch or sound
or any of his senses, one from another.
Not knowing what to do,
just as desire might bind and
draw him into entering
another body in another birth, he came
and entered the pavilion.

162. 3325

As if he had gained the realm of Freedom
that gives, like a mother, everything desired
by those who have done faultless tapas
and had taken amṛta as well from the shark-filled sea,
he came to his cool bed of flowers
and soft lovely cooling shoots
which grew on green trees that are visited
by bees whose humming is like a rāga.

163. 3326

Swimming through the rich and smoky fragrance
of the hair of those women who wore
beautiful ornaments, the south wind that could bring
life back even to someone whose life
is over, like amṛta from the roaring ocean,
came to that lovely, fragrant
pleasing garden and remained there,
offering a feast of welcome to the God of Love.

164. 3327

As the south wind came sliding through the window,
he wasn't able to bear it. As if
he had seen a snake from the mountains
come and enter the house where he lived,
he stared with eyes flowing fire
and much blood and he grew fiercely
enraged and he began to sob
and summoned his servants to him and he said,

165. 3328

"Can it be that only a single one
    of the gods is able to make me
suffer, as if a tiny bit of water
    that seeps down into a well could flood
the world? How did the south wind
    enter here without my command?"
he said and then he said as well,
    "Bring the soldiers of the guard at once!"

166. 3329

Then, as soon as his servants had run
    and brought the guards to him there,
the burning Rākṣasa fixed them with his eyes
    so red and full of cruelty they were terrified,
and he said, "Did you make a straight road
    for the south wind?" and the guards replied,
"Since there is this opening here
    for him, there is no way to stop him!"

167. 3330

"If the gods have thought things through
    and have no fear of doing as they will,
it would seem my control and my power
    have vanished. Search him out instantly!
Travel," he said, "with a speed that will
    carry you far off into every
direction! Capture him and then
    throw him here into a great prison!

168. 3331

"And yet there's nothing to be gained
    through my uselessly hating the Wind God.
Death will come to me right now
    if I cannot win what I wish
to be mine—mercy, the true kind,
    from Sītā who has black eyes like spears.
Bring my ministers," he said, "with their capacity
    for judging what is to be done next!"

169. 3332

Commanded by Rāvaṇa, some of them
ran here and there and everywhere
and summoned his ministers who came,
when called, on sturdy chariots with banners,
in palanquins, on horses and on elephants from whom
the liquid of musth rained down
and, in their hearts, the holy men who are gods
of this world and the gods in the sky were anguished.

170. 3333

With the ministers who had come and in their faultless
minds had considered the situation,
Rāvaṇa, who was accustomed to act on whatever
thought happened to enter his consciousness,
his heart in confusion, went off
on his flying car moving through the sky
to where Mārīca was living and restraining
his senses with no one else nearby.

171. 3334

So full of fear as soon as he saw Rāvaṇa
arrived, Mārīca, his heart
deeply troubled, went out in terror
and faced him who was like a great
black mountain and Mārīca performed
all the proper rituals of welcome
for a guest and he looked at the lovely
faces of Rāvaṇa. Then he said,

172. 3335

"You are a ruler terrifying even Yama
as well as the king of the gods
who lives in the shade of kalpaka trees
that have lovely flowers
and are cooling! Why, as if you were humble, have you come
to this pitiful dwelling of mine
in this forest? Tell me!" he said
and was confused by his fear.

173. 3336

"Everything has happened! I am weak
        from holding on to my life!
My beauty is gone. I have lost
        my majesty along with my fame.
How can I tell you about it now?
        What am I now to do?
Oh this disgrace that makes me ashamed
        before even the gods!

174. 3337

"Men have become stronger than us!
        More than that, with a sword,
they have cut off your niece's nose!
        What disgrace can there be
worse than this to your ancestry
        as well as my ancestry?
Just think it over now, you
        whose spear is famous!

175. 3338

"If you consider that he drank up the days
        of our younger brothers who fiercely
fought him and who were ferocious in their rage,
        isn't our reputation for victory
shamed? Don't you have two hands?
        You with your strong spear,
living at ease, while your nephews have died
        fighting a single bowman!

176. 3339

"The burning in my heart has not been calmed.
        I grow thin and weaken.
It is below my dignity to fight him.
        Because of this, I have come
here to free myself, through you, of this shame!
        You will help me carry away
the vine with a red mouth that shames coral,
        she who lives with him!"

177. 3340

Before the Rākṣasa, after saying all this,
        could grow so angry
it would have seemed like lumps of iron
        from a burning fire
had been placed and pressed into his ears,
        Mārīca covered them and said,
"Horrible!" then, freeing himself of fear,
        spoke, with his heart enraged,

178. 3341

"King! You have, without judgment, ended
        your own good life!
Yet I know that it's not your fault,
        but due to old karma.
Though it may be painful, I will still say
        what is right for your welfare!"
Then he told Rāvaṇa all these
        things of which he was certain.

179. 3342

"Kindling and lighting a fire, you threw in
        your severed arms and legs.
For a long, long time you endured
        hunger and you wasted away.
Within you, the life waned and only
        after that you secured
your prosperous state! If you lose it,
        will it ever be regained?

180. 3343

"Did you gain your place by doing tapas
        according to the Order of the World
or from outside, hostile to it? Tell me now,
        you who know the Vedas
where words are examined! Didn't you win
        by following Right Order!
After that, do you intend to behave
        against it and to lose?

181. 3344

"Those who seize land from their friends
or exact taxes
beyond measure or take away the wife
living in another man's house,
you have seen that the god Dharma
will cut them down!
Lord! What evil beings who do
these things can escape?

182. 3345

"The ruler of heaven was blighted
by the beauty of Ahalyā
and how many others have, like Indra,
earned themselves disgrace?
How many women beautiful as Śrī
now enjoy your handsome self?
Without judgment, you propose what only
false counselors could advise!

183. 3346

"Even if you do it, you will gain nothing,
nothing but shame
and bad karma! Should you go there,
Rāma will be victorious
instantly and with his arrows like curses
from the god who brought the world
into being, he will cut down all
your army and your race!

184. 3347

"Why don't you realize what's happening!
What is all this?
With his single bow, he killed Khara
who had the rank of supreme
general over your army, and he destroyed
the army with its powerful
chariots. He intends in his heart
to utterly destroy us!

185. 3348

"Among the fierce, who was a fiercer
warrior than Virādha?
Ah! He has gone to the gods through
a single arrow of Rāma's!
And I keep thinking over and
over, 'Who of us
will escape?' and I suffer. Now what
are you saying to torment me?

186. 3349

"Those who have died have died. You should not
be doing work for the dead!
You should not! If you do, is there a way
for you to escape?
How many rulers have ruled? Those who do not
labor at Righteousness
will not be exalted. Not be exalted! All such
though living have already died!

187. 3350

"Faced with this warrior bowman who shot
one arrow that ended
my younger brother and my mother, faced with
his younger brother beside him,
the manhood in me vanishes and I feel
weakened and my heart
trembles! When I think that you would oppose him,
I am deeply troubled.

188. 3351

"You who know the truth! All
things that are alive
moving or fixed in place, will not
last and will vanish!
Do not consider performing an act
so low! Accept my advice,
lord! Now live forever and ever," he said,
"on your towering wealth!"

189. 3352

"Are you saying that my handsome, victorious, jewel-decked arms
with which I picked up, on a palm, Mount Kailāsa as well as him
who holds the Ganges in his matted hair, that they have become easy
for a man now?" he said, hot eyes burning, with frowning brows,
[enraged.

190. 3353

"You haven't considered what has happened! You don't fear the state
of my heart! You have shown contempt for me. You, sir, have praised
those who made the entire face of my younger sister look like
a dug-up mountain! Your offense is immeasurable and yet I bear it!"

191. 3354

Mārīca did not hold himself back by thinking about how
Rāvaṇa would become even angrier after hearing him but he said,
looking at that cruel being who was angry with him and unjust, "Your
[anger
is with yourself, your anger is with your race, not, after all, with me.

192. 3355

"If you think so much of the mountain you lifted, well when Janaka
[said,
'This is the mountain Śiva bent into a powerful bow. Bend it!' he
who has no equal picked it up, grasped it, attached its loud string,
and broke the mountain which is the very mountain that pierces the top
[of the sky.

193. 3356

"You don't know anything of him and you won't accept what I say!
Before Rāma the strong dons his garland of victory, lives will be taken,
won't they? Deluded, you think this is the body of a woman.
Is this Sītā's body? I ask you, isn't it the bad karma of the Rākṣasas?

194. 3357

"When I realize that you will not survive, nor your kin, my heart
beats like a herald's drum! You haven't noticed it! My life,
precious to me, feels terror! Is it good that those standing nearby and
[aware
should say, 'That's fine!' to those who are on the verge of drinking
[poison?

195. 3358

"The heavenly weapons Viśvāmitra gave him that can in one
moment devour the lives in all the worlds, even to that
of Śiva as well as the realms of the other gods, faultless
ferocious limitless weapons stand at Rāma's command!

196. 3359

"Can we imagine achieving the strength of him who took to himself,
through his fierce cocked bow, all of the victories that had been won
by the incomparable Paraśurāma who, with his axe, had wiped out,
in a flash, the life of that being who had a thousand powerful arms?

197. 3360

"You have grown thin because of the surging in you of the poison of
[lust,
bringing you pain. The words you spoke were evil. Would not acting
[on them
lead us to destruction? I, as your mother's brother and your elder,
have advised you," he said. "That idea of yours, sir, give it up!"

198. 3361

The king of the Rākṣasas, contemptuous of him who had told him to
[think,
even a little, about all he had said, spoke then, "You live in fear
of him who cut off your mother's life! Does it make any sense
to think of you as someone who is fit to be counted a male!

199. 3362

"Can the sons of Daśaratha torment such as me, who entered the [heavens
and setting fire to all their places made the gods lose their state
and the Elephants of Space go into hiding? I am sovereign
over all the worlds! Aren't these positive, persuasive words?

200. 3363

"I have succeeded in winning sole rule over the three worlds!
Is there anything more welcome to me than gaining enemies? Do
what I command! How is it right for you to assume the responsibility
of my ministers who protect me and who deliberate when I order it!

201. 3364

"If it should happen that you refuse me, I will cut you down
with my sharp sword and I will do what my heart desires. I won't flinch!
Give up this practice of tendering me contemptible advice! Behave
as I command you!" he said, "if you wish to go on living!"

202. 3365

As soon as the Rākṣasa said these words,
Mārīca understood and he yielded, thinking,
"They speak the truth who say that
the proud at heart perish and
nothing is more deluded than to believe
you can safeguard those deluded by pride,"
and he began to speak, as if he were someone
pouring water over molten bronze.

203. 3366

"I had in mind what would be best for you.
I advised you truthfully but I spoke out
not because of my own fear of death.
Isn't it true that what is good
may seem evil, when someone's destruction
is near at hand? You who
base yourself on what is vile!"
he said, "Tell me what I am to do!"

204. 3367

As soon as he said that, Rāvaṇa rising,
embraced him, gave up the anger
that had surged in him and he said, "You whose arms
are as thick as mountains! There is
more fame in dying by Rāma's arrow,
isn't there, than by the fiery arrow
of the Love God? Bring me Sītā
who made the south wind burn!"

205. 3368

As his leader said these things, he answered,
"Tell me what work I have to do,
I who came back in fear
when, with two Rākṣasas, I had entered
the Daṇḍaka forest to avenge the offense
I had suffered and the arrow that he shot
then pierced my two friends
who fell and rolled on the ground."

206. 3369

When he had spoken, the king of the Rākṣasas
said, "Sir, I am prepared
to quickly kill the man
who took the precious life away
from your mother. Why ask me
'What, sir, do we have to do?'
Isn't it clear that through deception
and by magic we will capture her?"

207. 3370

"What else is there," said Mārīca, "to say
commenting on this? It would be vile
to seize the queen of that protecting king
by deception rather than straightforward action!
That would seem the worthy thing to do!
If you will defeat him in battle,
you will make the record of your courage
grow very high, O king!"

208. 3371

When he spoke, the king of the Rākṣasas
said to him, smiling, "Am I in need
of an army to conquer him? The sword
in my strong hand is surely enough!
And yet if the others die and she is left
alone, won't she also die,
she who is human? Therefore,"
he said, "we will seize her by magic."

209. 3372

Mārīca thought, "My scheming when I spoke
with deception, intending that his heads
should be cut off by arrows
before ever he touched the queen,
has failed. Who can understand
the workings of fate? I have no choice
but to do what he commands.
There is nothing else that I can do."

210. 3373

"And what great magic must I
practice? Tell me," he said.
"Become a deer made out of gold
and enter the forest to deceive
that golden woman." "I will do it,"
agreed Mārīca and started out,
and the king of the Rākṣasas whose spear
glitters went off by another way.

211. 3374

Since he had seen the strength of their bows before
and was not ready willingly to practice magic,
he went because of the strong sword of him who said,
"Be a deer!" I will recount his thoughts and his actions.

212. 3375

He thought of his beloved kin and he felt pain
and he was afraid of the heroes and bewildered. He trembled
like a fish when the water in its deep pond
has been poisoned and the state of his heart was unimaginable.

213. 3376

Though on the day of the sacrifice he had been harassed
by Rāma, and a second time as well, he had never
been destroyed, but now, this third time, consenting
to die, he had entered the forest where Rāghava lived.

214. 3377

Taking on the shape of a golden deer, illuminating
earth and sky with the lightning of its glistening
radiance that was without equal, he set out
to search for her who was like a lovely deer.

215. 3378

The stags and all the other deer who saw it
came toward it with desire as great as the ocean,
like all those who fall to whores without love,
skilled at elaborately deceiving the heart.

216. 3379

Sītā was walking and her waist that people would speak of as
nonexistent grew thinner, suffering from the effort,
and she was gathering flowers with the flowers that had never
been gathered of her hands and their flawless bangles.

217. 3380

As those who are about to experience disaster see,
as they sleep, some shape that has never been in their minds,
just like that, she saw it, she who was on the verge
of suffering pain no one ever before had felt.

218. 3381

She saw it and, not realizing it was deception, desired it
for its beauty, which was not worth desiring. It was because
the days of life for Rāvaṇa were finished and the Order
of the World would be established on earth the day he fell.

219. 3382

When it stood before that woman with her forehead like the crescent
moon, she was overcome by full and flowing desire, she thought,
"I'll tell him to capture this and then give it to me!"
and hurried away to the hero who carries a victorious bow.

220. 3383

She bowed to him and said, "There is a deer formed
of the finest gold, shining with wonderful light
far into the distance! Its strong legs and ears
are made of rubies! It is something to see!"

221. 3384

At her words, she who was like a lovely deer, he did not
even consider that a deer such as this one was not earthly
nor wonder what it was. The Lord even of the god who sits
on a flower filled with nectar felt desire.

222. 3385

When Rāma answered, "You who are like a vine wearing
ornaments of gold! We will go and we'll find it!"
his younger brother thinking, "This isn't something we should do!"
spoke to learn the intention of him who gives everything.

223. 3386

"Because she described the deer as having a body
of gold, and legs, ears and a tail of rubies and yet
it's seen to leap, one has to think it some deception
or, at least, accept that it may not be real!"

224. 3387

"Even the learned," Rāma answered, "with precise knowledge
do not understand the state of the world that is always changing.
There are tens of thousands of millions of lives abounding
everywhere! Anything, young man, can exist!

225. 3388

"Thinking about it, what do you imagine it is?
Because we have listened, we understand there are various
kinds of animals! Don't you know how seven
beautiful geese were born with bodies of shining gold?

226. 3389

"The density of living things is endless, of unlimited
variety," said the Lord to his younger brother and then
his woman, in her uneasiness, said to him, "It will go
away along many different paths and vanish!"

227. 3390

He who was as dark as a mountain of collyrium
        thought about what she wanted and he said,
"You who are wearing lovely ornaments,
        show it to me," and he went off,
behind him his younger brother with anklets
        resounding and a mind deeply troubled.
The deer stopped and approached like karma
        that cannot be evaded and glanced their way.

228. 3391

He looked at the deer that was looking at him
        and, not weighing anything in his sharp mind,
he thought, "How very fine this is!"
        It is right to say what this meant.
It was that he had left his bed
        of the serpent and been born because
of the merit earned by the gods.
        And that, could it be in vain?

229. 3392

"My younger brother! Can we say what it resembles?
Just look at this! All we can say
is that it is like itself! Is there any simile
adequate to it? Its teeth are like many
shining pearls and its soft tongue
flickering over the green grass
is like lightning! Its spots glow
like silver on a body of reddish gold!

230. 3393

"O you who are expert in the Veda
of the cocked bow! who among men
or women would not feel desire
before the beauty of this deer?
Look! Their hearts melting,
all creatures that crawl and fly
swing toward it like moths
who have seen the spreading light of a lamp!"

231. 3394

When the noble being had spoken these words,
his younger brother, looking at the deer,
came to the realization that this
was nothing good and he said, "What affair
of ours is this? Hero
with a fragrant, lovely garland!
Even if we have seen a deer of gold
here, it is best that we go back."

232. 3395

Before he had even finished saying
these things, the beautiful woman spoke
to her handsome husband. "Man of victories!
if you should quickly catch and give me
the deer that makes minds melt,
it will be a precious thing that we will
enjoy in happiness when our stay here
is over and we return to our city!"

233. 3396

When the woman with a tiny, lovely waist
said these things, the Lord agreed
"I'll do it!" and his great brother
with clear insight said, "You'll see,
my elder brother, in the end, that this
deer is a stratagem that has been created
through magic by Rākṣasas who are strong
and cruel and wish to deceive us."

234. 3397

"If it is magic, it dies by the sword
and when it is dead, we will have accomplished
our duty through having killed something
fierce and raging. If it is pure,
we will catch it and bring it here.
Through either of these choices, can we
go wrong? Tell me," he said
who would lift the suffering of the gods.

235. 3398

"We do not know who may be standing
behind this deer," said Lakṣmaṇa, "We don't know
what kind of magic may be at issue
nor understand just what this is.
You in whose strong arms the goddess
Śrī rests! For you to begin hunting,
which was renounced by our lineal ancestors,
is not something worth praising!"

236. 3399

The father of Brahmā the Creator said
that day to his great younger brother,
"If we were to say that the Rākṣasas
are enemies to everyone, are numerous,
practice potent magic and therefore
we were to abandon the vows
that we have undertaken, wouldn't that
be absurd? And so this is right!"

237. 3400

Lakṣmaṇa said, "Lord! Shouldn't we consider
what's best for us to do next?
However many there may be who have
released this deer and stand behind it,
I will shoot them with the burning arrows
that are fitted to my bow. I will go
quickly and cut it down. And if not,
well I will capture it and bring it back."

238. 3401

Then she who was like a wild goose,
in a sweet soft voice slipping
from her red mouth as if it were pouring out
amṛta, with the sweetness of a parrot,
sadly said, "Husband, so it seems
you won't catch it and give it to me!"
and she went off angry, weeping as if pearls
were falling from red-streaked water lilies.

239. 3402

The king, feeling the lover's anger
she had left with, said, "Listen! I myself
will capture this deer and quickly return.
You who wear a handsome garland!
Stay here and protect this woman
who is like a peacock wandering the forest,"
and he picked up his bow and arrows
that laugh at spears and hurried away.

240. 3403

"Of those three who came in former times
to the sacrifice, one escaped. I suspect
this deer and think it may be Mārīca.
Lord! Consider this as well!
May you live long! Go!" said Lakṣmaṇa,
joining his hands in respect and, to protect
her who was like the goddess Śrī,
he stood outside the hut she had entered.

241. 3404

Not taking the words into his heart
that were true and had been spoken by his younger brother,
but taking account of the anger of her
whose face is a match for the moon,
he who had handsome shoulders
like mountains and a mouth as red
as coral, Rāma, smiling,
began to follow the deer.

242. 3405

It stepped so very very gently.
It sprang, timid, in fear,
and jumped, stretching out its ears,
gathering its hoofed feet to its chest,
and it seemed as if it were teaching
new lessons for the movement of the
wind that rises and of the mind
as they travel and spread far.

243. 3406

Rāma strode with those feet
on which he had stood and then, lifting them,
had measured the three worlds. Ah!
Is there any other world beyond
to which he could stretch his feet?
He made the deer run and, pursuing it,
revealed his true identity. Who can form
an idea of that speed on that day?

244. 3407

It climbed up hills. It leaped
among banks of clouds. If Rāma
approached, then it ran away, but if
he stopped, it would come near enough
to be touched. It seemed to stand close by
and then vanish! How it seemed like the hearts
of women with lovely, fragrant garlands
who offer their love for pay!

245. 3408

"Its body shows it in one way
but its actions in another. The thoughts
my younger brother shared before with me
were right. If I think this over,
I have no urge to follow it. The trouble
that I have undergone here has been magic
performed by Rākṣasas. They have done it,"
said he who gives everything.

246. 3409

"Now he won't
try to catch me. He'll try
to kill me
and send me to heaven with an arrow,"
the Rākṣasa
of illusion thought in his heart
and rose
very rapidly up into the sky.

247. 3410

And at that moment
the Lord shot one of his arrows
that was red
in color and as impossible to ward off
as the fiery discus
which is his and he said to it, "Go
wherever
he has gone and take away his sweet life!"

248. 3411

The arrow
with its blade like a long leaf entered
the deceiving heart;
and then, with his mouth wide open,
he called out
so that the sound of his voice went
out beyond
the eight directions and he toppled like a mountain.

249. 3412

As soon as
the cruel being fell along with his life,
Rāma thought
of the younger brother who had told him this
was nothing good:
"That lord, who is my precious life, is amazing,
amazing!
He amazes me who came with me to save me!"

250. 3413

Standing,
he closely observed the body of that low being
who had fallen
shouting into the distances of all the directions,
and he realized
that this was truly Mārīca who had once come
to that sacrifice
of Viśvāmitra whose great tapas has no flaw.

251. 3414

In his heart,
he was concerned as he thought, "When the arrow
pierced his chest,
this degraded creature assumed my voice
through magic
that he controlled and he called out! My poor woman
with her eyes
like clouds will have heard and be distressed!

252. 3415

"He who stayed
behind, he who knew beforehand
without doubt
that the deer was Mārīca, my younger brother
clearly knows
my strength. Therefore he will reassure
Sītā by
telling her that those words were magic."

## 253. 3416

He thought,
"He wouldn't have come intending to die.
There was something
he was scheming. Evil could arise
through his words.
It would be best for me to return
before
the evil happens," and he did turn back.

## Paṭalam Eight
## Jaṭāyus Gives Up His Life

1. 3417

I have related
what happened there to him whose body
is dark as the sea
that has no equal and is filled with conches.
Now I will tell
what happened here and to her
who was like a branch,
flowers filled with pollen in her hair.

2. 3418

When he opened
the cave of his mouth and gritted his teeth
and sent out
false words, the moment they reached
her hearing,
like a kokila that has dropped to the ground,
she beat
her belly and she fell down fainting.

3. 3419

And then said, "I've
been a fool! I've killed my husband,
my source of life,
by telling him to catch and bring me this deer!"
and she rolled
around suffering like a vine fallen in thick fire
or a great
strong snake broken at the sound of thunder.

4. 3420

"Do you stand here
near me?" she said, "Young prince! by yourself!
even now
when we have been told that our lord
who is utterly
faultless has gone away, has fallen
through magic
performed by cruel and hostile Rākṣasas?"

5. 3421

"Would those who are wise say there is anyone in this world
of higher strength than Rāma? The words that you say
come from being a woman!" he answered her, speaking
as one who knew the truth, to make her know it as well.

6. 3422

"Could Rāghava, even alone, give way in any battle with swords
to the meager strength of those miserable beings who inhabit
the seven oceans, the fourteen worlds, the seven mountains
around this world, woman! or anywhere near them?

7. 3423

"Earth and Water, Wind, Space and Fire,
if he grows angry and tells them they must alter,
they will alter! Who do you think he is with his lotus eyes
dark as rain clouds, that you let yourself sink into this pain?

8. 3424

"Would Rāma defeated by the Rākṣasa summon us as anguish
overcame him? If he were to summon us, the great universes
that swarm above and below us would be shattered and
all living things from Brahmā on down would perish!

9. 3425

"What words can express it? The bow that powerful Śiva
strung, then stood and shot when he burned the three
strong cities was broken so that heaven and earth gave praise!
Did it have strength to match the strength of our lord?

10. 3426

"If this had happened now and our protector had suffered as
you think, it would be the end for all the three worlds,
and the gods who are highest and the holy men and all excellence
would perish and the right Order of the World would disappear.

11. 3427

"Why go on talking? When he who is a god shot his arrow,
the Rākṣasa—as it struck him there, as he fell and was losing his
strength—cried out. It was he who used these words. Do not
feel distress or grief about this. Wait here," Lakṣmaṇa said.

12. 3428

And when he had said these things, she with her rising anger,
suffering as if she had taken a death blow, with her heart
seething, said, "It's not right of you to just stay here like this!"
and she went on further then, with great cruelty and hostility.

13. 3429

"Even those who've known someone for a day may give their lives
for that someone, while you, though you hear your elder brother in
[pain,
do not fear for him and remain here. What else can I say? Now
I will plunge at once into fire and here I will die."

14. 3430

As she moved toward a fire blazing and smoking in the forest,
like a wild goose who would leap into a field of lotuses,
the young man with his protecting bow stopped her and spoke,
embracing the broad earth before the tiny flowers of her feet.

15. 3431

"Why should you die? You've spoken words that make me
afraid. I will not refuse you. Put away your worries
and wait here. I who am your servant am going.
How can we defeat fate which is cruel and angry?

16. 3432

"I am your servant. I will go. Evil will come of it.
Ignoring the king's order, you tell me to go
and you will be left here alone," he said to her, then
took his leave and went away and his heart was burning.

17. 3433

"If I stay here, she will not be, she will die in the fire,
and if I should go to him who is like an immovable mountain,
evil will arrive without fail and unfold. What should I do,
who seem to have some great desire for my dear life?" and he wept.

18. 3434

"If the god Dharma is able, he will make it come out well.
Rather than have her die, I will dare to do this, leaving
her here and going. I am an ignorant man, I feel this
suffering because I was born, because of actions in some other life!

19. 3435

"I resolve to go. If anything is to happen, the king
of the vultures who guards her will see it and he will do
what he can to protect her," he said; and because the gods
had done tapas for that purpose, the great being went off.

20. 3436

Once the young prince had left, he who was waiting with curved teeth
for him to leave so as to carry out his deception held up
three joined sticks of bamboo and took on the form
of an ascetic who has cut off the three attachments that are his enemies.

21. 3437

His body so dried out you would say there was no flesh
and his movements pained as if he had traveled a very long way,
like someone learned in music who beats out his own time,
he was singing the Sāma Veda as sweetly as a veena.

22. 3438

He walked like the petals unfolding on a flower. His steps
were skittish as if there were fire spread across the earth.
His legs and arms were trembling unable to stop.
He was so old, old age itself despised his age.

23. 3439

He had a garland for tapas of threaded lotus seeds.
His backside was like a tortoise, with his body bent over.
He wore the thread of good fame on his chest and ah!
he approached the place where she was, pure-minded as Arundhatī.

24. 3440

He came near the doorway of that hut without flaw
and he said, the words trembling as his tongue completely stumbled,
"Who are you living inside this place?" he whose body
seemed to be so real as to deceive even the gods.

25. 3441

And the woman beautiful as a peacock thought, "This is a man
of tapas, no doubt of it, and the thoughts of such are faultless."
With her words like liquid sugar, she, like a vine of coral,
said to him, "Come here!" and she came out toward him.

26. 3442

With his body sweating like the flowing musth of an elephant,
like an ocean of desire crossed by rolling waves of love,
he saw her with his own eyes, she who was an ornament
to beauty itself, repository of fame, the queen of purity.

27. 3443

When he saw the form of her whose beauty surpassed
the women of the gods and whose bright words were like the singing
of the sleepless kokila, what can I say of his thoughts as he felt
longing? His heroic shoulders grew thin and wasted away.

28. 3444

Why say his row of eyes were as ecstatic as a swarm of bees
whose humming is music when they settle and drink from a spring
full of flower nectar, at her beauty as lovely as a
peacock in the forest? No! They were as ecstatic as his heart!

29. 3445

"Are twenty eyes enough here for me to look at the body
the color of a ruby of her who has left her home
on the lotus with its red petals. I have no thousand
eyes that never blink!" he said and he felt pain.

30. 3446

"Are all the thirty-five million lives that I have gained
through my faultless tapas enough," he thought, "for this lovely
ocean of beauty without any shores, this woman
standing here with a row of bangles on her wrist?"

31. 3447

And he thought, "Now I am saved. I will carry out her orders
while she rules, as she should, over all the three worlds,
and the gods and the Asuras together with their wives will be
slaves to her, their duty only to do what they are commanded!

32. 3448

"If she has this radiance in her face as she suffers pain,
what must her smile be like with the tender leaves of her teeth
glistening?" he thought, "I will give my kingdom away
to the younger sister who drew me to this woman with loosened hair."

33. 3449

As soon as she saw that being who kept to no rules,
in whose heart desire had swollen and risen as he was thinking
such things, the woman of purity wiped away the tears
from her eyes and she told him, "Come in please," and she spoke
[sweetly.

34. 3450

She bowed to him and, as soon as he entered, she said, "Sit here,"
and offered him, in the proper manner, a seat made of cane
and the deceiver set his great Tridaṇḍaka there
beside him and sat down inside the hut that was lovely.

35. 3451

The mountains and the trees trembled and the birds, their tongues
reined in, were quiet. The animals were afraid. The snakes
shrunk up their hoods and cowered, because all of them had eyes
that could see the Rākṣasa in his cruel and sinful action.

36. 3452

Sitting there, he said, "What is the name of this home?
Who is the man who lives here and you, who are you?"
and the woman with the large eyes began to speak to him,
thinking, "He has just come here and doesn't know this place."

37. 3453

"The leader of the ancient line of Daśaratha, honoring
a command from a mother of noble descent, lives here
without suffering, along with his younger brother. You,
majesty!" she said, "will know the name of such a man."

38. 3454

"I have heard of him but never have I seen him. I was once
in that land rich with the waters of the Ganges. But whose
beautiful daughter are you, with your eyes like flowers
large as swords, who spend your hard days in the forest?"

39. 3455

"Holy man! You who follow the great path free of sin!
My name is Jānakī, elder daughter of Janaka, who in his heart
recognized no gods other than men like you, and I
am the wife of Kākutstha," she said, whose purity was flawless.

40. 3456

And once she had declared these things, the woman with lovely
[ornaments
said to him, "Enduring this painful path, you who have grown
so old and intend, through this path, to cross beyond
both good and bad karma, from where have you come here?"

41. 3457

"There is a king even over Indra, one who is so handsome
a painting cannot picture him. Born to the line of Brahmā,
he rules over all the worlds, heaven among them,
and his tongue sings the mantras of the precious Vedas.

42. 3458

"He was strong enough to seize the great glowing mountain
where Śiva rules and lift it even to its tiniest roots,
and his arms ground the fighting tusks into powder
of the elephants who support the directions with their great energy.

43. 3459

"Those who crowd at his threshold are gods while words
are not adequate for the description of his might. In his hands,
he holds the kalpaka tree and other treasures. His beautiful home
is the golden city of Laṅkā encircled by the great waters.

44. 3460

"Menakā, Tilottamā, and other women like them,
leaving heaven, have come to him because of his majesty,
and their work is to do such things as hold his stainless bag
of betelnut, rub his feet and polish his sandals.

45. 3461

"Those beings called the moon and the sun will abandon
their paths if he wishes it! Shining Indra
and the other gods stand as guards for his palace
which is in this world and rises up to block the clouds.

46. 3462

"All the pleasant, faultless things from the golden city
of heaven and from the ancient and lovely city
of the Nāgas and from all the cities that are part of
the great earth are found now in his fine city.

47. 3463

"His life is of endless days granted him by the god
who sits on the stemmed lotus. He holds in his strong hand
the sword of the god who includes a woman. He has thrown
the fierce constellations into his jail. He has eminent virtues.

48. 3464

"His conduct is free of cruelty. His learning is broad.
He is impartial and so handsome that even the God of Love
is bewildered by him. He has taken on the full majesty
of the three gods whom all those living call their lords.

49. 3465

"How many beautiful women there are throughout the world
who desire his love! They think about him and they melt.
But he will not agree to be of help to them. He
is searching for a woman who will be sweetness in his heart.

50. 3466

"I wished to do it and so I committed myself to staying
a few days in that city where the king I have described rules
enthroned. But I didn't have the heart to leave. I drew out
my visit, then returned," he said, weaving his deception.

51. 3467

"Not wishing for the Vedas or the grace of those who practice
the Vedas, for what reason did you stay in the city of the Rākṣasas
who are sinful, who consume the lives of beings that feel
and think? O you who consider even the body as without significance!

52. 3468

"You did not stay in the forest with the men of great tapas
nor think to enter a city of pure people in a beautiful land
full of water," she said. "You lived among those who do not believe
in the way of the Order of the World. What have you done?"

53. 3469

When he who had gone beyond all limits
 heard the words of the young woman, he then said,
"Because I realized that the Rākṣasas
 with their cruel swords have no faults
I wasn't afraid. If you look at the truth,
 you whose face is as bright as the moon!
the Rākṣasas are no more evil than the gods
 and, toward people like us, they seem to be kind!"

54. 3470

When he had spoken, the woman with lovely ornaments
 said, "Even those who have good reputations
and follow the ancient ways are pure
 no longer if they associate with evil
beings," and because she did not realize
 that Rākṣasas with their skill at magic
were able to take on any form they
 might wish for, she did not suspect him.

55. 3471

In his heart, he felt she was suspicious
and, thinking he would make all of her doubts
vanish, he chose a different approach:
"How can all those who are living
in the three worlds where things are seen
clearly ever accomplish anything
unless they act in accordance with
the nature of those who hold power?"

56. 3472

Since he knew her character, he spoke
these words in deception, and she
who was so rich in virtues said,
"In these times when he who gives everything
and teaches Righteousness is carrying out
the difficult tapas of living here, the Rākṣasas,
distant from Righteousness, will die. Their clan
will be finished. There will be no suffering in the world."

57. 3473

While the woman like a doe was speaking,
he said, "If men could conquer
Rākṣasas and cut them down at the root,
O you whose eyes glitter like fishes!
then a baby rabbit could kill a herd
of elephants without a survivor, and more!
a tiny fawn could kill a tiger
that is male and has curving claws."

58. 3474

"It seems," she said, "that you haven't heard
anything of the battles where Virādha
whose hair was like gathered lightning or Khara
the Victorious followed by his hordes
all died," and as she spoke and thought
of what had happened to them on that day,
she began to pour out tears
that fell like waterfalls of rain.

59. 3475

"The tiger is He Who Gives Everything,"
she said, "and the Rākṣasas are a herd
of deer such as you mentioned. Tomorrow
you will see them perish with their kin
as the gods rejoice! Don't you understand,
you who are flawless! Can sin
overcome that which cannot be destroyed,
the very Order of the World!"

60. 3476

As that string of language, sparse and
sweet as honey that has been mixed
with amṛta, entered his ears,
the flesh on his body bristled
and swelled up. A terrifying pride
seized hold of him. Because she had said
that mere men possessed such power,
he became enraged at her words.

61. 3477

In his anger, he said these things:
"Since you have described how a man
put an end to those lowly beings
of insignificant strength, tomorrow
you will know better, when the north wind
of those twenty strong arms
blows and then Rāma will die
as lightly as a silk-cotton flower!

62. 3478

"If you want to rip out Mount Meru,
if you want to break apart the sky,
if you want to mix the ocean water with mud
or quench the fire below the sea,
if you want to lift up the earth,
among all these acts, what is impossible
for Rāvaṇa? Woman of few words!
Who do you think you are discussing?"

63. 3479

And she answered, "Is someone strong merely
because he has many hulking arms
to protect him? Didn't one man with two arms
in a moment cut the whole forest
of hulking arms belonging to the hero
with anklets on his legs who had once imprisoned
the king of Laṅkā which is surrounded
by waters full of tiny cormorants?"

64. 3480

As she was saying this, at those words,
his eyes burned, his hulking arms
shot out into all the directions,
his diadem touched the sky and
his strong hands slapped each other.
His rows of teeth gnashed together
like thunder and, with anger boiling up,
his covering of illusion dropped away.

65. 3481

Just as she was thinking, "Can it be
that this person is not a superior being
who has abandoned good and evil acts?"
as she felt doubt, not knowing anything
and wondering, "Who could he be?"
he appeared, like a cobra with fierce poison
seething in terrible, swollen anger,
rising up and spreading out its hood.

66. 3482

Considering the agony she felt now
who had already suffered so cruelly,
how could one imagine it greater?
There were no words she could form
before him, nothing she could do.
She trembled, as does a life
when Death, whom no one commands,
comes and is near at hand.

67. 3483

"Witness my heroic strength through which
I conquered and the gods do my bidding!
When you said that men have power
who live like worms in the mud,
not because you are a woman did you survive!"
he said, "I would have decided to crush you
into a handful of food and chew you up,
but had I done it, I would have lost my life.

68. 3484

"Don't tremble! Woman like a wild goose!
I will uphold you tenderly, like a crown,
on my ten heads, one by one,
that have never bowed before to any being.
As, numberless, the ornamented women
of heaven will linger at your feet,
fulfilling your orders, you will live
with the wealth of ruling over the fourteen worlds!"

69. 3485

Tightly she closed up her ears
with her hands like shoots and spoke,
"Rākṣasa! What have you said to me,
to the pure wife of victorious Kākutstha
with his cruel and lovely bow in hand!
You who behave wrongly on the earth
like a dog who desires the oblation
pure men offer into the rising fire!

70. 3486

"Would I permit my noble purity
to be destroyed out of fear of losing
my sweet life which anyway passes
quickly as the dew on a blade of grass?
Run and hide yourself," she said,
"if you want to save your life
before the cruel arrows come,
angry as thunder, like blazing lightning!"

71. 3487

She said these things but that Rākṣasa
who had no mercy remained there and said,
"If your husband were to shoot an arrow
that would reach my chest which destroyed
the force of the strong hard tusks
of those elephants like mountains who uphold
the directions, it would be like an arrow
of flowers shot into a hill.

72. 3488

"You who appear to be a goddess
for the goddess Śrī to worship! Give me
life! My body has withered as the sickness
of my desire for you seethes in me!
Accept a state that will be higher than
the women of heaven with their massive earrings!"
he said, bowing, whose arms were stronger
than the mountains that support the earth.

73. 3489

As he came and bent to the ground at her feet,
she cried out in grief, "Lord! Young prince!"
beautiful as endurance itself, like someone whose life
is quaking below a descending bloodstained sword.

74. 3490

Then, right there, in his evil, without touching her
whose ornaments were lovely, remembering the curse that he was
never to seize a woman, he dug out a *yojana* of earth below
and around her with his strong arms high as columns.

75. 3491

He lifted it onto his tall chariot and the woman
with dense bangles, her precious life obscured,
fainted away like lightning fallen to the earth.
Then he hurried to fly off across the sky.

76. 3492

"Drive the chariot!" he said, and she writhed like a vine
burnt and destroyed in blazing fire. She was exhausted,
frenzied, and she stood up quivering and weeping in her pain.
"O Righteousness!" she said, "Save me quickly from this!

77. 3493

"Mountains! Trees! Peacocks! Kokilas!
Stags! Does! Bull elephants and cow elephants!
Know me as I am, with a life that cannot last!
Go! Tell it to him whose strength is indestructible!

78. 3494

"It is you who know where my noble lord is!
Clouds! Gardens! Deities of the forest! If you
are gracious, if you tell me not to fear and that
I am saved, would that cause you any harm? Speak to me!

79. 3495

"Won't you come like a dark blue cloud
shooting your streams of arrows so that the Rākṣasas
perish! Generous Lord! Young prince! Faultless Bharata!
and his younger brother! Will you take on such shame?

80. 3496

"Godāvarī! You who are so cool and so gentle!
who are like a mother to me! Won't you run and go to him,
he who knows clearly, without being told, what is in my heart!
Tell him how I stand, who have behaved badly!

81. 3497

"Mountain springs here before me! Lions in the caves!
May you laugh when you see how the twenty hands,
which seized me with this earth, and the ten heads
are battered, ruined, felled to the ground!"

82. 3498

As she went on saying these many things,
    yearning to run, raving in tears,
he said to her, "You whose soft breasts
    are the color of gold, you who wear
golden earrings! Will those men in battle
    kill me and rescue you? Let them try!"
He laughed and slapped his strong, hard hands,
    he who was uselessly wasting the days of his life.

83. 3499

Answering him then, she said to him,
    "Through magic, you created a deer
that was only deception and he who will be
    your death, who will consume your precious life,
you made him go away and then
    skulking up, you seized me and have gone off.
If you know how to defend yourself, if you know
    how to fight, then stop this chariot!"

84. 3500

And she kept on talking, saying more:
    "Are you a hero? You, even when you heard
that the men who cut off your sister's breasts
    and her nose are still in the forest,
the same men who killed your fellow Rākṣasas
    swiftly, all you did then was
work this magic! Wasn't that
    because you were overwhelmed by fear?"

85. 3501

"Woman!" he said, when she had finished,
    "Listen to this! Were I to accept
a fight with men who are contemptible,
    whose bodies have no strength, these arms
would draw shame to them. And they once lifted
    the silver mountain of the god with the third eye
in his forehead! Deception will give me
    a far better result than battle!"

86. 3502

Hearing that, she who was as beautiful
as a carved image, said to him, "It seems
that it is sinful to stand against the enemies
of your clan, and that combat with the sword
is shameful! But is it right to have
the strength for deceiving pure women?
Is there any fault, is there
any shame for the merciless Rākṣasas?"

87. 3503

Then, as she was speaking, Jaṭāyus
appeared and said, like the thunder, "You!
Where are you going? Where are you
going? Stop! Stop!" The flames
of his anger spreading through his eyes,
his heroic beak shining like lightning,
his body like huge, golden
Mount Meru coming through the sky.

88. 3504

His two wings beat the air
as when a world ends, and the fierce wind
blows through the entire universe,
uprooting all the broad, strong mountains
till they rise in the sky and smash
one another to dust falling,
and the sea, swelling, surges up to be one
with the earth and both are destroyed.

89. 3505

Trees with strong leafy tops curved down while
the clouds above soared high in the sky to avoid him.
"Up there! The great cruel Garuḍa is coming!" the cobras
thought, shrunk their hoods, skulked off and were deeply troubled.

90. 3506

Elephants and yāḷis and every other sort of animal,
great trees from the forest and bushes and rocks
were torn away by the wind from his two wings
and sent soaring so that the sky seemed like the forest.

91. 3507

"Where are you going? Where are you taking the wife
of the highest on your towering chariot along with
part of the earth? Now I will cover the sky, all the directions!"
said he whose nature was to spread his protective wings.

92. 3508

He came, the king of the vultures, his legs and head reddish
as Mount Kailāsa with its caves when, at day's end,
the red sky veils it, and he was meaning to block
the evil one's finely crafted chariot on its way.

93. 3509

Then he was there and said to the woman, "Don't be afraid!"
but realizing that Rāvaṇa had not touched her,
the anger that had flared in him and was rising did not
reach its height, but he began, again, to speak:

94. 3510

"Foulness! You have burned away life for yourself
and for your clan! Why have you done this?
If you understand that you are lost, release
his wife! Go off! Then you will not die.

95. 3511

"You have made a mistake in your ignorance! In your obsession,
what did you think she is? she who is mother
of the great world! You have shown no judgment!
Who is there now to offer you protection?

96. 3512

"Don't you know, sir! that the God of Death just
filled his hands with food and ate a banquet
of your people's precious lives honestly offered him
by Rāma who fought them and did not let them escape?

97. 3513

"Do you want to launch a ball of mud, throwing it
at a cruel raging elephant coming to kill you?
Though you might not know that it can kill, think
what would happen to your life if you ate poison?

98. 3514

"All the worlds and Indra and the three gods
beyond him and even Death are like deer
at the sight of a tiger! Do any of them have
the strength in them to defeat those bowmen?

99. 3515

"In this world, there is nothing worse than this
savage action, destroying you and yours in this life,
leading to rebirth in a terrible hell, hard
to escape. What birth did you think it would gain you?

100. 3516

"These men are incarnations of that god who is
first cause and substance of the three highest gods.
You who do not think! With what gods would you think
to compare them? You are crazed and so have gone astray!

101. 3517

"The favors you have received through grace of the god
on the bull, he who fought and burned the three cities,
as well as all your other magic skills only have power
till the Truth shoots arrows from the bow he carries!

102. 3518

"If the son of him who lives well in heaven were to come
by himself with his bow bent, then you would not
be able to withstand him! I will, myself, return
the woman whose forehead is lovely. Go! At once!"

103. 3519

The king of the Rākṣasas heard him. Fire poured
from the glittering bright pupils of his eyes. He pursed
his mouth and he angrily said, "Don't spit your
words at me! Quickly, show me those you mean!

104. 3520

"You have come, vulture! Move now! or I will pierce your chest
with an arrow and open a great wound! Even if water
eaten by red hot iron could reappear, know that she
whose voice has eaten sugar will never reappear away from me!"

105. 3521

Fear twice as strong as before overwhelmed
        Sītā when he said this,
and Jaṭāyus, seeing that woman who was like a wild goose
        so distressed, spoke to her:
"The Rākṣāsa's body will be dismembered instantly!"
        and he said, "Because the son
of the king has not come with his bow, do not
        be anguished, my mother!

106. 3522

"Don't worry! Don't grieve! so that teardrops,
        like descending pearls
fall upon your breasts! Today you will see
        me offer his heads,
like a thick cluster of palmyra fruit,
        as my sacrifice," he said,
"to the ten directions that this being
        claims to have conquered!"

107. 3523

He flapped and beat his great wings
which roared like thunder
and dashed Rāvaṇa's row of crowns to the ground
as he rushed forward
swiftly to bite at him with his snapping beak
which seized and broke
Rāvaṇa's tall and lovely banner marked with a veena
and the gods above blessed him.

108. 3524

Then the Rākṣasa with his eyes reddened
like melting lac,
he who had never before suffered
humiliation like this,
laughed so as to make the seven worlds
tremble, and he curved
his eyebrows and, with his hands, the bow,
large as a mountain.

109. 3525

As the rain of streaming arrows that were shot then
by Rāvaṇa with the curving
cruel teeth bright as the crescent moon
came at him, he beat
some of them down with his wings, broke some to pieces
with his sharp talons
and, with the weapon of his beak which even Death fears,
he ripped up Rāvaṇa's bow.

110. 3526

Jaṭāyus stretched out his great beak that was
like the weapon of the discus
toward Rāvaṇa's powerful heads and it was as if
he were Garuḍa attacking
the cruel-eyed cobra Ananta. When Rāvaṇa then
bent the bow
he held in reserve, Jaṭāyus snatched his jeweled earrings
and soared up in the sky.

111. 3527

As he rose, Rāvaṇa rained seven arrows
and then seven more,
which he wasted without penetrating the strong chest.
The Rākṣasa roared
and poured out more gleaming arrows. The gods,
in fear, with the thought
that now Jaṭāyus the warrior would surely fall,
breathed hot sighs.

112. 3528

As the blood flowed like fresh water from his wounds,
the shining king of birds
seemed like a white cloud shining in the sky
that had drunk up
the lake of blood which Khara and those others
had left on the earth,
having mistaken it for the ocean but now, on seeing the mistake,
vomiting it out again.

113. 3529

So he was but suddenly took a fresh breath,
grew angry and plunged
into the great row of Rāvaṇa's twenty arms,
snapping with his beak,
gouging with his claws, striking out with his wings,
and he cut through the links
of Rāvaṇa's armor that lay across the chest adorned
with a necklace of pearls.

114. 3530

And the Rākṣasa sank a hundred arrows
into the broad chest
of him who had cut through his armor. As he did that,
the gods were fearful
and troubled, but before their trouble could grow,
the king of birds
plucked away Rāvaṇa's bow with his beak, and the assembly
in heaven cheered.

115. 3531

As he seized the bow in his beak of that being
who had with the strength
of his arms lifted up the glittering silver
mountain of Kailāsa
along with Lord Śiva, Jaṭāyus shone like a great
towering cloud
raising a rainbow. Who could present the power
of his shoulders in words?

116. 3532

The beloved friend of Daśaratha let fall from his beak
the bow of Rāvaṇa
who had harassed thousand-eyed Indra with arrows
so that the god whose chest
never shrinks back had run away in the sky. The close
companion of that Rāma
who had broken the bow of Śiva with his bare hands
broke that bow with his feet.

117. 3533

When that being, ravager of the world, saw that
the shaft of his fine bow
which matched his strength was broken, his courage
was undaunted. Rage
in his heart, he seized and hurled a trident
like the single arrow
with which Śiva whose neck is stained by the poison
destroyed the three cities.

118. 3534

The king of the vultures repelled that three-headed spear
with his chest and said,
"See my strength, so you don't imagine that I
am not strong enough
for this!" and the gods, without revealing themselves,
said, "Who will ever
do such a thing in the future?" and they slapped
their backs and shouted.

119. 3535

That trident was flung back like glances from the eyes
of men who are impoverished
and can merely wish to delight their senses with women
whose intent is gold
or the glances of respectable guests who have come where
they are not regarded fondly
or those of women with gentle eyes married to yogis
intent on the Self.

120. 3536

Before Rāvaṇa, who had lost his trident, could take hold
of another weapon, Jaṭāyus
plucked the head from the driver of that chariot
with its shining horses
so tall that it hid the sky and, by throwing
the head into the faces
of that creature insane for the woman of great purity,
he drove Rāvaṇa wild.

121. 3537

Looking at Jaṭāyus who had hurled the head,
he realized the strength
of that heart. Enraged, he lifted up a battle
staff of gold
and struck a blow. Sparks and flames
shot up densely.
The king of the vultures fell to earth,
like a mighty mountain.

122. 3538

He fell to the earth and, as he was falling, Rāvaṇa
by himself drove
his chariot with the shining horses, flew upward
so that watching eyes
could never follow him, and, while he was rising,
the delicate woman
rolled on the earth, quivering, as if blazing fire
had been thrust into a wound.

123. 3539

Seeing how the woman soft as a tender shoot
was wailing and fainting,
Jaṭāyus said, "Mother! Do not drown in your
suffering! Don't fear!"
He took new breath, went soaring up and said,
"You! Where are you going
now?" and fell upon Rāvaṇa's chariot as the gods
shouted with joy.

124. 3540

He darted forward, snatched away the staff adorned
with its many jewels
and flung it away. Then, with the strong, unyielding sword
of his beak, he dealt out
destruction, attacking the sixteen horses of the bright
decorated chariot, and they grew
weak, were broken and destroyed. Death took them,
clapping his hands.

125. 3541

He destroyed the mighty chariot. Hanging there
on the strong back
of Rāvaṇa were quivers so dense that they covered
the sky and, since he
could not shoot arrows now in close, difficult
combat, they were full
like the vaults of misers and Jaṭāyus seized them
in his powerful claws.

126. 3542

Like a great kingfisher he dove, then reared up
and beat his wings
on the Rākṣasa's chest and shoulders. Rāvaṇa
fell into anguish,
lost his breath, and his head was hanging.
Jaṭāyus said to him,
"Now you are finished. Is this all
the strength you have?"

127. 3543

Then that Rākṣasa who carries a savage spear
grew enraged,
unable to bear what had been said and, in his rage,
seeing no other weapon
he could launch, thinking, "Now I will consume
this one's sweet life,"
he drew his long sword that cannot fail
and hurled it at Jaṭāyus.

128. 3544

Lack of strength did not defeat him. It was the sword
of Śiva, divine,
irresistible, preeminent in destruction; and it was
that the days of his life
had reached their end, when they must vanish;
and so he fell like
one of the mountains that had its wings severed when Indra
threw his thunderbolt.

129. 3545

He fell, wide wings first, to the earth
and the gods fled
while multitudes of holy men, saddened, said,
"She has lost her protector,"
and those who reside in the spacious heaven
of Viṣṇu showered
down a rain of fresh, yellow flowers. Sītā
watched in dread.

130. 3546

The Rākṣasas, who had felt shamed, now shouted,
filled with his pride,
and the sound spread through the great sky but Sītā
suffered like a deer
caught in a net. She tried to think of what to do,
heavily breathing in pain;
she saw no one to rely on and she was shaken like a vine
falling when its branch breaks.

131. 3547

"The king of vultures came to offer me his strong protection
and perished. What refuge can there be for me, from this day on?"
she spoke and oh! cried out like the beautiful mate
of an aṉṟil bird in the pain of separation from her sweet companion.

132. 3548

"I was a fool. I would not listen to any advice
from Rāma's younger brother and I sent him hurrying away
and then this king fought for me but his wings were cut off
and I am desperate! What more is there that fate can do to me?

133. 3549

"Has this good being been defeated who came as I was suffering
and said to me, 'Don't fear!' Has that one won the victory
who is only fit for hells? Did evil win? Are the Vedas
false, the Order of the World nothing?" she said, in her grieving.

134. 3550

She mourned, "O my lords who went off because of my words!
How shameless I am! Come see him who so loved your father.
Jaṭāyus who was the linchpin of all those who stand
for the Order of the World which does not vanish!" and she wept.

135. 3551

"You who turned the wheel of the law! You live in the heaven
of light! Will you welcome this lord who followed the Order
of the World given in the teachings, who performed his beneficent,
difficult duty, worthy of your friendship?" she said, in tears.

136. 3552

"It is my duty," she wept, "to resist violation. And yet,
even so, shame has come to the bow of Rāma with his skill
in battle, to the strong bow with its imperishable beauty.
Shame has come to the clan in which I, this sinner, was born!"

137. 3553

The Rākṣasa looked at her standing there, in tears, all alone,
and looked down at him who had lost his wings. Then he snatched
up Sītā on the length of earth he had carried in the chariot,
put her and that soil on his shoulders, and went off through the sky.

138. 3554

With the speed of that cruel being passing through the heavens
Sītā's mind and her eyes whirled, and she lost the awareness,
that fills the heart. The pure woman was conscious
of nothing. Forgetting even herself, she writhed on the earth.

139. 3555

The Rākṣasa went off and the king of the vultures came back
to his senses as the ferocious suffering that had stunned him
abated a little. He looked at the sky and there, on his swift way,
saw the cunning being. Feeling the anguish within him then, he spoke:

140. 3556

"My sons have not come. Fate has not been willing to grant me
the true glory of dispelling my daughter-in-law's fierce
suffering. Instead it has brought down the wall that was meant
to defend the Order of the World! Now what will happen?

141. 3557

"If those conquerors had been here, could this ever have been done
to the woman with golden bracelets, her waist as thin
as lightning? Nor can I even tell them what has taken place.
Has the treachery of their stepmother now carried them to their deaths?

142. 3558

"Rāma is that god the dark color of collyrium
who lies on a snake as if it were a bed of cotton.
Then how could he be defeated by a fiercely raging Rākṣasa?
Rāvaṇa must have used cunning and worked his deceiving magic.

143. 3559

"My son will defeat the Rākṣasas, cutting them off at the root,
ridding himself of this burning shame while this Rākṣasa will not dare
to touch the noble being's wife because of the unfailing curse
spoken by him who, from his beautiful flower, created this great world."

144. 3560

So said he who once had giant wings, and he thought, "She is suffering,
imprisoned, escape will be hard," but then he realized, though he had
no wings to fight for her, that her purity, as if it were a great wing,
would shield the woman who was like a myna bird and his pain left him.

145. 3561

As the river of blood from the loss of his lovely wings flowed away,
ever lessening, and his heart filled with shame because he had not saved
the woman beautiful as a vañci vine, his love went out
toward his children. Awareness slipped away from him. He slept.

146. 3562

Meanwhile the Rākṣasa, with his fear of directly touching
the beautiful body of the woman lovely as a vañci vine,
quickly took her to the Śiṃśupa Forest and placed her there
in confinement guarded by Rākṣasa women who were like poison.

147. 3563

I have described, in this way, the actions of Rāvaṇa.
Now I will tell what happened to Lakṣmaṇa after the woman
ordered him away, saying, "Find out what has happened
to my lord who went off, following after the golden deer!"

148. 3564

Distressed, a great pain growing in his heart as he thought
of how the incomparable woman would be left alone, Lakṣmaṇa
had committed himself to a search like that of Bharata when he left
his wealthy city, in anguish at separation from his elder brother.

149. 3565

He went as swiftly as a boat floating on cool waves
and when he saw him who seemed to be a black cloud
descended to the earth and marked with a great flowering forest
of red lotuses, his eyes were as pleasured as his heart.

150. 3566

And he of the dark body thought, looking at his younger brother,
"Since she must have heard that unsettling cry from the Rākṣasa,
the woman lovely as a peacock will be shaken at heart and troubled,
in pain, confused, like an innocent woman," and his mind was uneasy.

151. 3567

And he thought, "It was because I who feel this pain paid no
attention to his words that he is coming,
in deluded obedience to the foolish woman's insistent command,
who did not understand, in her anxiety, that those were words
from the gaping mouth of a Rākṣasa adapted for so low
a use of language, for that reason, in disobedience to my orders,
coming, as I see him, with a troubled mind and all
alone, to find out how I am, is the young hero!

152. 3568

"What does fate have in store for me now?" thought the lord while
[Lakṣmaṇa,
the hero who held a lovely bow in his strong hand,
bowed to his handsome feet as he stood there. Then Rāma
quickly embraced him and they hugged each other,
handsome chest to chest that were crossed like lightning
by their sacred threads and, Rāma's heart flowing out
toward him, the great being, standing back, asked him,
"Why have you come here, with what in mind?" and Lakṣmaṇa
[answered:

153. 3569

"When, with you away, the cruel outcry of the Rākṣasa was heard
and she who is like a vañci vine became anguished,
though I told her that these were only the words of a Rākṣasa
with the gift of skillful speech, she would not believe me
and, in her distress, she said to me, 'Don't stay here!
Go and find out what's happened!' She would not recognize
the strength of your giant arms, though I told her, but she stood there
and heard what she heard, resolute in her anger and quivering.

154. 3570

" 'If you insist on staying here,' she said, 'if you will not go,
then I will throw myself into the fire,' and she began
at once to run toward the great forest while I, who have gone
against my pledge to you, felt fear in my heart,
and I thought that if I remained, if I refused to go, then she would not
survive, and then I thought how that would be wrong, how
it would go against the Order of the World for her to die, and so
I have come here," he said, and then the Faultless Being
[understood.

155. 3571

"This has happened because he had to prevent her from taking her own
[life!
That is nothing for me to question! But that she,
because of her pain, would not allow his explanations to reach
her heart! Trouble will come to her now since she
has no one to protect her! It is all part of a plot through which
someone has planned to lay his hands on her
without anything going wrong for him, and to take her with him
far away, while this other was assigned to draw us apart!"

156. 3572

And Rāma said to Lakṣmaṇa, "No fault clings to you for having come
nor was that innocent woman wrong in what she did,
telling you to go, disturbed as she was. No! things have turned bad
for no reason other than that decision which I, to my misfortune,
made when I followed the deer and I did not let you stop me,
even though you realized the truth." And Rāma, after speaking,
began thinking all this over and could not stop thinking. In his heart
which had never known the feeling of anguish, his anguish grew.

157. 3573

"But what good is it to stay here and delay any longer!" he thought.
"Only if I can see her who is like a kokila or a myna bird
that has learned how to speak, only then and in no other way will
my pain vanish!" He quickly set out on his path.
Though far away from her, he covered the great distance
as fast as an arrow that has been shot from a bow.
Rapidly he approached the shining grove where she should be whose
[skin
was the color of the gold needle that tests the quality of gold.

158. 3574

He arrived at a run but did not see her
with her wavy hair adorned
by blossoming flowers that he had given her
from the grove near the hut.
He stood there as if he were life
that is precious and had been
separated from a body and comes
searching for it in vain.

159. 3575

His mind turned bitter, not seeing
the woman with heavy earrings—
like a man standing in amazement
when a great treasure buried
underground as a help for his old age
has been taken by thieves
and now there is no wealth left for him
to spend and survive.

160. 3576

The earth whirled and the great mountains
    whirled and the minds
of wise men whirled. Heaven
    whirled and the seven seas
that rise into waves whirled.
    Even the Vedas whirled
and the eyes of Brahmā whirled
    and the sun and the moon!

161. 3577

Everything in this world trembled
    and thought, "Will he be angry
at Righteousness, at mercy, at the gods?
    angry at holy men,
angry at the violence of the evil,
    will the great being be angry
at the teaching of the Vedas, wondering
    'What worth are they now?' "

162. 3578

As great Rāma with his dark body
    was troubled in mind,
everything there is, impossible to number,
    was overturned. What was
above fell, what was below rose,
    and it seemed the time
when, together with its creating god,
    all the universe ends.

163. 3579

The young prince bowed to him and said,
    "We've noticed tracks
of a chariot. We've seen that, afraid
    to touch her, he left
with a piece of the earth. Why stay here,
    uselessly questioning
as if we were weak? Let us follow
    before they go far!"

164. 3580

"Yes, that's what we should do now," said
the Pure Being and they took
their quivers of long, shining arrows
with their other arms and they,
so strong, went so fast they made great
lovely trees and mountains
sway down by the long trail of the chariot
where Rāvaṇa had crossed the earth.

165. 3581

They came to a place where the trail
of his passing chariot
vanished as if risen into the sky.
His heart pierced with pain
like a spear into the raw burn on a body,
Rāma said, "What
do you think that we should do now,
my younger brother?"

166. 3582

"It is clear," the young prince said,
"that this massive chariot
went south. Lord! with your thick arms
ready for wrestling!
The sky is not too far away
for an arrow from your bow!
Why should we stay on here
in astonishment and indecision?"

167. 3583

Rāma said, "Yes, we should do that,"
and they moved in that direction,
going some two yojanas until they came
on the pole of a flag
that showed a lovely veena and was lying
on the earth like a giant
bamboo broken in the air
by an assaulting wind.

168. 3584

They saw this and they wondered whether
there had been fierce battle
between the hosts of the gods and their enemies
over that woman. But then,
when He Who Protects realized that the sword
had been a beak which broke
the shining staff, a flood of tears came
into his lotus eyes and he spoke:

169. 3585

"If you will look here, you will see
it was broken by the beak
of Jaṭāyus, he who is like your father
and must have come here quickly,
fiercely attacking. How can we know
what may have happened
in battle? He was alone, his body thin
from the long passage of years."

170. 3586

Lakṣmaṇa said, "This is good news!
He is so strong that nothing
would make him tremble! We can go
and join him. Surely
he will be steadily holding them back!
He may win and rescue her!
Why should we stay here, delaying, thinking
thoughts that do not matter?"

171. 3587

The great one answered, "Yes, we should
keep after them." They moved
as fast as the wind that sails
like a kite over the earth,
and they saw a strong and cruel bow
lying there like a broken
rainbow or like a wave towering
high upon the sea.

172. 3588

"The bow that lies here, Lakṣmaṇa,
    is mighty as Mount Mandara
with which the gods churned the ocean.
    It seems, resting there,
like an entire digit of the moon.
    Just think of what
he is who bit and broke this," Rāma said,
    standing and looking at the bow.

173. 3589

After that, they went close together,
    crossing a long way.
Then they looked and saw a great,
    massive, three-bladed
trident and they saw two quivers
    that lay there like
two hills filled with many arrows
    like rain and they were amazed.

174. 3590

And on they went and saw the armor
    plucked and thrown down
from the chest of the king of the Rākṣasas
    lying there as if all
the lights that shine and move
    their brightness across the sky
were gathered together here, covering
    the forest ahead of them.

175. 3591

And they reached the place where the horses
    that had been swift as the wind
lay shrouding over portions of the forest
    and they came to the charioteer
lying there and then to the chariot
    lying like a cloud
on the earth and, near it, lay flesh bright
    with the blood of Rāvaṇa.

176. 3592

Their shining hands trembled as they saw
a heap of ornaments
set with fine gems and so many
jeweled earrings it seemed
as if the many circles of the sun that appear
with outspread rays
when a universe ends had abandoned the sky's
beauty and lay on the earth.

177. 3593

"There are many ornaments for the arms," said Rāma,
"many piles of earrings
that are glistening with light and many
jeweled crowns. He is alone,
he who is like our father, and all
the days he has lived through!
Young prince! Many must have fought him
who were as strong as yāḷis!"

178. 3594

The husband of Śrī spoke, and the lion,
the son of Sumitrā, answered,
"Considering the many arms as long
as trees and the many heads,
I would say no more than one
being fought against
our father for so long a way
and that being is Rāvaṇa!"

179. 3595

Accepting the words of the young prince,
garlanded with petals,
Rāma moved quickly on, looking ahead,
as the fire flew
from his strong eyes. Then he saw him
who seemed their father lying
on the bright blood spreading from his body like
Mount Mandara on the milky ocean.

180. 3596

He was shaken. His eyes like the finest
of red lotuses wept tears.
He wiped them away and then the pure
exalted being collapsed
on the handsome body of that father who gave
everything, who was precious to him
as life itself—like a hill of collyrium fallen
over Śiva's silver mountain.

181. 3597

For a moment, he did not breathe
and his younger brother, wondering
whether he had fainted, raised him up
in his lovely hands and sprinkled
water on him from a waterfall fed
by recent rains. Then
he opened his lotus eyes and, as the weakness
slowly left him,

182. 3598

Rāma said, "What sons ever before have killed their own father?
First one father died. O my father Jaṭāyus! have you
ah! have you died also for my sake! How I am now someone
who does everything wrong! Become only irresistible Death!

183. 3599

"Paying no attention to the fact that you were alone, you did your duty
as kin to calm the suffering of a woman, while I, a fool,
had no idea of what would happen to her! Why do I, not able
to do my duty as a kinsman, suffer so now, O my father!

184. 3600

"I feel dead. Yet I have undertaken a vow I accepted to meet
the requests of Brahmins. For that, I will put up with living.
I stand here tall as a tree but my actions are low, useless.
I don't want this worthless birth, this great illusion! I don't want it!

185. 3601

"You who are so noble rose up to oppose him when he seized my wife
and he who has killed you remains alive while you lie there
cut down. I hold my strongly built bow. I carry an ocean
of arrows but stand and stand and stand here like a tall tree!

186. 3602

"Has there ever been anyone spoken of as I will be now, I who suffer
from ancient karma? My wife looked on as, armed, he killed you
and escaped, winged one! with your many teeth! while I, who carry
a bow stood idle. A conquering warrior, is that what I am?"

187. 3603

Things of this kind he said over and over and he wept and he was
confused, He Who Has No Equal, and his younger brother was the
[same.
The king of the birds, coming slowly to consciousness, his thoughts
[clearing,
drew his difficult breaths and opened his eyes upon the two of them.

188. 3604

He whose breath was heated, as his life was perishing and he had not
[known
what had become of them, saw the victorious ones and his heart cooled
[down
as if he had been given back the two wings cut from him, his sweet life,
and the seven worlds, and he said to them, "Now all my shame is gone.

189. 3605

"It is my good luck today that as I abandon my useless, shameful
[body,
I have seen you, bringer of good, come to me," he said, and with the
[beak
through which, in attacking, he had torn the crowns from the Rākṣasa's
[heads,
he drew in the smell of the hair of Rāma and then of Lakṣmaṇa.

190. 3606

"I have already thought in my heart that Rāvaṇa must have come and
[taken her
through deception," he said, "but nevertheless is it true that the two of
[you,
with your faultless strength, left her alone, the woman who is like
a peacock that speaks beautifully, she who is chaste as Arundhatī?"

191. 3607

When he had spoken, the younger prince related
in full what had happened, how things stood,
not leaving anything out from that moment
when the magic deer appeared, with its strength and its powers.

192. 3608

As the strong prince, obeying Rāma, related these things,
the king of the vultures heard them and understood them,
turned them over in his mind and thought, "It will be better
to console them, or their hearts may fill with irremediable pain."

193. 3609

"Does anyone cause what is totally unexpected? Unless
we accept that, in this life not worth praising, joy
and suffering," he said, "happen through the power of fate,
can we ever, with the force of the mind, overcome fate?

194. 3610

"When suffering comes but one knows it must,
it is foolish to let the mind sink down and be defeated.
For fate—which cut off a head of Brahmā, the creator
and separator of the worlds—is anything impossible?

195. 3611

"On the day when pain or pleasure happen,
is there sense in thinking we can obstruct them?
Not by reason of his tapas did the god whose arrows pierced
the three cities beg with Brahmā's skull as his bowl!

196. 3612

"The raging snake planet, the cruel killer, swallows
the god with blazing eyes who flowers in the sky
but then withdraws. The moon, which lights, with its lovely rays,
the great world of beautiful spaces, waxes and wanes.

197. 3613

"You whose arms are handsome! The coming of troubles
and their disappearance both are due to ancient karma.
Can you count all the misfortunes that happened to Indra
though he hears the truth from Bṛhaspati, skilled in mantras?

198. 3614

"Indra, holding the thunderbolt in his hand, was shamed
by the Asura Śambara, base in actions but whose strength
was too great to block. Master of arrows and the bow!
Your father, with his thick arms, wiped away that shame!

199. 3615

"You are separated from her who is like a parrot
with the sweet voice of a child only because
the Order of the World has been set aside
and the gods are suffering. Root out
the weed of the Rākṣasas who are traitorous
in battle. And live on! You whose spear
coated with flesh is like a mother
to the birds and to the ghouls without mind!

200. 3616

"As Rāvaṇa passed, carrying her,
with her eyes like slices of mango
and her long hair, together with a portion
of the earth, I stood against him
and I blocked him as much as my strength
could do. He struck me down with the sword
Śiva gave him under pressure of tapas.
I fell here. It was today that it happened."

201. 3617

Before the words that had been spoken even
could reach Rāma's ears, his fine eyes
filled with blood, he breathed breaths
like red fire. He raised his eyebrows
and raised them more. The lights in the sky
fled. The globe of the earth
was split open everywhere and
all the mountains were broken apart.

202. 3618

The condition of the earth was changed
and of great mountains rising from it
and the waters of great extent and
the wind along with the lights in the sky
and heaven protected by Indra and even
Brahmā who is beyond all other
realms. On that day it was clear
that the hero was all things, innumerable.

203. 3619

As all the worlds remained confused,
terrified as they fearfully thought,
"Toward whom is this fierce anger
that he feels?" Rāma began speaking
and a flashing scowl appeared
on his face from which fire
burst forth, spreading wide
and spitting out sparks and smoke.

204. 3620

"All these worlds to the eight directions
which did not tremble at the time
an ignorant Rākṣasa with a spear
seized hold of a single woman
who had remained alone and went off
as you were killed and those gods
also who looked on just now,
you will see them all destroyed today.

205. 3621

"Watch the stars fall, the incomparable
light of the sun become
dust and bright fire appear
in the great vast sky while
the earth and the waters and the wind
and everything that moves or is rooted
in place is destroyed without
exception and the gods will die!

206. 3622

"See how the fourteen worlds
that exist and seem so enormous
may be extinguished in a moment, how
even worlds beyond the globe
of this earth that encloses the directions
will catch on fire and burst
like a bubble in the water!" he said,
and while he was speaking in anger,

207. 3623

the god of the burning rays began
to retreat on his path and disappeared
beyond Meru, while the elephants of massive strength
who stand in the directions ran away.
Why bother describing how all
the worlds were in fear? Even the young prince
with his brave heart felt afraid.
Could there be any limit to the fear in others?

208. 3624

As this was happening, the king of the vultures
spoke, "O excellence! Do not be angry
with anyone! May you live long!
Hero of fierce strength! The gods
and the holy men think that only
through you can they prevail and remain
happy! Otherwise by what strength
could they overcome the acts of Rāvaṇa?

209. 3625

"In me you see the valor of Rāvaṇa's arms
    whose faultless strength was granted them
by the lord who sits on the blossomed lotus.
    Need anything more be said! Brahmā
who rests on a lotus that is red
    at the height of its stalk, he and the rest
of the gods are slaves to those ten heads.
    Who is there to maintain the Order of the World?

210. 3626

"In this world that the clear waves circle,
    the gods are living like women
waiting on their enemies. Isn't this
    how it is with the gods? Had they
never drunk amṛta from the ocean
    of milk on that day when the god
who had once measured the earth gave it
    to them, would they be living on this day?

211. 3627

"You left her alone in the forest,
    the woman who is like a vañci vine
and binds up her breasts. You went off
    after a deer with horns and disgraced
your clan! Gentlemen, don't you hold
    in your hands cocked bows that shoot
arrows? Think! Is there any blame
    to this world? No! The blame is yours.

212. 3628

"And so you should not be angry
    but remedy the suffering of that woman
who loves you and is as chaste as Arundhatī
    and bring to pass what the gods wish,
establish all things as ordained
    in the books of the Vedas. Destroy
everything else evil," said he who had reached
    the lotuses of Viṣṇu's lovely feet.

213. 3629

He whose skin was the color of a storm cloud
then accepted into his heart the words
spoken by that pure being. Rāma thought,
"These are the commands of Daśaratha. Why
be angry at others? The destruction
of the race of Rākṣasas becomes
at once my proper course of action,"
and he calmed the anger that he had summoned up.

214. 3630

After this, Rāma who has no flaws
said, "Lord, is there anything else
I can do but obey the words
from your mouth that enjoin me
to be calm. Tell me now, where
was that Rākṣasa going?" but the king
of the birds was weak, his awareness fading.
He said nothing and abandoned his life.

215. 3631

Jaṭāyus saw the feet of that being—
the hero whom even Brahmā sitting
on his cool lotus and the rest of the gods
cannot see, nor do the Vedas see him
for, though he is manifest, he is also hidden—
and entered the realm that is not destroyed
even when the five great elements
perish that have once become form.

216. 3632

When he had gained Freedom, Brahmā
with the other high gods and the king
of men with his younger brother wept
and mourned. The trees in the forest
and the animals and the stones melted
and sank down while those who live
in the highest world raised and joined
their palms over their heads to welcome him.

217. 3633

"I have lost my manhood," Rāma said,
"through the act of a Rākṣasa who does not honor
the Order of the World! Should I give up everything
and practice tapas, or should I rather
abandon my life? Tell me!
This father to whom I was son has died
because I was born and received by him. I live on
still! Young prince! what should I do?"

218. 3634

The young prince bowed to that lord who had spoken
and he said, "You who are always and everywhere
and are victorious! There is no shame in what
has happened, since it came about through fate.
Is this the only misfortune we have suffered?
What good is it to stand here and ponder?
After killing the Rākṣasas who did this harm,
we can sink into our own fierce, burning pain.

219. 3635

"My lord! What is the use of my talking?
If you really intend to give up
your poor woman whose hair is long
and lovely, if you grow cool,
if you are not determined to take the life
from him who took your father's life,
if your resolve is such as it seems,
then doing tapas, for you, is the right thing."

220. 3636

When the youth spoke that way, Rāma,
suddenly aware again, lost his weakness
and thought, "It is foolishness for me
to remain as I am, to consider such things,"
and, restraining his hot tears, he said,
"My younger brother! We will perform all
the proper rites in the finest manner
for our father who is now dead."

221. 3637

He went and built up a heap
of black akil wood and of sandalwood,
fire logs so fine as to arouse wonder,
and spread the darbha grass and strewed
the flowers that were required. Having made
this perfect altar in the sand,
he sprinkled sweet water and approached it,
lifting his father in his strong hands.

222. 3638

He carried him with his own two hands and raised him
onto the pyre. He scattered flowers
and sandalwood powder and water. Near
Jaṭāyus's head, he kindled a fire
and Rāma, skilled in the sacred knowledge
of the mantras which abound in the beneficent
books of the Vedas, closely then
followed the order of the rites.

223. 3639

He who was dark as a storm cloud bathed
his eyes with a flood of tears,
the streams flowing like droplets of nectar
from red lotus flowers in the midst
of dense, dark green shoots.
After bathing in the river and offering
the good water he had brought from it, he forgot
his pain in his furious hatred of the Rākṣasas.

224. 3640

What more is there to say? It was as if
all creatures that are found from Brahmā down,
the high and the low, drank up
that water and were drunk with it.
Rāma offered it on his palms joined
in reverence to the king of the birds,
saying, "Accept this now," and it was
as if the Lord himself drank that water.

225. 3641

When the hero in his youth had completed the many
    rites and many sacrifices of the Vedas
and stood then concentrated on victory,
    the burning sun reached the ocean
and plunged into the water, grieving
    for Jaṭāyus who had been born in the sun's
ancient line, and it seemed he was performing
    all the rites for the good of the afterlife.

# Paṭalam Nine
# Ayomukhī

1. 3642

When the evening twilight reached them there,
the two of them left and they went
to rest on a black mountain, of which
the summit was turning red, and then
the wide darkness began to spread
as a source of cruel pain and it seemed
like the rising up of the Rākṣasas who have
never submitted to Indra.

2. 3643

As the forests and the mountains flowed
with flower nectar and the waterfalls flowed
with water, it seemed as if they were all
shedding tears under pressure of the night,
as if in anguish. Shame and fury
and the death of their father tormented
the hearts of the sons in the same way
as true knowledge when it struggles against suffering.

3. 3644

The night that swelled up was as hard
to dissipate as births that arise
from ignorance, which bring karma
and bar knowledge so that the truth
is not realized. For them who could do nothing,
whose long sighs rose and spread
like a fire with ghee poured into it, there was
no end to be seen of that night.

4. 3645

We cannot know whether it was because
they had lost the woman, divine
and lovely, sweetly smiling Jānakī,
or because they could not see the full moon
of her face—whatever the reason—
the red lotuses which were called
eyes of the hero with the fragrant garland
did not close, even in the night.

5. 3646

What Rāma thought within his faultless heart,
because of the error that had parted him from her
who was so beautiful, who was like a lamp
of the shining nature of woman,
we cannot know. The eyes of the Pure Being
called Rāma never closed for an instant,
like the open eyes of that one with
strong arms who was his younger brother.

6. 3647

The lovely white moon, which makes
the sky glow, then spread
over the hillside where the murderous snake
of the cool sweet south wind
slithered, and it made Rāma show
his love for Sītā, saying, "I have seen
the bright face of Sītā shining
in the heavens, she whose garland hums with bees!"

7. 3648

The flood of moonlight that illuminated
all the world turned the night
clear in which Kāma hides,
who steals and betrays; but it burned
Rāma as if it were the poison
flowing from the hollow fangs
of the venomous snake that for others
was this mass of the deepest darkness.

8. 3649

As the darkness grew and the white moonlight
        spreading out like poison burned him,
he was obsessed by his sense of shame,
        and he kept thinking of her, alone,
she who had a yoni as lovely
        as a cobra's spreading hood, whose voice
was as sweet as flowing milk,
        whose eyes were large and wide.

9. 3650

He tightened
        his lips but then began to sigh.
His shoulders
        swelled but then shrunk up.
He kept thinking
        of her who was like a branch of cool
budding shoots
        and flowers broken by a rutting elephant.

10. 3651

"Is she looking
        down the long road in both directions
and thinking,
        'He will come, he with the long bow
will come!' "
        and his sighs thickened and lessened
like waves
        spreading across the surging sea.

11. 3652

"Is it right
        to imagine that she doesn't think of me!
When he came
        like an animal with teeth that terrify
even the lightning
        and said, 'Don't go! Don't go away!' to her,
then what
        did she think?" he thought in pain.

12. 3653

"As she shrinks
like the moon in the treacherous mouth
of the huge snake
whose fangs pour out poison,
is she in doubt,
wondering whether Rāma may fear
the cruelty
of the Rākṣasas with their burning anger?"

13. 3654

The pride
that was his ornament and the love he felt
for Sītā,
which could not leave him, urged him on,
lingered with him,
burning his precious life between them
again and again.
He thought, "What good is my bow?"

14. 3655

Looking at his bow,
he laughed and he laughed again looking
at the mountains
of his great swelling shoulders. He thought
of the shame
that would in the end be his and he laughed
whom all contemplate
when meditating on the goal of the ancient Vedas.

15. 3656

He considered
cruel death that is like the north wind
in the cold season.
He sighed like an elephant calf
and he thought,
"Is Sītā gone from me now
whom I married,
following the rituals of the Vedic sacrifice?"

16. 3657

"I have resolved
    to remain here and to protect many lives
but have no power
    to soften the pain of my woman
whose ornaments
    are beautiful, whose family is noble.
Wonderful,
    wonderful is my strength!" he thought in shame.

17. 3658

He lay down
    but the bed of tender leaves carefully prepared
by his younger brother
    scorched him and, as it burned him, he sat up.
With pain
    and anguish, he considered his life;
and his mouth
    and heart drying up, he was bewildered.

18. 3659

Was it because
    of the separation or because of the love
he had for her?
    We cannot know, but he who passes
a thousand *kalpas*
    with a blink of the lovely flowers of his eyes
did not move
    and could not imagine an end to the night.

19. 3660

"Young prince
    whose hands hold a victorious spear!
You have lived
    and seen that all the days before this
were not marred.
    They were like each other," he said,
"then why
    is this great night now so long?"

20. 3661

In that evening
which went on, he said to the full moon,
"You have always
grown thinner and thinner and been ashamed.
Now you shine
with intense brightness because
the glowing face
is gone of that woman adorned with ornaments.

21. 3662

"Has the sun
who crosses the sky in his incomparable chariot
departed from
this country ashamed because ceaseless
disgrace
has come to his line with its fame
as bright
and wide as the long light of the moon?"

22. 3663

He felt faint
and thought how interminable the night was
that burned him.
"Has the Rākṣasa with his sword," he said,
"blocked the sun,
bound him along with that great lord,
his lame charioteer,
and locked them up in his massive prison?

23. 3664

"If she whose waist
is like the narrow middle of a *tuṭi* drum
does not appear,
this night as long as a *kalpa*
and deep black
will grow even longer before it ends.
The immense world
circled by rich waters would then perish.

24. 3665

"If they who live
with violent courage force their will on holy men,
inflicting
torments through their strength, wandering and
consuming
the lives of those who inhabit the earth,
what now
can be accomplished through the Order of the World?"

25. 3666

The God of Love,
hero whose flowers of combat are released
from a flower bow
with a string of bees that is long and lovely
and divine,
stood in the sky and thought of shooting
at the Pure Being
but remained motionless, could not attack, and felt bewildered.

26. 3667

That god suffered,
thinking of how he had lost his body
because of the anger
of Śiva practicing intense yoga.
How could he
have had the strength for his natural duty
while such pain
was his because of his former anguish?

27. 3668

As these thoughts
tormented Rāma like a trident,
the night
came to an end as if this were
the moment
at the end of a universe when Brahmā
the First Cause
who is seated on the lotus perishes.

28. 3669

He had left his pleasant sleep on the ocean of milk
where the flood roars and he had entered the ocean
of chastity that was her, she who wore a garland
of flowers where bees and dragonflies would hum.
The birds sounded for him and the grove resounded
and the waters rushed and the ornaments that she
would wear sounded in his mind but in truth
they did not and so how could he keep on living?

29. 3670

He saw a peacock wandering along with its mate,
a doe tenderly coming to meet with a stag,
a male elephant and his loving elephant cow
arriving together and roaming. He was separated
from her whose speech had an essence sweeter
than the voice of the kokila bird, than sugar or rich honey,
the flute or the *yal̠*, thick jaggery sauce or amṛta
that is a delight to drink. How could his suffering stop?

30. 3671

The sun with its hot rays appeared before the Udaya mountain
and its summit looked as if a crown had been set down upon it,
while the sun seemed to be opening lotuses for that hero
who could not hear the soft words of the woman lovely as a
[parrot,
though he saw dawn coming for the old dense night as if
the sun were letting him know: "She who is like a wild goose and
[lived
before this as Śrī upon a red lotus cannot
be found within the fresh fragrant lotus I closed when setting."

31. 3672

He looked at the grove and he looked at the birds
that lived in the grove and at the loveliness of a branch
in flower and he looked at the beauty of a young peacock
while thinking of her hair, she who was the very nature
of womanhood, and he thought of the hills of her two breasts
and of the decorations that had been drawn with sandal paste
to decorate those hills and he himself looked down then
at his empty arms and somehow passed the day.

32. 3673

Then the young hero said, bowing at his feet,
"Great being! Will it make our fame grow to remain
here without searching for that woman who is like gold?"
and he whose fame was great answered his brother,
"We will follow. We will find the place where the Rākṣasa
lives whom Jaṭāyus described to us," and they went off
with their flashing bows into the forest that was blazing
with sun, where there lay a chain of mountains.

33. 3674

They who were like the great elephants that uphold the directions
passed through many forests that were dense with green leaves,
then crossed a river, climbed up and down a mountain that
was perfect of form, and traveled for a distance of eighteen yojanas.

34. 3675

They searched for her but they did not find her, she
with her garland full of nectar who was born because of tapas done
by the Earth, and they entered a large, cool grove inhabited
by birds, as anger surged up in them along with their sighs.

35. 3676

The sun with its burning rays, knowing of the pain in the hearts
of those noble beings, searched everywhere for the woman, went on
searching, wandering throughout the great world but then
disappeared again behind Mount Meru, and the darkness followed.

36. 3677

As thick darkness like columns of collyrium spread everywhere,
inspiring fear so that people shrank in on themselves,
the ten directions took on that darkness as it came,
like the minds of men who have not achieved clear knowledge.

37. 3678

In a grove where the bush myna, whose sweet voice is like the dominant
in a rāga, teaches the parrot to speak, in a grove
surrounded by kiṃśuka trees, they saw a ledge of crystal
like the circle of the bright flawed moon, and there they stopped.

38. 3679

Rāma the Lord, when he had come there, spoke to the young warrior
who resembled a fierce bull. "Warrior!" he said to him,
"Search around and bring us water," and he whose bow
in battle drives enemies to retreat went off alone.

39. 3680

He went searching everywhere but found no source of water,
and while he was wandering alone, as if he were a lion,
a Rākṣasī with cruel eyes, whose name was Ayomukhī,
saw him and desired him, there, in that forest.

40. 3681

She followed him like a snake that does not retreat even
when venerated mantras are uttered by men of excellent knowledge,
and her pride and her cruelty softened and dwindled within her
as she thought in her heart that this was the God of Love.

41. 3682

The Rākṣasī, her heart set on him, came with a love so great
pain rose up within her. She halted, across from him. She thought,
"With this anguish that torments me now, how could I do anything
[except
embrace him? How could I ever consume him?" and she was weeping.

42. 3683

"When I approach him, if he will not consent to what I ask of him
but refuses himself to me, then I will seize him and go to my cave
where I will make love to him as much as I wish," she thought,
and she who was fiercer than fire came quickly then, closer to him.

43. 3684

She exhaled fire in her breath and she could chew up a herd
of elephants with her teeth and swallow them into her stomach
with pleasure. Her breasts were bound with a rope fit for tying
a strong cruel mountain snake. Her eyes were sunken.

44. 3685

She had selected an anklet made of strong lions and of yāḷis
which she had captured and lashed together with a snake. Her face
was like the enormous sun that rises on that day
when the universe is destroyed and all things come to their end.

45. 3686

Her mouth was a huge cave like a ladle that could be used
for drying up the ocean in a single scoop, while her red hair
spreading out around her and moving in waves resembled
the look of the fire that blazes at the end of a universe.

46. 3687

She wore strips of fat clinging to guts and intertwined
with many heads and chunks of flesh that all hung down
to graze her feet. Around her waist she wore a hooded snake
which touched the ground, and she was gnashing her teeth like thunder.

47. 3688

Her glances seemed to say, "These eyes are like the burning eyes
of Śiva!" but the flaming of her teeth made the eyes seem cool.
She staggered the world, displacing mountains and uniting oceans.
As she walked, the faultless earth felt shame at being a woman too.

48. 3689

She had filled her wrists that hung low with bangles of long snakes.
The necklace she wore was of male tigers with a snake linking them.
Her *tāli* was formed of many yāḷis all tied to one another.
Her earrings, that were dangling down, were made of murderous lions.

49. 3690

There she stood. Her eyes flowing with tears of desire
seemed like red crab's-eye seeds but grew tender as she looked at him.
Her teeth quivered and glowed like lightning. And Lakṣmaṇa saw her
even in thick darkness, he who was like a roaming murderous lion.

50. 3691

He realized that she was of the same nature as Tāḍakā
and the other one of great strength who suffered when she lost
her nose, before. This was a woman with bright bangles belonging
to the race of Rākṣasas, they who are thorns to the world.

51. 3692

"Because the actions of these Rākṣasa women are evil, because
they are without higher virtues, they desire us," he thought,
and he said to her, "You who come through the forest where animals
prowl in the great darkness, quickly tell me who you are!"

52. 3693

He spoke to her and she, who was not ashamed to speak out before
a strange man, said to him, with her heart aching and swaying
within her like a swing, "I am Ayomukhī and I have come
in happiness to you, out of my desire, with a faultless love."

53. 3694

And she had more to say: "O great, handsome hero!
Give me back my sweet life quickly by pressing
my breasts which no one ever before has touched
to your broad lovely chest that is like gold!"

54. 3695

After she had spoken, with her heart still cooled in tenderness,
he who was like a murderous lion growing enraged, said,
red-eyed, "If those words once more sound from your mouth,
this long arrow, indomitable, will cut your body in two."

55. 3696

Even when he said these things, she was not angered at heart
but she raised her two hands over her head in respect and said,
"Conqueror! If I can even cause you to come and take
my life, then I will be truly born today as a woman!"

56. 3697

And then she added, still without her cruel burning anger,
"Great being! If what you are searching for here is good water,
then all you need do is just say to me, 'Do not fear!'
and I with these two hands will bring water at once from the Ganges!"

57. 3698

Sumitrā's son, not able to bear listening to these
words she was saying, responded, "Go away! or else
I will cut your nose off as well as your two ears!"
She heard him without blinking, stood there, then thought:

58. 3699

"Once I have taken him, gone off, shut him up within my cave,
and rid him of this heat of his, then he will consent to me,
and I will at once have something very fine. And so it's right
to act with resolution now!" and she moved nearer to him.

59. 3700

She summoned up a magic power called "Bewilderment" that was hers
and used it. Then the fierce woman seized him who was like
a tall mountain reaching into the heavens and she went off
through the sky like a dark cloud carrying along the moon.

60. 3701

She seemed to be Mount Mandara dipped in the ocean of milk
or she was like the black cloud that Indra would ride
across the sky or like the peacock mounted by the hero
Murukaṉ who killed Cūr with his spear of blazing power.

61. 3702

Held as he was then between her chest and hands, that powerful
being with his long bow and anklets engraved with flowers
seemed like Śiva within the skin of the huge elephant that had been
fiercely angry, cruel in battle, dripping the liquid of musth.

62. 3703

As she went off in this way, Rāma, on his side, was thinking,
"He who is like a great mountain, who gives my life strength,
went looking for a source of water. He has not returned,"
and the hero then, his whole body on fire, hurried off.

63. 3704

"Was it that sweet water could not be found
in the burning forest, or was it something else?
He has the speed that he needs to come back quickly.
He would not delay, not come back. What is happening?

64. 3705

"I told him to go this way, look for water and find it
and bring it and return and yet he hasn't returned
this long time. Has he been fighting with those who seized
my woman with the band around her breasts? Something is wrong!

65. 3706

"Has Rāvaṇa captured him, the Rākṣasa who before
deceived my woman who is like a parrot with a lovely voice,
or has he died through the treacherous actions of Rāvaṇa
whose heart is so cruel, and through the force of his own fate?

66. 3707

"He who carries a cocked bow in his hand and is to me
like my precious life has not come back. Tormented,
burning with anxiety for me who have lost my woman
because I would not listen to him, has he lost his life?

67. 3708

"He has been the eyes for me who am alone
in this black darkness that has arisen. I have
no other eyes. I feel anguished! My heart is wounded.
I cannot even think! How will I find him?

68. 3709

"You who have been the incomparably precious life for me
whose actions must bear their fruit! Have you gone into hiding,
alone? Child! Great being! You have made a mistake.
The world will not accept it. How wrong this is!

69. 3710

"You who can remove even irremediable
sufferings when they come! You have given me pain
that will not leave me. Hero to whom enemies bow!
Do you hate me so? To stay away this long? Return!

70. 3711

"I have become separated from the father who made me,
from my mothers, from her with the gold earrings who is
like Śrī. I live on, I survive only because
I have not been separated from you and you give me life!

71. 3712

"As I endure suffering, searching for her who wears
shining lovely earrings, golden earrings,
do you replace that pain now with the suffering of my search
for you? Young elephant bull who came and searched me out!

72. 3713

"I will not live through this day. And all
of our own will surely perish when someone
tells them I am dead. You are cruel! You have killed
all of your kinsmen together! Is this too a virtue?

73. 3714

"When I gave up becoming a king in the line of kings
that begins with Mandhātā, those who were truly
connected to me each left me but when I was alone,
you went with me. Have you left me now and gone?"

74. 3715

He said this and rose to his feet but fell back again.
Sitting there and thinking, he was deeply confused.
More than one trouble had happened. "It does not thunder without
[lightning.
How will it end in this darkness?" thought he who is the only Lord.

75. 3716

He searched for him everywhere, in many places. He ran
and he suffered as he called out his brother's name. He grew
so tired that his life was ready to wither and vanish. He was bewildered.
He seemed a great elephant charging around in the ecstasy of rut.

76. 3717

"Would he who never even blinks his eyes when protecting
my life and the life of that patient woman, would he
delay so long? Is life no longer for me with my karma
that makes me wander, burdening the earth? I do not know.

77. 3718

"If my karma is good and Lakṣmaṇa is to be born again,
let him be born as my elder brother!" He drew
out his sharp fierce sword and he was fixed on
bringing about the end of his firmly enduring life.

78. 3719

His younger brother escaped from the powerful magic.
He freed himself from her, gripped her nose and cut it off.
She went faint and the cry she uttered reached as far as
Rāma's ears and sounded there. The divine Rāma understood.

79. 3720

He thought, "This is no sound that rises up when Rākṣasas
attack in cruel and difficult battle and their many anklets
resound within the forest strewn with pebbles. It is the cry
of a woman who has been wounded and it seems to be a Rākṣasī."

80. 3721

He then took into his red hand the great weapon
that was his arrow of fire, and as the black one held it,
the swollen darkness retreated beyond the world
and the night shone within the forest as if it were the day.

81. 3722

Rāma hurried to the attack, his speed three times that
of the fierce wind. Great mountains turned to powder.
Tall towering trees cracked. The Earth Goddess trembled
and a sound of roaring rose everywhere around him.

82. 3723

The younger brother saw his older brother who had always
been of such great help to him, looking as if the black ocean
had risen as one and poured onto the earth at the end of a universe,
and said, "You who give everything! Do not be troubled! Do not be
[troubled!"

83. 3724

And he addressed him then, to let Rāma know, "I have come,
I who am your servant! Do not grieve within your limitless heart!"
He bowed at those feet that were lovely and soft as shoots,
and the act made Rāma feel he had lost an eye that now reappeared.

84. 3725

Rāma stood there, his eyes flowing like springs with his tears.
He was like a cow who had been suffering, standing and calling out,
not able to bear that her calf had been separated from her,
her cool udders flowing with milk as now, with difficulty, he returns.

85. 3726

Rāma embraced him many times and washed his golden body
with the tears that were streaming from his eyes, and he said,
"You who have arms that are like crossbars or like mountains!
I was grieving, because I thought in my heart that you were lost!"

86. 3727

"What happened out there? Tell me," Rāma said to him,
and when Lakṣmaṇa had recounted all of it so that his brother
now knew, Rāma felt pain and felt happiness too, He
for whom nothing existing is higher than Himself.

87. 3728

He said, "Should someone in the midst of the great and mysterious
ocean be troubled every time a towering wave arrives?
Should we who are caught in the cruel prison of births
due to evil acts feel weak because of suffering, because of pain?

88. 3729

"Even if all the three worlds and the three gods
were to come against me, unapproachable enemies,
who of them could conquer me? My younger brother, when you
are with me, you are my strength. Do I need a fortress now?

89. 3730

"Let all who would leave me go away! Let everything
come that comes with great pain! Hero with your strength
in battle who wear the long anklets of a warrior!
Always calmed by you, don't my troubles go away?

90. 3731

"Hero fierce in battle! You have told me you defeated
the Rākṣasī with her power in war and you returned.
Even in your anger at what the base woman had said,
it seems that you did not kill her. Tell me why!"

91. 3732

The young prince said, "When I cut her ears and they fell
along with her nose and when I had rid her of
her breasts that were tied up with a band, then it was
that she made that noise, screaming," and he cupped his hands in
[respect.

92. 3733

"You did not kill her though she followed you to kill
in the thick darkness but you cut away and rid her of her nose!
You have acted with grace, you of the line that begins with Manu!"
and sobbing and weeping for happiness, Rāma embraced him.

93. 3734

For the hero and his younger brother, it could be said their immense
[pain,
hard to dispel, had for the moment lessened. They waited
for the dawn, chanted the Varuṇa mantra, drank the water it brought
from the sky, then stopped on a mountain that upholds the earth.

94. 3735

In that forest of wastelands where the trails were rock,
on a bed made of shoots and flowers, on fine sand,
the hero lay down, his pain again without limit,
and the young prince massaged the soft feet of Rāma.

95. 3736

From the moment she was gone, who was as lovely as a peacock,
he had not eaten a thing because of the pain of his disgrace
nor had he slept, given such suffering. Can his state
be described? He felt his life swinging among his sighs.

96. 3737

"Everywhere I turn my eyes throughout the whole forest,
I seem to see Jānakī's form! Is it because
I cannot forget the body of that lofty woman
even for a moment or is it the Rākṣasas' magic?

97. 3738

"When she who has black hair and eyes with lovely red lines,
who is the ornament of pure women, comes and sits by me,
out of desire I embrace her body whole but cannot
feel her touch. Is her form as elusive as her waist?

98. 3739

"I can taste the amṛta from her mouth like coral
with its beautiful glowing red like a toṇṭai fruit
and the nectar of a red lotus just blooming,
yet she is not here. Can I dream with open eyes?

99. 3740

"Is the night that is longer than earth, than sky
or the other three elements, and longer than thought and
cruel because it causes pain, is it longer than the eyes
of the noble daughter of Janaka, with her cool fragrant hair?

100. 3741

"Has the burning sky broken out in blisters all over
its body, scorched by the hot spreading rays
of the fire of universal conflagration which is called the moon
and pleasant, rising from the ocean full of glittering fish?"

101. 3742

The king of kings, who had his strength destroyed,
said all these things and he was confused in his heart.
The god with red rays saw him in this state
and thought, "How this man suffers!" then appeared.

# Paṭalam Ten
# The Killing of Kabandha

1. 3743

At dawn, as the wandering birds cried out and seemed to be weeping,
Rāma and Lakṣmaṇa set off at once to search for her,
the woman who was as beautiful as a peacock, of the highest purity,
and so patient that even the Earth would call her truly patient.

2. 3744

Then for fifty yojanas they were wandering
    through places encircled by the wilderness
and the sun reached the middle of the sky.
    The two men went on with their bows
that unleash arrows and they arrived
    at the forest inhabited by Kabandha
who stretches out his hands and surrounds
    all the living and buries them in his stomach.

3. 3745

Every being that breathed in a body suffered and grew weak
from the elephant all the way down to the ant,
and they were full of terror, their eyes were glazed,
they were trapped in a net it was not possible to escape.

4. 3746

Rāma and Lakṣmaṇa saw how they were all trembling,
crowding together and scattering, racing around in distress,
bewildered, like creatures living in a country that is ruled
without skill, or honor, or clearly established distinctions.

5. 3747

Great mountains went rolling there and the great trees
fell that had been uprooted, trunks and all. Forest rivers
and the heights above them turned into level plains
while the clouds pregnant with water shriveled and collapsed.

6. 3748

The two of them entered between his hands which encompassed
the directions, like oceans rising up on the last day of a universe,
as the roaring wind swells up from the four directions and those oceans
come roaring, engulfing, spreading through all the world.

7. 3749

And they felt happy, thinking that, due to the power in purity
of the woman with the sweet voice, an army of Rākṣasas
had come and, to their own grief, surrounded Rāma and Lakṣmaṇa;
but they were within the walls of his hands, weighty as Mount Nemi.

8. 3750

Rāma looked at the young prince and he said, "The city
where Rāvaṇa lives, the tormenter of my woman, must
also be here. You realize, sir, that our great pain
which up to now has only been growing must be over!"

9. 3751

But the young prince stood before him, bowed down, and said,
"Were this an army of Rākṣasas resounding around us,
there would be a sound of royal drums being beaten, of conches
being blown! Since there is no music, this is something other.

10. 3752

"Is it the snake with white fangs who was pulled by the gods
so as to raise the clear amṛta from the sea? or some other snake?
Eternal being! It seems to have surrounded us with its head,
and its tail that we can't repel, while we are caught inside!"

11. 3753

The Lord, who was walking ahead, weighed these words
his younger brother had spoken and thought well of them,
then went forward, within, for one or two yojanas,
and there, straight before him, Kabandha stood like a mountain.

12. 3754

He had burning eyes so that it looked as if Mount Meru
had two blazing suns placed upon it and between
each of his teeth there was a distance of two *kātams*
in the mouth that seemed a shark-filled ocean on his belly.

13. 3755

His hands stretching down were as long as the great snake
pulled at either end by the gods and by the Asuras when,
assembling together, they looped it around the divine
churning rod of the great mountain resting on the moon.

14. 3756

Fire with its banner of smoke sprayed from his nose
like a bellows pumped by a blacksmith who works masses of fire.
His curling tongue was like a sprout of flame from the consuming
fire that drinks up the great ocean, its rightful enemy.

15. 3757

He had fangs that were shining as if the white full moon
had been cut in two after plunging into a mighty cave
within a great mountain full of waterfalls, entering for refuge
but remaining there in fear of the snake planet's slithering attack.

16. 3758

It seemed as if his life had not been composed
out of the five elements: earth and cool water and the rest,
but rather that his body had been massed together
of the five great sins enunciated by the tradition of the Vedas.

17. 3759

The openings of his ears were so enormous that the fierce serpents
who consume the burning sun and the cooling moon could sleep
there in idleness. His belly was even worse than the hell
for low, deceitful men whose cruelty has been limitless.

18. 3760

As he seized and destroyed every living being that surrounded him,
scooping them up in his hands, his mouth seemed as if it were
the gate of victories in the city of the God of Death, given
the sight of them pouring in to be eaten, in immense numbers.

19. 3761

The sound he made was like the drumming of the ocean's roaring.
His body was as dark and as glowing as the Hālāhala poison.
Like the Asura Kālanemi whose head was severed by the discus
of dark Viṣṇu, this monster had the form of a headless trunk.

20. 3762

Those two, going their way, who had penetrating knowledge
of the Vedas, saw him, his body like Mount Meru
after it had lost its highest towering summits under
the assault of the wind whose onslaughts cannot be calmed.

21. 3763

They saw a huge gaping mouth into which the earth encircled
by the Nemi Mountain and the great ocean of water could enter.
They thought, "Is this the gate of entry to an ancient
fortress of the Rākṣasas not even malevolent gods can enter?"

22. 3764

Then the younger of them looked very closely and he said,
"This is a huge, raging monster. He seizes and engulfs
living beings in his hands and crams them into his mouth.
Master of the bow, what should we do now?" and the Lord answered:

23. 3765

"You who are as strong as the boar that dug up and lifted
the Earth! This is a true demon! Its body spreads out
so that the earth encircled by the oceans seems insufficient
for it! Look how far its hands reach, to the right and to the left!

24. 3766

"The woman who is like a peacock is gone from me. My father
Jaṭāyus has died. I do not want to go on carrying
this cruel torment of guilt! So I will become food
for this creature now," he said, "Young prince! Leave me.

25. 3767

"Although I am strong enough to live with the shameful guilt
of making my parents suffer, giving my younger brother pain,
and pain to those who are noble, can the great shame of this pain
that stays with me now vanish, unless I give up my life!

26. 3768

"Must I say, 'The woman you gave to me, she who is like a vine,
whose words are sweet, whose character suits her for the home,
she is now in the house of the Rākṣasa!' when I, holding
my bow, my quiver like a mountain, go to the king of Mithilā?

27. 3769

"I would not have people saying that I could not protect her,
she who wears a garland of blossomed flowers, that I need
to be shielded by my younger brother! Better that they say
'He has gone to the other world.' It is right that I die."

28. 3770

When the Lord had spoken in this way,
    the hero, his younger brother,
said to him, "What good would there be
    for me in my returning
and not ending my precious life
    before death touches you
since I have chosen to follow you here
    where this suffering has arisen?"

29. 3771

He spoke and then he added these words,
"Those truly are heroes
who conquer suffering. When a man does not
die before those as close
as his mother, his father, his elder brother
perish at the hands
of their enemies, won't the good name
of that man vanish?

30. 3772

"Could there be anything worse than people
saying of Lakṣmaṇa,
'He came back without them,' in answer
to anyone who would say,
'When his elder brother lived with Sītā,
that doe of a woman,
in the mountainous forests, he stood near defending them,
never closing his eyes in sleep.'

31. 3773

"My mother said to me, 'Agree with
anything commanded
by your elder brother! Don't shrink back
before pain, but accept it!
Should he of great fame be destroyed,
you should die before him!'
I cannot make her words into lies
and stay an honest man.

32. 3774

"In no way have my mother and I
been false to the purpose
of your mother and of yourself and we
have received the abiding
praise for it which the good desire!
You whose arms are adorned
with fine gold! Would I give that up,
craving my precious life?

33. 3775

"You who do not perish at the time
a universe is ending,
when even the gods die who praise
the Vedas which do not perish!
Consider this, does it make any sense
that you should seem to die
slain by a monster in this forest who
lives by eating elephants?

34. 3776

"Those who hear will not believe. Those who see
will not accept it. Could there be
worse said of you than that you died unable
to prevail in battle
rather than gaining great fame in the tumult
of war, by rescuing her
with the long hair, with the garland of flower petals,
and ending her suffering?

35. 3777

"If you think that he cannot be vanquished
with this fine sword, surely
you are wrong! Though the monster is as fiery
as poison, he is not worth
respecting! Watch how I, without fail,
will cut off his gorged
cavernous mouth and the hands that encircle us.
Do not worry yourself."

36. 3778

The young prince spoke and moved forward,
then the elder brother ran ahead
of the younger, and the incomparable young prince
then sped ahead of him.
There was nobody with them to prevent them
from behaving as they did.
Ah! The gods saw it and they suffered
and they broke into tears.

37. 3779

As the heroes with their large, resounding anklets
moved forward
in this way like two eyes within a face,
Kabandha
asked them, "Who are you coming now because
of bad karma?"
They weighed his words in their hearts, not blinking, and stood there
in fury.

38. 3780

"They do not panic," he thought, "They show contempt,"
and he burned.
As his anger came swelling up, sparks flashed
from the hairs
of his body. Rising into the sky, he rushed them, shouting,
"I will eat you!"
The heroes, with their swords, cut off his towering arms,
then threw them down.

39. 3781

The body of Kabandha, with no arms, as his blood,
burning,
poured down in rivers, resembled the great beauty,
beyond compare,
of a majestic mountain with foothills while, flowing
on high
and below over the rocks of its slopes, mighty
streams flood.

40. 3782

Through a touch of the lovely hand of the Lord who rules
all beings,
the old bad karma that had brought a curse upon him
was ended.
He gave up his flawed body from which the arms
had been severed
and flew up into the sky, like a bird released
from a cage.

41. 3783

He stood there in the sky and, in his mind, he realized,
"This is he
who stands there before the eyes of Brahmā and all
the other gods!"
He opened his mouth and he praised the endless virtues
of that being.
Can anything be impossible when good karma leads
to its fruit?

42. 3784

"Shall I say that you are the universal creator, that you are the witness
of all good and limitless Righteousness, that you are the only object
of the tapas of the gods, that you are the root from which the highest
[three
unfolded? You have come and freed a great sinner from his painful
[curse!

43. 3785

"O cause without origin! Whatever form that you may conceive and
[assume
is beyond understanding! Are you the banyan tree that appears when a
[universe
ends? Or the leaves of that tree? Or the boy who lies sleeping
among the leaves? Or the breadth of the primeval ocean? Let me know!

44. 3786

"You are the eye for those that see and for all things that are seen!
Here you remain as if attached, you who are attached to nothing!
In your majesty you can swallow and hide the world when a universe
[ends!
Are you male? Are you female? Are you both? Of what sex are you?

45. 3787

"You are Brahmā, cause of the world, and that highest who existed even
before him! And if there is anything earlier than the beginning
you are that too! Since the Vedas men recite call you the shining
mass of light, aren't those other gods humbled before you?

46. 3788

"The place where you exist is the seed within the lotus bud that
never opens, beyond the three spheres that offer their beauty
to all the great palace that is the universe, rising with fourteen
levels of worlds and the eight directions for its strong walls!

47. 3789

"You consume the noble Sacrifice with its towering flame that is exalted
in men's minds, whose culmination no one can see as it is offered
by the Brahmins who are gods on earth, and you feed that Sacrifice!
How can it be understood that you are both? O highest, tell me!

48. 3790

"Like bubbles that form and rise in the great abiding surge
of the waters and then disappear again, the worlds rise
in their abundance, appear within you, and then disappear!
Can anyone easily comprehend this? O ultimate beyond the ultimate!

49. 3791

"Were the vast Vedas conceived after witnessing your acts? Or were
your actions based on those ways which they prescribe?
What have I done in my past births that you have given me this great
treasure which those who act with cruelty cannot pursue?

50. 3792

"My Lord! You cut through the enmity I showed you in my ignorance
when I had the appearance of a demon! You have freed me from
[delusion,
from this treacherous birth, and given me a faultless body and brought
[me
over the ocean of suffering! What good has a dog like me performed?"

51. 3793

All that he said he murmured softly because he was thinking,
"For this to be openly known may not further the welfare of the gods!"
and there he was in the sky like a calf who has seen his mother,
where the Lord who appears before all those on the path of knowledge
[saw him.

52. 3794

And Rāma said, "My younger brother, look there! The one who fell has become a great being, utterly other, and his nature is immense radiance! He is there in the sky, facing us. You must go and learn about him!" Lakṣmaṇa, obeying Rāma, said, "Who are [you?"

53. 3795

He answered, "Hero with a garland
as lovely ornament! I am a Gandharva
and my name is Danu. Because of a curse,
I have undergone this lowly birth,
but when you came, and your hand like a flower
touched me, I regained the form
I had before! O more father to me
than my father! Listen to what I will say!

54. 3796

"Though no protectors can exist for you
who carry bows ready for their arrows,
it would be best to have followers you can command
to search out that woman without equal.
For anyone who does not have a boat,
it is very difficult to cross the ocean.
Just so, the country of your enemies cannot
be ravaged and destroyed without help.

55. 3797

"Can anything be said against the manliness
of Lord Śiva who exists without blame
and destroys all beings who have drawn
life from the greatly noble Brahmā
sitting enthroned on his lotus?
But surely you know that Śiva lives
with his endless hordes of followers,
his Bhūtas of unconquerable strength?

56. 3798

"It is this that you must do,
thinking of the Order of the World,
allying yourself not with the evil but
with those who are good. First
you will meet Śabarī,
who is of greater help to living beings
than a mother and you will go on the route
she enjoins and will climb Antelope Hill.

57. 3799

"And when you meet him who is
the bright color of gold, the son
of the sun, embrace him with love
and stay with him at your ease
and then go searching for the woman
with arms smooth as tall bamboo.
So you should proceed," he said, and the heroes
who wear resounding anklets agreed.

58. 3800

Then he bowed to them and praised them
and went off into the sky. The young men
who had been born in the line of Manu
went on their way as he had directed,
passing through forests, over mountains,
till they reached the place where the sage
Mataṅga lived, a stamping ground for elephants.
There darkness came and remained.

# Paṭalam Eleven
# Śabarī Escapes Rebirth

1. 3801

Just as the Wish-Granting Trees give
    anything desired, that grove,
fragrant, filled with richness,
    offered whatever came into the mind
and it was like a paradise where those
    live whose actions have been pure,
where no suffering exists but only
    the pleasures imagined in this world.

2. 3802

Such was the place that Rāma
    approached now, where she was, and he met
Śabarī who had performed tapas
    through endless time, thinking only
of him and, in his mercy, he spoke
    pleasantly to her and he said,
"I hope you are well," who has
    no root imaginable, nothing preceding him.

3. 3803

And with love then, she praised him,
    her eyes waterfalls of weeping,
and she said, "My delusion of attachment
    is gone! The achievement of all the difficult
tapas I have done for endless time
    is here! I have come to the end
of my lives!" and she gave them what
    they needed and, as they were eating the meal,

4. 3804

she said, "My father! Śiva came
    and Brahmā who sits on the lotus
and all the gods. Indra himself,
    here, looking at me with happiness,
then declared, 'The goal of your faultless
    tapas has arrived. Worship
Rāma as he should be served. That done,
    come to our world!' And they left me.

5. 3805

"I have remained here, my father,
    because I knew that you would come.
My pure actions have today
    flowered!" He looked with love
at that empress of difficult tapas
    when she spoke and he said, "You
are a woman who has lifted away our trouble
    and pain, may all go well for you!"

6. 3806

He Who Has No Faults and the young prince stayed
    for the day, then she who had performed
tapas such as destroys karma
    looked at Rāma with true love
and, remembering, told him the whole
    unimaginable way, requiring care,
to the indestructible mountain where lives the son
    of the fiery god in the swift-horsed chariot.

7. 3807

He who is the essence of the amṛta
    which those whose ears have been fully
opened to enlightenment drink down
    with their knowledge, listened to everything
she said, as if he were hearing
    a sage who was there presenting,
in her revelation, an awareness of the way
    of truth which leads to Freedom.

8. 3808

After that, she gave up her body,
in culmination of her yogic powers
gained through her efforts and, by herself,
with joy she reached the heavenly world.
Seeing her, the heroes felt
measureless admiration and set out,
with their anklets of gold resounding
on the great route that she had described.

9. 3809

They moved ahead, putting cool forests
and hills and rivers behind them
and they entered Lake Pampā which was like
pure actions melted to liquid
by the great fire kindled there every day,
as countless people from across the earth,
through their bathing in that lake, burned away
evil acts that had clung to them.

# Notes to the Translation

## The Invocation

It is customary to begin a work in India with some sort of auspicious verse, usually one that invokes a god. The purpose is to ensure success in the endeavor that has been started. Kampaṉ begins his whole work with such an invocation and continues giving an auspicious verse (called "the praise of god" in Tamil) at the beginning of each of the Kāṇḍas that make up his *Rāmāyaṇa*.

The first line means literally, "[He] is not different from the differentiated forms that arise undifferentiated [from their own essence]." G. says that by essence is meant the heat of fire, the coolness of water, etc. It is the quality that makes, say, a table a table rather than something else. According to some schools of Indian philosophy, this quality is unchanging but is connected with the changeable object in which it inheres. Kampaṉ plays on a common paradox expounded by Indian devotional literature: that God is hard to know, yet he is inside us and so close to us that, if only we have enough love for him, he is the easiest of all things to know. For "gods," the text has literally "those of whom the first is [the god] Brahmā." For "knowledge for our knowing," G. comments "the object that is known by our knowledge," but this seems unwarranted.

It would appear that Kampaṉ wrote this invocation with the Forest Book in mind. More than any of the Kāṇḍas of the *Rāmāyaṇa*, this book turns on contrast and difference. Its major theme is the encounter between the Rākṣasas and the world they rule on the one hand, and Rāma and the Hindu Dharma that he represents on the other. In this stanza, Kampaṉ says that, no matter how different appearances may be, ultimately such differences are illusory, that they are *māyā*. The only reality is God, and he is awareness itself, not the Vedas or the gods or any of the other components of the Hindu world order. Kampaṉ sets out in this invocation the paradox that will pervade the entire book: the tension between the world of appearances, in which Rāma is only a man, and the world as it really is, in which Rāma is Divinity itself.

## Paṭalam One

2. 2607

See "Elephants of Space" in the Glossary.

4. 2608

The commentators remark that the clothes, jewels, and sandal paste are given to Sītā by Anasūyā. The name "Anasūyā" has been added for clarity.

5. 2609

This stanza, and the following passage, describe the demon Virādha. For more on demons, see "Rākṣasa" in the Glossary.

6. 2610

Rākṣasas have bright red hair and black skin.

8. 2613

Men would commonly smear their chests with sandal paste for coolness. The word used here for sandal paste is *ceccai*, which can also mean "coat" or "shirt," which is the meaning that Crit. takes. The interpretation of G., followed here, seems better.

10. 2615

The text does not actually mention fingers; it is supplied at G.'s suggestion. Crit. says the elephants were not between his fingers but on a spear; the original is unclear.

11. 2616

G. notes that although this stanza has been variously commented upon, none of the interpretations really work. This version follows Crit. G. says that the hood-jewels are compared to the chariots of the gods: "the chariots of the gods that [glittered as if] one had snatched away the hood-jewels of the leaders of the snakes."

12. 2617

The defeat of Indra, king of the gods, is used here to glorify Virādha: if he can defeat Indra and take the ornament of his elephant, then he can defeat anyone.

13. 2618

"Final age of a world"—Kaliyuga, the last of the four *yugas*, when men and others in the world are at their most corrupt. "Poison and glowing fire, the worst evils . . ." is G.'s interpretation; Crit. says "a great sin like poison and fire."

14. 2619

See the Glossary under "Elephants of Space."

15. 2620

According to the *Tamil Lexicon*, the calañcalam conch is said to be surrounded by (and, presumably, produced by) a thousand right-twisting conches. As most conches twist left, these themselves are very rare; if it takes a thousand to produce one Calañcalam conch, it must be rarest of all.

16. 2621

For the beginning of this stanza, Crit. uses an inferior and less well attested reading, and, with some difficulty, construes, "he moved across [the forest], his leg-rings jingling, which he had put on [and which were so lovely and large] that they vied with the great silver mountain and the gold mountain."

23. 2628

Hindu cosmology sees the universe as consisting of three layers: the nether world, where the snakes (Nāgas) live; this world; and the upper world of the gods.

25. 2630

The commentators disagree on the interpretation of the word *vaṭa*. G., who is followed here, takes it as "the horse [named] *vaṭa*[*vā*] [which means 'Underwater Fire']"; Crit. takes it as "necklace": "the ocean that is like a bright [pearl] necklace [of the earth goddess]." The Underwater Fire, according to the *Tamil Lexicon*, is "in the form of a mare's head, believed to consume the world at the end of a *yuga*." Here, it appears to issue out of a mare's mouth and to drink up the northern sea, just as the blade of Virādha's trident drinks up the ocean of an opposing army.

26. 2631

See "Churning of the Ocean," "Elephants of Space," and "Seven Mountains" in the Glossary.

27. 2632

Comets are considered extremely baleful omens.

28. 2633

"That had humbled gods" is G.'s interpretation of *cūr oṭuṅku*; Crit. construes, "which contained an evil god [*cūr*] in it." It was believed in South India that drums and certain weapons had in them a spirit or god that gave them their power.

30. 2635

In Hinduism, gods have many names, and these names are important. One of the most prominent Vaiṣṇava works is the *Viṣṇusahasranāma*, "The Thousand Names of Viṣṇu." Viṣṇu is supposed to rest on a many-headed snake floating on the primal ocean of milk, which he leaves to reestablish the Order of the World as an incarnation such as Rāma.

36. 2641

In an Indian temple, devotees often circumambulate the deity, keeping him (or her) on their right. See "Meru" in the Glossary.

37. 2642

According to Crit., this refers to a story about Krishna's nephew Aniruddha. He abducted Uṣā, the daughter of the demon Bāṇa. Subsequently, Krishna and Balarāma came with Garuḍa to the prison where Bāṇa had locked up Aniruddha and freed him.

39. 2644

It is common in Indian literature to describe a woman as having a very thin waist with large breasts and hips. Often, the waist is said to be so thin it is virtually invisible, or, as here, as thin as a streak of lightning.

42. 2647

The snake planet (Rāhu) is supposed to cause the eclipse of the sun and the moon when it devours them. See "Rāhu" in the Glossary.

43. 2648

"Made his plan"—literally, "who had good schemes [*eṇ*]." G. takes this differently: "who is in everyone's thoughts [*eṇ*]."

44. 2649

A central part of the Vedic ritual was pouring ghee into the fire. The idea here is that those who love Rāma are like Vedic fires, and Rāma is like the ghee that is poured into them and makes them flame up. This is G.'s interpretation. Crit. says, "after they drink the ghee [that he pours down] having become a faultless sacrificial ladle."

45. 2650

The story of how Tumburu was cursed to become a Rākṣasa is given in this Paṭalam, 61 ff. Hindu cosmology is complex and has many different stories about the beginning of the world. One is that the world sprang from an egg; another is that Brahmā created it. Here, these two stories are put together, and G. remarks that Viṣṇu created the waters and the egg upon them, then created Brahmā to create creatures.

48. 2653

The story here is that once there was a Pandyan king who was a great devotee of Viṣṇu. One day while he was doing *puja* (worship) to Viṣṇu, the sage Agastya came there. Immersed in his ceremony, he did not give the proper greeting and respect to him. The sage became angry and cursed him to become an elephant. Yet even as an elephant living in a jungle, he was devoted to Viṣṇu and every day offered him puja with a thousand lotuses. One day he went to a lotus pond to get flowers for his puja. As he descended into the pond a crocodile took hold of his foot. Now, the crocodile was actually a Gandharva named Hūhū, who had been cursed to become a crocodile because he had taken hold of the foot of a muni named Devala and pulled it. As the elephant could not pull his foot away from the crocodile, he cried out to Viṣṇu, who came mounted on Garuḍa and cut the crocodile in two with his discus, granting *mokṣa* (release from the cycle of transmigration) to the elephant and release from his curse to Hūhū.

50. 2655

"Where they were completely free"—literally, "where they had renunciation as their occupation [and so gained freedom]." According to the commentators, the point of this stanza is, "Why then do you, who are Viṣṇu himself, appear like an ordinary man totally unaware of your identity?"

51. 2656

"Religion" is an inexact translation of *camayam*; it can include not only such different religions as Buddhism and Jainism but also different sects of Hinduism. The *Bhagavad Gītā* says that, whatever god you worship, whatever religious system you belong to, Viṣṇu takes the form of that god and is actually the deity who is worshiped (IV.11).

52. 2657

"World's Order" translates *dharma*.

53. 2658

"Religions"—see the note on 51 above. "None of them fully comprehending your nature": *āyāta*; G. says this means "[religions] that are hard to comprehend."

54. 2659

"O you who are already here when you come" is *vārātē vara vallāy*; literally, "O you who can come without coming." In 6.10.9, the *Tiruvāymoḻi*, the most important Tamil scripture for Śrīvaiṣṇavas, says that this means "you who come even though you seem not to come." The *Īṭu*, the most important commentary on the *Tiruvāymoḻi*, comments that while God makes it seem to those who worship him that he is hard to attain, he is actually inside of everyone.

56. 2661

"Always in deep yogic sleep, you are awake!"—literally, "You sleep like those who do not have even one act, O you who never sleep." G. says the sleep referred to is *yoganidrā*, the sleep of a yogi. The *Gītā* says, "That which is night for all creatures, in that the restrained one [i.e., the yogi] is awake. In that [night] when all creatures are awake, that is night for the sage who [really] sees" (II.69).

57. 2662

The primal snake is Ādiśeṣa. The boar is Varāha, the boar incarnation of Viṣṇu; the dwarf, Vāmana, another incarnation (see "Śeṣa," "Varāha," and "Vāmana" in the Glossary). Śrī is, of course, the wife of Viṣṇu.

58. 2663

Śiva, jealous because Brahmā also had five heads, cut one of the rival god's heads off. Because of this sin, the skull stuck to his hand. To atone, Śiva had to go about begging with the skull until it was full; unfortunately for him, however much he begged, it did not fill up. Finally, he went to Viṣṇu, whose alms filled it, whereupon it immediately became unstuck.

59. 2664

See "Varāha" and "Māyā" in the Glossary. G. notes that this stanza contains the doctrine of Viśiṣṭādvaita (later expounded by the famous theologian and philosopher Rāmānuja) that creatures are both different and not different from God.

63. 2668

This is G.'s reading. Crit. says, "I live in the sky [i.e., heaven] that belongs to Kubera [the god of wealth]." G. transposes this and the next stanza.

64. 2669

G. reads *ūṭal*, "lovers' quarrel," for *ūṭu*, "because of," and construes, "A quarrel having come, I made love [with her to conciliate her]." See the notes to 3490 for Rambhā.

65. 2670

The sin of Tumburu, according to the commentaries, was that he neglected the work he was doing for his master, Kubera, the god of wealth, to make love with Rambhā. For this he was cursed by his master to become a Rākṣasa. The *Meghadūta* of Kālidāsa is about a Yakṣa who was cursed by Kubera to spend a year in the Vindhyā mountains away from his wife.

67. 2672

For circling a temple, see the note on 36 above. The Tamil word for "circumambulating," *valam ceytu*, means literally "making it [to the] right," i.e., circling it with one's right side toward it.

68. 2673

"Stubbornly" is *niṉṟu*—literally, "consistently." G. reads *tiṉṟu*, "eating" for this—"I have followed evil, eating [all manner of creatures as a Rākṣasa]."

69. 2674

The end of this stanza is translated according to G.'s interpretation. Crit. says, "Today I am no longer confused because I was touched by your feet that . . . wear [as ornament] the book of the Vedas that abides so all desire it, [and this happened] because my old deeds were sent away."

71. 2675

"Who was famous for fighting the gods" is G.'s somewhat forced meaning for *tēvu kātal*. Crit. takes *kātal* in its more normal sense of "love" but comes up with a meaning that seems to make little sense: "who was distinguished by his love for the gods." The U.V.S. edition construes, "he whose excellence was such that even the gods would desire [*kātal*] it."

72. 2676

The grove is an ashram, where ascetics who have given up worldly life live. Such men commonly go to the forest in order to be away from the world. They are conventionally considered to live lives of peace and contentment. One of the greatest sins of the Rākṣasas is that they were troubling the lives and rituals of such forest ascetics.

## Paṭalam Two

2. 2679

Normal lotuses close in the evening and only open again at the first rays of the morning sun.

4. 2681

The veena is a classical stringed instrument still played in South India. For "garlanded," G. reads "whose body was black."

5. 2682

G. remarks on the belief that anyone who performs a hundred Aśvamedha sacrifices will be born as Indra in his next birth. The Aśvamedha is a Vedic rite in which a horse is allowed to roam free, guarded by the king's men, for a year, after which it is sacrificed. The point is to demonstrate the king's power and the extent of his dominion by showing that his horse can wander at will unmolested.

6. 2683

Airāvata, the elephant on which Indra rides, is white; hence, Indra atop his white elephant is compared to Śiva atop his mountain, Kailāsa, which is made of silver. The wife of Indra is Śaśi.

7. 2684

One of the emblems of an Indian king is his umbrella. In the early Caṅkam poems of Tamil, the king's umbrella, which is white, is often compared to the cool moon. The point appears to be that those who live under the protection of the king are guarded from the sunlike heat and suffering of misfortune and experience only the coolness and pleasure of happiness.

8. 2685

Another emblem of an Indian king is a chowry, or white yak's tail, with which the king is fanned. In classical Indian literature, fame is conventionally said to be white, which is the point of this stanza. See "Asuras" and "Elephants of Space" in the Glossary.

11. 2688

As early as the *Ṛg Veda*, Indra is a god of rain. The rainbow is called in Sanskrit *indradhanus*, "the bow of Indra."

12. 2689

"A sword that . . . had the shape of a fish" is G.'s interpretation. Crit. says "and he had the swords that are the eyes of heavenly women which have high victory and are [shaped] like fish." This, he explains, means that the heavenly women could not take their eyes off him.

17. 2694

For "with your pure wife [*nallāḷuṭan̠ē*]!" G. has, "O you who are good, [go] at once [*nallāy uṭan̠ē*]."

18. 2695

"When their color fades"—literally, "whose workmanship decays."

20. 2697

"Every being" is *pūtam*, which could also mean "element," i.e., the five great elements of earth, water, fire, air, and space (see "Great Elements" in the Glossary). The great wind is the hurricane that comes at the end of time, after the *kalpa* is over. "A place of total purity" is literally "which does not deviate from the *guṇa* [of *sattva*]." This refers to the theory of the three *guṇas*, or strands, expounded by the *Bhagavad Gītā*. See "Guṇa" in the Glossary. The state meant is *mokṣa*, the ultimate and total release from transmigration.

22. 2699

The elephant is Airāvata, Indra's white elephant. See "Airāvata" in the Glossary.

24. 2701

The sun causes lotuses to open in the morning.

25. 2702

"Those who are holy" is *antaṇar*, which can mean either Brahmins or ascetics. "A form of the highest lord" is based on G.'s interpretation of *āḷ nātan̠* as a Tamil equivalent of the Sanskrit *puruṣottama*, a Vaiṣṇava term for Viṣṇu as "the supreme being."

26. 2703

Crit. takes "like one who did not know" as referring to Rāma, who, he says, stood next to Śarabhaṅga like one who did not know what was going on; but this is forcing the meaning.

28. 2705

"No before and no after" could also mean "no front and no behind." "Dark sleeper on the ocean of milk" is interpretative for *karuṅ kaṭalil kaṇ vaḷarāy*—literally, "O you who sleep in the black [or great] ocean." G. remarks that the great ocean of milk appears black as it reflects the dark color of Viṣṇu; hence this translation.

29. 2706

See "Brahmā" and "Churning of the Ocean" in the Glossary. One Hindu creation story has it that as Viṣṇu slept on the ocean of milk, a lotus containing the Creator Brahmā grew from his navel and that Brahmā subsequently created the world, buzzing around the lotus like a bee.

30. 2707

For the Hindu notion of aeon, see "Kalpa" in the Glossary. The concept that God is the creator of both good and evil is one of the basic areas in which Hindu thought differs from Western ideas.

31. 2708

The difficulty with this stanza is that no one seems to know the story on which it is based. G. tells a nice story that makes him take *eriyōṉ*, which should mean "fire," as "Śiva": The seven sages, wishing to find out who was the highest god, decided the criterion would be the *guṇa* that each manifested. Their chief, Bhṛgu, visited Śiva, who could not see them because he was making love to Pārvatī for seven days. When he found out that Bhṛgu had visited and had become angry at not being received, he went to Bhṛgu, who said, "You are impure—don't touch me." Śiva tried to burn him with his third eye, but the sage intercepted the fire with a flame from his big toe and cursed Śiva to be a god unfit for Brahmins, as he showed *tāmasa guṇa*. He then went to Brahmā, who, feeling that fathers should not bow to their children (he is the grandfather of the world), refused to return Bhṛgu's bow, thus showing *rājasa guṇa*. Bhṛgu cursed him to have no temples. Finally he went to Viṣṇu in Vaikuṇṭha, the paradise and world on which Viṣṇu dwells. When he kicked that god on the chest, the god got up and said, "Did your foot hurt? My chest is honored by being touched by your foot. Forgive me for not knowing you were coming," and thus he showed *sāttvika guṇa*. In this way Bhṛgu learned that Viṣṇu is the highest god. G. takes *vallai* as "quickly" and construes it with *tiṇṭi*: they quickly went to Śiva.

34. 2711

G. has a different interpretation for the last line: "he [Rāma] was happy, as if he were engaged in his yogic sleep on the ocean [of milk]."

36. 2713

The end of night goes with the sage's attainment of liberation. The violence of the sun imagery prefigures the violence of Śarabhaṅga's entering the fire.

39. 2716

G. has a different reading: "the ecstasy that [came to him because] he was about to leave his body."

40. 2717

"As had to be" is *pukaluṟu viti.* This could mean "[now that you have come] by fate, which should be praised."

41. 2718

G. rearranges the words a bit and gets the meaning, "Indra came and when he said, 'Brahmā has given . . . until the time of the end [of the universe].' "

43. 2720

G. has a different reading and interprets, "The gods and others, who have as their leader Brahmā, who is on his great fragrant lotus and who knows the future."

## Paṭalam Three

3. 2724)

The Vālakhilyas are sixty thousand beings the size of a thumb who sprang from Brahmā's hairs.

4. 2725

Amṛta is ambrosia, the substance that conferred eternal life on the gods. See the Glossary.

6. 2727

"The Rākṣasas from whom they could not hide" is literally "the Rākṣasas whose acts cannot be concealed." G. suggests this may also mean "Rākṣasas whose evil acts are done in full view of everyone."

9. 2730

"A cloud that has just drunk water" is literally "a shoot [i.e., a beginning] of a cloud." Since clouds conventionally begin in Indian tradition by drinking water from the ocean, G. says that is meant here.

14. 2735

The six duties enjoined for a Brahmin are teaching (the Vedas), reciting (the Vedas), sacrificing (a Vedic sacrifice), conducting (a Vedic) sacrifice (for someone else), giving, and receiving. Any Vedic sacrifice involves pouring an oblation of ghee into the sacred fire.

15. 2736

It is a convention to compare the king's sovereignty to a wheel. Aśoka's wheel of law is on the Indian flag.

17. 2738

The royal line of Rāma is supposed to have been descended from the sun.

18. 2739

The sense of this stanza is that Rāma was fortunate to go into the forest, even though it entailed the suffering of so many, because it gave him a chance to help the ascetics there.

20. 2741

The quiver, bow, and arrows will no longer be so heavy because Rāma finally can use them to good purpose, so they are not mere dead weight.

22. 2743

See "Murukaṉ" in the Glossary.

23. 2744

Ascetics carry a trident staff, the three branches of which symbolize, according to G., the *trimūrti*—Brahmā the Creator, Viṣṇu the Preserver, and Śiva the Destroyer.

24. 2745

This threefold world consists of heaven, earth, and the underworld. G. has a different reading for the end and says, "The Veda, our tapas, and [our] great knowledge is witness to it."

30. 2751

The line of Brahmā includes everyone and everything, as he is the grandfather of the whole world. "Ancestors" is *munṉaiyōr*, which Crit. takes as "the first [*varṇa*, i.e., Brahmins]," but this meaning is not attested in the *Tamil Lexicon.*

31. 2752

For *kāṇikkai*, the synonym of *takkaṇai*, the word used here for "offering," the *Tamil Lexicon* says, "voluntary offering, commonly in money, gold, fruits; gift to temple or church; present to a guru or other great person."

35. 2756

Crit. construes, "waterfalls that shine with a sweet taste like honey squeezed from the honeycomb," but this seems neither correct nor felicitous.

36. 2757

The sage Agastya is supposed to have received Tamil grammar from Śiva himself and to have given it to the world from Mount Potiyil (Skt. Malaya) in the south. See "Vāmana" in the Glossary for the story of how Viṣṇu measured out the world in three steps.

37. 2758

This story is given by G.: when Vṛddhāsura and other Asuras hid from the gods, their enemies, in the ocean, Indra and the other gods came to Agastya and asked him for his help. He scooped up all the water of the ocean in one hand and drank it down. After Indra had killed the demons, he regurgitated the water back into the ocean.

38. 2759

G. tells this story: There were two Rākṣasa brothers, Ilvala and Vātāpi. The elder, Ilvala, would take on the form of a Brahmin every day and, saying he was having a ceremony for the dead (*śrāddha*), would invite Brahmins. His younger brother would take on the form of a ram, and Ilvala would kill him and offer his meat to the Brahmins as part of the rite. After they had eaten, he would cry out, "Vātāpi! Come out!" and his brother would come to life, rip open the stomachs of the Brahmins who had eaten the meat, and emerge. The two brothers would then eat the bodies of the dead Brahmins. The sages asked Agastya for help, and so he went to one of Ilvala's celebrations. After he had eaten the meat of the ram, Agastya cried out, "Vātāpi! Be digested!" and so destroyed the demon. When the enraged Ilvala came at him, he burnt him with his glance and so killed him also.

39. 2760

Once, the Vindhya mountain, wanting to become taller than Mount Meru or any other mountain, grew up into the sky and blocked the passage of the sun and all the other planets (the sun is a planet in Hindu astronomy). The gods, sages, and others asked Agastya for help and went to the mountain, which bowed down in salutation to him. He said, "Remain bowed over as I go south, and until I return to the north again." He went south (where he gave Tamil to the world) but never returned; thus, the mountain has been curved over ever since.

40. 2761

When all the gods went to Śiva's wedding on Mount Kailāsa in the north, the world went out of balance, the north sinking and the south rising up. To correct this, Agastya went south and remained on Mount Potiyil (Skt. Malaya).

41. 2762

See the note on 36 above for how Agastya gave Tamil to the world. G. interprets "Rising to great heights by study of the four Vedas" quite differently: "[Tamil] that is higher than the four Vedas." Crit. points out that Naccin̠arkkin̠iyar, a medieval Tamil commentator who was a Śaiva Brahmin, gives a list of the four Vedas quite at odds with our own: the Taittirīyam, the Bauḍikam, the Talavakāram(?), and the Sāma Veda. See "Veda" in the Glossary.

42. 2763

"Or within great wisdom" is Crit.'s interpretation. G. says this means "in great hearts" and adds "he says this . . . because he comes quickly into the hearts of those who think of him with love and stays enthroned there."

43. 2764

"Their attendant *śāstras*" is literally "the other ancillary [*iyainta*] books." G. points out that this simile is particularly apt for Agastya, as he is known as a physician and would be accustomed to grind things.

44. 2765

See "Gods" in the Glossary for the four characteristics of the gods.

46. 2766

Agastya is supposed to have brought the Kāvēri, the major river of Tamilnad, in his ascetic's pitcher.

47. 2767

See 36 above for how Agastya gave Tamil to the world.

51. 2772

Śiva wears the crescent moon and the Ganges river in his hair.

53. 2774

The laws of Manu, *Manusmṛti*, are the most famous set of Hindu laws. The seven worlds are placed one on top of the other; they form a different conception from that of the three worlds, which is more commonly encountered. See 24 above and "World" in the Glossary. For the wheel of law, see 15 above.

55. 2776

"Viṣṇu" is literally "the cause of the universe" here. According to G., Viṣṇu's bow was made by Viśvakarman, the architect of the gods, was kept by Viṣṇu for a time, and came into the keeping of Paraśurāma. He gave it to Rāma, who gave it to Varuṇa for safekeeping. That god, realizing that the time had come for the destruction of the Rākṣasa Khara and the others, brought it to Agastya so he could give it to Rāma. For more on Paraśurāma and Viṣṇu's bow, see the notes to 3149.

56. 2777

See "Śiva" in the Glossary for the story of the destruction of the three cities.

58. 2779

"Golden woman"—*poṉ ivaḷoṭum*—is taken by Crit. to mean "Sarasvatī," since one of the names of that goddess of learning is "gold" on account of her light color.

## Paṭalam Four

1. 2781

A *kāvatam* is about ten miles. G. interprets "regions where the growth was dense" as "forests following [one on the other] and thick." See "Jaṭāyus" in the Glossary.

2. 2782

The Eastern Mountain is the mountain behind which the sun and moon are supposed to rise. Crit. construes, "He shone as if the [young] sun, rising from the summit of the Eastern Mountain, like melted gold [in color], were spreading through the directions its shoots of thick rays that illumined all the directions." This translation follows G., who reads *ciṟai*, "wing," for Crit.'s *ticai*, "direction."

3. 2783

See the "Churning of the Ocean" and "Mandara" in the Glossary.

5. 2785

"Of time and space" is added to clarify "distances" at G.'s suggestion. For "who consider and investigate and then know," Crit. interprets, "so you would say he is a learned man in a learned court."

6. 2786

For Indra's elephant, see "Airāvata" in the Glossary.

7. 2787

The nine planets whirl around the Polar Star (Dhruva) in a circular pattern that is compared to a wheel. According to G., the wheel is likened to the necklace of Jaṭāyus, while the nine planets are likened to the central ornament of the necklace, made of the nine jewels.

8. 2788

See "Aruṇa" in the Glossary for Dawn.

10. 2790

"In anger" is *ceyirttu*. G. says "in doubt" for this, but this meaning is not given by the *Tamil Lexicon*.

13. 2793

See "Kāma" in the Glossary for the God of Love.

14. 2794

There are several bodily characteristics by which one can recognize a Cakravartin, or universal monarch. Among these, according to Crit., are an appearance like that of a mountain, a broad chest, and naturally red eyes (described in the next stanza).

15. 2795

Rāma is black in color, while Lakṣmaṇa is light-skinned—said to be red by Hindus. The friend Jaṭāyus mentions is Daśaratha, the father of Rāma and Lakṣmaṇa.

21. 2801

For Wish-Granting Tree see "Kalpaka" in the Glossary. The king's generosity is more than the kalpaka tree's, his umbrella is cooler—and more life-giving—than the moon, his patience is greater than the earth's, who bears all burdens set upon her.

22. 2802

"Freed it of death" is literally, in G.'s version, "that gave life." Crit. reads "that gave amṛta [the drink that confers immortality]" for this.

23. 2803

G. gives the story of Śambara: A demon named Śambara fought with Indra and took over heaven. Indra, defeated, asked Daśaratha for help, and, with Jaṭāyus as an ally, he defeated the demon. In gratitude for his help, Daśaratha told Jaṭāyus, "[We are so close that] I am the body, you the life."

25. 2805

See "Asura" in the Glossary. The commentators are not much help with the genealogy given in this and the next few stanzas. We have Sanskritized the names (in keeping with our practice) where possible; however, it was not possible to discover Sanskrit equivalents for Kaḻai (possibly Kalā) and Aruṭṭai. Kampaṉ's purpose in giving this genealogy is evidently to impart a feeling of the primeval quality of the great bird who is speaking. The Dawn is Aruṇa.

26. 2806

G. reads, "Surabhi gave birth to, in addition to the cows, all other [creatures] that move or are stationary." Dānavas (a matronymic) is another name for Rākṣasas. The four classes of humanity are the four *varṇas:* the Brahmin, the Kṣatriya, the Vaiśya, and the Śūdra (see "Varṇa" in the Glossary). See the Glossary for "Gandharvas."

32. 2812

G. suggests that the "virtues" mentioned in line 1 are the *kalyāṇaguṇas*—the auspicious qualities—that the Śrīvaiṣṇavas attribute to Viṣṇu.

35. 2815

" . . . us who, because of meeting you, have lost the pain . . . " is literally "us who thought that, because of meeting you, we had lost the pain . . . "

38. 2818

For *katir*, "gleaming," G. reads *kaṟai*, stain, i.e., bloodstained.

41. 2821

"Inner lotuses" is *alli*, the inner flower petals of a flower. Both Crit. and G. say this word has no force—Crit. says it is simply a characteristic of all lotuses, like "white" in "white moon"; but it seemed warranted to us to bring out the force of this rather nice word. "Kissed his hair" is actually "smelled [his head]," a common way of expressing affection in Indian literature.

43. 2823

For Tāḍakā see "Mārīca" in the Glossary. Rāma won Sītā by breaking the bow of Śiva when she chose a bridegroom. Crit. remarks that the mention of this event answers Jaṭāyus's question in the previous stanza about who Sītā is. "Sleeping in the forest" is literally "staying in the grass." G. says it merely means "staying in the forest," while Crit. suggests it refers to the time when Rāma, on his way to his exile in Daṇḍaka forest, had to sleep on the grass on the banks of the Ganges. He writes, "Rāma, who should have slept on five three-ply mattresses, after he set out for the forest, slept on a bed of grass laid down among the rocks. When Guha showed this to Bharata, it was an occasion of great suffering; hence, it describes how [Rāma] had to stay in the forest."

44. 2824

"You who have left your wealthy land behind you" is G.'s interpretation. Crit. says it means, "You have left behind your wealth. [Stay in this forest] as if in [your own] country."

45. 2825

"Beautiful" is *maṇi*, which could also mean "which has jewels [that it carries along with it from the hills]."

46. 2826

"Bathing place" is *tuṟai*, one of the most difficult Tamil words to translate. Among the relevant meanings in the *Tamil Lexicon* are "seaport, harbour, roadstead," "sea," "river," "place where washermen wash clothes," "ghat, bathing ghat," and "frequented place, place of meeting, rendezvous."

## Paṭalam Five

(In the notes to this section, the various changes of meter are analyzed and discussed.)

1. 2829

This beginning section follows a pattern of one *viḷam* plus two *mās* plus one viḷam plus two mās. Here is the first line of stanza 1, broken up according to metrical feet rather than word and meaning (this practice will be followed with all metrical illustrations of Kamban̲'s verse):

˘ ˘ ˘ ˘ | ˘ ˘ - | - - |
*puviyin̲uk kaṇiyā yān̲r̲a*
˘ ˘ ˘ ˘ | ˘ ˘ - | - - |
*poruṭantu pulattir̲ r̲āki.*

The long even line suits the quiet and elaborate description.

"The five landscapes of poetry," *aintiṇai.* This is a reference to the five landscapes (*tiṇais*) of Caṅkam love poetry (*akam*), each associated with a particular stage of love. They are characterized by the names of flowers and trees that grow in the respective areas. The five are: *kur̲iñci* (representing the mountains and associated with the premarital union of lovers), *mullai* (the forest, associated with the patient waiting of lovers), *neytal* (the seashore, anxious waiting), *pālai* (the waste land, separation), and *marutam* (the agricultural riverine country, infidelity). Each element in the original of this stanza refers both to the river and to "the poems of the great poets," *cān̲r̲ōr kavi.* There are seven points of comparison, enumerated below. Here, "1" gives the attribute of the river, "2" of the poem. 1. an ornament to the earth, 2. an ornament [i.e., object of beauty] for [i.e., praised by] the earth; 1. giving much [or excellent] wealth (*poruḷ*), 2. giving excellent meanings (*poruḷ*) [G. says this means "telling of the *caturvarga* (the four aims of life)," but this hardly seems necessary]; 1. having fields, 2. being a repository of wisdom; 1. having watering places (*tur̲aikaḷ*) which are places (*akam*) [to escape from the] heat (*ava*) [so G.; Crit says "having the sorts (*tur̲ai*) [of sacrifice] where the oblation (*ava*) is food (*aka*)]," 2. having the subdivisions (*tur̲ai*) [of a *tiṇai*]; 1. going along (*ner̲i*) the five tracts (*aintiṇai*), 2. having the [grammatical] types (*ner̲i*) of the five *tiṇais*; 1. clear in a lovely way, 2. clear so that it is lovely; 1. having a cool flow, 2. having a cool [i.e., sweet] flow.

4. 2832

See "Cakravāka" in the Glossary. The description of the conjugal love between Rāma and Sītā is meant to contrast with the lust of Śūrpaṇakhā that forms the main subject matter of this Paṭalam.

5. 2833

"Sudden" is *putiyatu*—literally, "something new."

6. 2834

"Red lotuses," *alli am kamalam*—literally, "beautiful lotuses with interior petals." Rāma's body is black like the water lilies, with red hands, feet, and eyes, like the lotuses.

8. 2836

"Fatal disease"—this is based on the belief that the fatal disease which will take one's life is already fixed at birth.

9. 2837

Rākṣasas have black skin and red hair. Both commentaries point out that "copper" could also be understood as "red dust." For "swollen full of burning lust past measuring," G. has a different reading that he has to struggle to make sense of: "with a body that grew so incomparably that Rāhu would grow angry." See "Rāhu" in the Glossary.

10. 2838

"The instrument of a cruel fate" is a problem, and neither commentator seems to know quite what it means. The two basic interpretations for this phrase are "having a cruel purpose, willingly she stayed in that forest," and "moved by a cruel agency [i.e., fate], she stayed in that forest." Taking the first interpretation, G. writes, "When her elder brother Rāvaṇa killed the Asura named Vidyujjihva, who was her husband, while he was defeating Kālakeya during his conquest of the world, she became a widow, was enraged at Rāvaṇa, and, at his request, went to the place called Janasthāna with Khara and other warriors, and wandered as she wished through that whole forest." He also remarks, with more sense, that her cruel purpose may have simply been to bother ascetics.

11. 2839

"The Lord" is, of course, Rāma, an incarnation of Viṣṇu, who left his sleep on the ocean of milk, where he lay on a serpent.

12. 2840

In Tamil poetry, it is conventional to begin an erotic encounter in this way: the person who is falling in love wonders whether the other person is a god or a human being or what. One of the most notable uses of this convention is in the *Tirukōvaiyār* of Māṇikkavācakar, where the man, who represents the soul, wonders whether the woman he sees (who represents God) is a goddess. He decides she cannot be a goddess, since her feet touch the earth.

14. 2842

See "Elephants of Space" in the Glossary.

15. 2843

Golden Meru is the wrong color to resemble the black arms of Rāma.

17. 2845

In Indian literature, the moon is thought to have a blemish. This blemish is supposed to resemble a hare; thus a common name of the moon is *śaśāṅka*, "he whose mark [or blemish] is a hare."

19. 2847

The words "swaying" and "graceful" have been added to establish the Indian view of the great beauty in an elephant's gait.

20. 2848

G. reads "of him who has a sword at his waist" for "whose smile is like glistening moonlight."

22. 2850

Ascetics wear garments of bark as a sign of their humility.

23. 2851

An ascetic smears mud on his hair until it becomes clumped and matted. A warrior in ancient South India would wear a tuft.

24. 2852

The text just says "king of jewels," which Apte says is a ruby. G. says the text merely means "an excellent jewel," while Crit. says it refers to the Kaustabha, a jewel obtained when the ocean was churned and worn by Viṣṇu on his breast.

25. 2853

Brahmā not only created the world; he ordained the place of everything in it. Śūrpaṇakhā says he erred by making Rāma a humble ascetic wandering through the forest, while he made Indra, who in appearance is not worth the dust on Rāma's feet, king of all the worlds.

26. 2854

"Purity," *kaṟpu*. This is a very important term in Tamil tradition, in which a woman's chastity is considered to have magic powers. For a discussion, see George Hart, *The Poems of Ancient Tamil* (Berkeley, 1975), pp. 96 ff. and *passim.*

28. 2856

"I will make love with . . ." is literally, "I will unite with the broad chest of . . . "

31. 2859

This is one of the most famous passages in Tamil literature. The rhythm changes, to catch the Rākṣasī's sensual movement, into a pattern of two *kāys*, a *viḷam*, and a *mā*:

¯ ˘ ˘ ¯ | ¯ ˘ ˘ ¯ |

*pañciyoḷir viñcukuḷir*

¯ ˘ ˘ | ˘ ˘ ¯ |

*pallava maṉuṅkac.*

A rough equivalent of this in English would be:

'xxx 'xxx 'xx x"

where ' indicates a sound that is long and stressed. The red cotton and cool shoots are likened to the color and softness of her feet.

32. 2860

"Flowing gold" refers to the golden pollen that drops from the lotus on which Śrī rests. "Jeweled chariot," *maṇit tēr*, a metaphor for the yoni. "Myna bird" is *pūvai*, which G. takes as "parrot."

33. 2861

"Vine of heaven" has been added, as the *Tamil Lexicon* says for *vaḷḷi*, "a fabled creeper of gold that twines around the celestial Kalpaka tree." See "Kalpaka" in the Glossary. A creeper cannot grow without something to climb on; thus the tree "gives life" to the creeper. A famous story in Caṅkam literature concerns Pāri, a king who saw a jasmine vine with nothing to grow on and gave it his chariot for a support so it would not die.

35. 2863

"Once he has entered the mind" translates *eṇ aruḷi*—literally, "having given the thought [of himself]." G. takes *eṇ* as "heart" and interprets, "having conceived grace [*aruḷi*] in his heart." Crit. remarks, "Because she is infatuated with Rāma, [Kampaṉ] says she comes so her large, beautiful breasts are visible."

36. 2864

See the notes on 12 above. "Is there any limit to the beauty within her?" is G.'s interpretation. Crit. says, "With whom [else] does beauty attain its fullness?"

38. 2866

"With all your excellence"—*cēyōy*—could also mean "O you who are red [i.e., light-skinned]." For "Source of the Vedas," G. interprets, "who are proclaimed as the cause of the universe in the Vedas"; Crit. agrees with our interpretation. In a formal Indian situation, one must know the caste and position of a person before having dealings with him.

39. 2867

The meter changes back to the pattern of one *viḷam* plus two *mās* plus one viḷam plus two mās (see note to stanza 1). See the Glossary for all the names here. "Granddaughter of Brahmā" is literally "the daughter of the son [Vajravasu] of the son [Pulastya Prajāpati] of the one who is in the flower [Brahmā]." Crit. suggests that she is hiding the fact that she is a widow. "The overlord of the three worlds" is, of course, Rāvaṇa.

40. 2868

"Whose eyes blaze" is literally "whose eyes are red." G. elaborates: "from anger."

41. 2869

"Righteousness" is *aṟam*, the Tamil word for Sanskrit *dharma.*

44. 2872

According to Crit., "this will come clear" refers to the idea that the thoughts of women are not easily understood; according to G., it refers to Śūrpaṇakhā's intention.

45. 2873

"My troubled life" is interpreted by G. as "my life that [should be] happy." In Tamil, the first half is involuted, probably to reflect the devious mind of Śūrpaṇakhā: "saying that [women] themselves telling the desire they feel is right is not befitting for women of noble families."

46. 2874

"Feelings," *ēṇ*, is translated according to G., who says it means "states," a meaning not given by the *Tamil Lexicon.* Crit. says this means "strengths," but that makes no sense. Another meaning in the *Lexicon* is "boundary," from which G. evidently gets his "states."

48. 2876

"Hours," *poḻutu*, which is literally one of the six four-hour divisions of a day. Crit. reminds us that the purpose of being a woman is to live with a husband.

49. 2877

"He who gives everything"—literally, "the generous one." Rāma says that he, as a Kṣatriya (the second *varṇa*), cannot marry a woman who is a Brahmin (and belongs to the first *varṇa*).

50. 2878

"The Vedas" here is *āraṇam*, from *Āraṇyaka*, used to mean all the Vedas. Śūrpaṇakhā's point is that even though her father is a Brahmin, her mother is an Asura, and so she is not really a Brahmin. Underlying this and the previous stanza is the notion that sexual union itself is a form of marriage, called a Gandharva marriage.

52. 2880

So Crit. G. has a different reading for the first part: "I am a Vidyādhara woman [see Glossary], hard to describe; not investigating my birth, [your] saying that I am Rāvaṇa's sister is pure ignorance." For how she worshiped the gods, see 41 above.

54. 2882

See the note on 50 above.

55. 2883

"All who do tapas"—i.e., ascetics in the forest. The text here is *muṉivar*.

57. 2885

"In the eyes" could also mean "that hurts the eyes." Crit., taking the first of these meanings, clarifies, "Rāma who shows favor standing as light in the eyes of everyone." "Of the trees" is added at the suggestion of the commentaries. "A jeweled vine rising from the earth" is literally "like a vañci [vine] that came as [a mass of] jewels from [or on] the earth." Crit. says this refers to Sītā's birth from a furrow (see the notes to 3241). "For the salvation of the gods" is literally "because of a good boon gotten by the gods."

58. 2886

"As if burned by hot meat"—this is not entirely clear. The text has no "as if"; we have added that for clarity. G. interprets, "whose mouth gaped [open], yearning to cook meat," while Crit. says, "whose mouth gaped open as she suffered because meat [just taken from the fire] burned [her mouth]." Both commentators take this as a sign of Śūrpaṇakhā's meanness and cruelty. Crit. adds that it shows her stupidity, as she lacks the sense to make sure food is cool enough to eat before putting it in her mouth. This is a good example of the punditry of Indian commentators.

59. 2887

Once again, a character wonders whether someone is a god or not. See stanzas 12 and 36 and the notes on 12.

60. 2888

"Beyond the limits of its creators"—i.e., if there seem to be flaws in beautiful things, that is the fault of the people who made those things, not of beauty itself.

61. 2889

"The god in the lotus" is Brahmā. "Myna bird" is *pūvai*, which G. construes as "parrot."

62. 2890

For "is like gold," G. has "glistens like gold." Śūrpaṇakhā's idea is that Rāma, as an ascetic, could not have his wife with him in the forest.

63. 2891

Śūrpaṇakhā is speaking, telling Rāma that Sītā is really a Rākṣasī.

64. 2892

G. interprets "Your obvious virtue has made this clear to your mind" as "It's obvious you have a good heart."

65. 2893

In Tamil, a woman's arms are often compared to bamboo, the point of comparison being roundness and suppleness.

66. 2894

"A bolt" is added for clarification. For "her waist thin as lightning," G. reads, "she whose lightning-[thin] waist was like a vañci vine." Sītā is light-skinned, and so she appears like lightning against the black body of Rāma.

68. 2896

The names Brahmā, Viṣṇu, and Śiva have been added.

70. 2898

"He has no affection for me at all" is interpretative for the literal "he is not fit," a phrase that can be construed as "he is not fit for me [i.e., is beneath me]" or "he is not fit [for my love, as he does not return it]." This last interpretation seems best here. For "No room in his heart for me," G. says, "No sense of helping me [who need him so much]."

71. 2899

"Golden pollen" is *poṉ*—literally, "gold." It could also mean "loveliness" here.

72. 2900

Śūrpaṇakhā's lovesickness is described in a rhythm of one ***mā*** plus three *viḷams:*

˘ ˘ - | - ˘ ˘ | - ˘ ˘ | - ˘ ˘ |

*aḻinta cintaiya ḷāyayar vālvayiṉ.*

In Tamil, night is conventionally the time that those separated from their lovers suffer the most. "Newly molted" is the interpretation of Crit. for *vaḻinta.* G. takes this as "[whose poison] flows [in abundance]."

74. 2902

Śūrpaṇakhā, angry at the moon and the god of love for tormenting her, wishes to eat them (as Rākṣasas are wont to do to their enemies), but the pleasant wind from the south fills her with anguish and keeps her from fulfilling her intention.

75. 2903

This is a very old image in Tamil, occurring in Caṅkam literature itself, where a young woman's innocence is suggested by describing how she grew angry at the ocean when it took her doll away and tried to fill it with sand (*Aiṅkuṟunūṟu* 124).

77. 2905

For "beyond my reach," G. reads, "is not well-disposed." For the snake that swallows the moon, see "Rāhu" in the Glossary.

78. 2906

The image of "butter . . . on a hot ledge" occurs in a famous Caṅkam poem: "Like butter placed on a hot ledge scorched by the sun, desire spreads . . ." (*Kuṟuntokai* 58). None of the commentators explains how Śūrpaṇakhā obtains ice so readily.

79. 2907

"Arrows" is Crit.'s interpretation of *kaṇ*. This meaning is not given in the *Tamil Lexicon*; G. glosses as "nature." "Love" is Anaṅkaṉ (Skt. Anaṅga), "the bodiless one," a name for Kāma, the god of love.

80. 2908

"By the moon's touch" has been added for clarity. Śūrpaṇakhā is reminded of Rāma by the color of the dark cloud and the dark sapphires. For the moonstone, see "Candrakānta" in the Glossary.

81. 2909

Mountain snakes are considered to be especially venomous. Crit. makes two points: first, Kāma would not come to such a cave, since the snake is an ornament of Śiva (who destroyed the body of Kāma); and second, since the wind and moonlight cannot come into the cave, Kāma cannot see her there.

82. 2910

Rolling on a bed of tender leaves is a traditional recourse (in Indian ornate poetry) for lovelorn women. For the beginning, G. has a different reading: "As the south wind with its great fire became three times more [painful] than before . . ."

85. 2913

For the hot fire at the end of the world, see "Kalpa" in the Glossary.

86. 2914

For "suffering," G. has "desire."

87. 2915

"Darting fish" is literally "Kayal fish."

88. 2916

“Fire,” *aṉal*, is based on G.'s reading. Crit. has *allāl*, “unless” and construes, “Does Kāma who destroys not touch the bodies [of people] unless they feel desire?”

90. 2918

The meter that begins Sūrpaṇakhā's morning and will describe her mutilation begins here. It is a pattern of one *mā* plus three *viḷams* plus one *mā:*

˘ ˘ – | – ˘ ˘ | – ˘ ˘ |
*viṭiyal kāṇṭali ṉīṇṭuṭaṉ*
˘ ˘ ˘ ˘ | – – |
*ṉuyirkaṇṭa veyyāḷ.*

See the notes on 72 above for the meaning of night for a person in love. For “that form that he loves,” G. reads, “[living with] him who is the very form of her love.”

93. 2921

“Thick hair” is a translation of G.'s reading *cil al ōti*—literally, “hair that is not sparse.” Crit. reads *cil val ōti*, “strong sparse hair,” which makes less sense. In Caṅkam literature, the conventional phrase *am cil ōti*, “lovely, sparse hair,” is often used for women's hair. Its meaning seems questionable, as beautiful women are supposed to have thick hair. George Hart's Tamil teacher, Rama Subramanian, said it meant “with five braids.” Crit. says that “welling out like a glowing fire” refers to the redness of the Rākṣasī's hair, while G. says it only suggests its ampleness. As there is no mention of Śūrpaṇakhā's having abandoned her disguise as a beautiful woman, G.'s suggestion seems better here. For “pulled her” (*īrttu*), G. reads *vayiṟṟu*, “stomach,” i.e., “kicked her in the stomach.”

94. 2922

An interesting difference from the Vālmīki *Rāmāyaṇa* is the addition by Kampaṉ of the breasts to the act of mutilation.

95. 2923

“Seemed to be melting the earth with its touch”—literally, “As the bloody fluid flowed . . . , the earth itself grew soft.”

96. 2924

“For killing his enemies”—*kolai tumittu*—is taken by G. as “having refrained from killing [her].”

97. 2925

Khara and the Rākṣasas under his command will be killed by Rāma in the subsequent paṭalam.

98. 2926

"Faint away" is *uyir cōrum*—literally, "grow weak in her precious life."

99. 2927

For "press her nose back on," both commentators say that she tried to tie it on with her dress.

100. 2928

The word used for Death is *kūṟṟu*, often used in Caṅkam literature.

101. 2929

For Śūrpaṇakhā's outcries of pain and rage, Kampaṉ uses four *kāys*, producing long rolling rhythms:

˘ ˘ ˘ ˘ – | ˘ ˘ ˘ ˘ – | – ˘ ˘ – | – ˘ ˘ – |

*nilaiyeṭuttu neṭunilattu nīyirukkat tāpatarkaḷ.*

For the story of Rāvaṇa lifting up Kailāsa, the mountain of Śiva, see "Śiva" in the Glossary. This section is reminiscent of the *Kaṇṇaki Vaḻakkurai* in the *Cilappatikāram*, where Kaṇṇaki, her husband, executed unjustly, calls out for revenge. It involves Tamil beliefs about the power of woman: here as in the *Cilappatikāram*, subsequent misfortune stems from the mistreatment of a woman.

102. 2930

The three gods who are highest are Brahmā, Viṣṇu, and Śiva.

103. 2931

"You saw the back"—a conventional image of victory and of the opponent's disgrace. G. says this stanza is addressed to Indrajit, Rāvaṇa's son, an interpretation that is quite awkward, as the stanzas on either side are clearly addressed to Rāvaṇa. While the encounter between Indrajit and Indra is well known (see "Indrajit" in the Glossary), there is no reason to suppose that Rāvaṇa never encountered the god. See stanzas 3175 and 3532.

104. 2932

"Wind, fire, and water and Death" are construed by G. as the gods Vāyu, Agni, Varuṇa, and Yama, who serve Rāvaṇa in his court—

see 3178, 3181, 3177, and 3180. See "Śiva" in the Glossary for the story of how Rāvaṇa got his sword.

105. 2933

See "Kāma," "Elephants of Space," and "Śiva" in the Glossary.

106. 2934

One of the characteristics of the gods is that their garlands never wither. G. suggests that by "the meat of whose bodies is meant as food for our race" Śūrpaṇakhā means that men's bodies have no strength; Crit. suggests she means that men are good for nothing but food for Rākṣasas.

107. 2935

"You whose hands . . ." is *karaṉēyō*, which G. says is a call to Khara: "O Khara, who are so strong . . ." This makes the whole stanza addressed to Khara instead of Rāvaṇa. In light of the succeeding stanzas, which are clearly addressed to Rāvaṇa, this interpretation seems weak.

108. 2936

The beginning of Paṭalam 7 ("The Killing of Mārīca") describes how the various gods serve Rāvaṇa. See the notes on 104 above.

111. 2939

The nephew is Indrajit, "Conqueror of Indra," Rāvaṇa's son (see "Indrajit" in the Glossary).

112. 2940

"In chains" —not in the text but supplied by the commentaries of both Crit. and G.

113. 2941

Dūṣaṇa is one of Rāvaṇa's generals. Kumbhakarṇa is Rāvaṇa's brother. Kumbhakarṇa did tapas along with Rāvaṇa to get boons (see "Rāvaṇa" in the Glossary), and, after Brahmā granted Rāvaṇa the boon to be killed only by a man, the gods were afraid that Kumbhakarṇa might get an equally powerful boon. They had Sarasvatī, the goddess of speech, dance on his tongue, so that, instead of *nirdevatvam*—absence of gods—he asked for *nidratvam*—sleep. Henceforth, Kumbhakarṇa slept for six months of the year.

114. 2942

"Beautiful earth" is *poṉ tuṉṉum paṭi.* Crit. takes *poṉ* in its more literal meaning here: earth [covered with] gold [dust]. "The full morning rites of his tapas"—Crit. suggest this is *sandhyāvandanam*, the morning prayers, and that they are obligatory for Rāma because he has become a forest ascetic.

115. 2943

To beat one's belly is a traditional expression of grief.

116. 2944

It is inauspicious for a woman to have her hair spread out and disarranged. G. remarks that since Śūrpaṇakhā has been disfigured, she is so ugly that Rāma cannot recognize her as the same woman who came the day before.

117. 2945

"Who holds . . . by his cruel spear" is literally "who holds . . . and has a cruel spear."

118. 2946

"The Rākṣasas with all their power" is literally "the worthy Rākṣasas." Crit. clarifies: "The Rākṣasas who have all the power you mentioned."

119. 2947

"Was it you walking . . ." is literally, "Oh, so are we the one who walked . . ." "Lovely fishes:" literally, "red kayal fish."

121. 2949

"Rākṣasas" is added for clarification at the suggestion of the commentaries.

122. 2950

"Where . . . a pregnant frog . . ."—this is a comic version of a Caṅkam *uḷḷurai* ("inscape"—A. K. Ramanujan's translation) in which a visual image from the natural world mirrors some aspect of love. This particular *uḷḷurai* belongs to the *tiṇai* of *neytal*, which uses the landscape of the seashore (see the notes on stanza 1 above). The situation suggested here is more commonly found with the *tiṇai* of *marutam* than with *neytal.* It concerns the conduct of a husband who, when his wife is pregnant or after she has had a child, often becomes involved with courtesans. Such poems can be placed in the mouth of any of the characters involved. According to G., in this *uḷḷurai*, the frog's mate suspects him of having copulated with the conch.

123. 2951

"Who fight in their strength against the weak" is literally "strong in cowardly battle." Crit. remarks that the Rākṣasas are cowardly because they fight enemies weaker than they are. "Forest where truth is sought" is literally "forest of truth." Crit. interprets differently and says this means that the forest has truth because ascetics who always speak the truth stay there.

125. 2953

"Cultured gentleman" is *nākarikar*—literally, "person associated with a city." The word *nākarikam* is used even today for "civilization." "Barren ground" is *pulliṭai*, which G. takes literally as "in the grass" (taking *iṭai* as "in"); however, *pul* often has a connotation of lowness and worthlessness; hence Crit.'s interpretation "dirty place" and our translation.

126. 2954

Both commentaries change the word order and interpret, "If you protect me, I will protect you; if not, who will protect you? For, because there is that Rāvaṇa, the gods . . . protect their own heads."

129. 2957

Literally, "Won't you tell me . . . who is fit to be compared with me . . . in their family, their excellence, their ability to bring whatever things they want, their knowledge, their form, their youth?"

132. 2960

Brahmā has four faces, each of which faces a different direction.

133. 2961

The Paṭalam concludes with a meter that lengthens the previous one, four *kāys* plus two *mās*:

- ˘ ˘ - | ˘ ˘ ˘ ˘ - | ˘ ˘ - - |

*poṉṉuruvap porukaḻalīr puḻaikāṇa*

- ˘ ˘ - | ˘ ˘ - | - - |

*mūkkarivāṉ poruḷvē ṟuṇṭō.*

The last line reads literally, "It's because I knew that, isn't it, that my love has doubled. Don't I know?" Crit. says she means that she is not so stupid that she would love someone who tried to hurt her.

135. 2963

See the Glossary for "Tāḍakā." G. interprets "live in this forest" as "born on this earth."

137. 2964

The Yakṣas are mentioned because their king, Kubera, is also Śūrpaṇakhā's brother. See "Yakṣa" in the Glossary.

139. 2967

"Intricate" is *poṟiyiṉ*. The word *poṟi* can mean the five senses, knowledge, and machine. Crit. here takes the second of these meanings; hence, "intricate." G. takes the first and construes "machines that cheat like the [five] senses."

140. 2968

"Him who has imprisoned the sun and the moon"—Rāvaṇa. G. has a different reading and interpretation: "[If you think you should keep Sītā, and if you intend battle, then] coming and joining the three [of us together] with the thought, 'We will take the field,' you should realize, 'after killing the [Rākṣasa] heroes who have strength and are cruel, she will not draw back before him who put the two planets in jail,' [and so] you should marry me to the young king [Lakṣmaṇa]."

141. 2969

"A woman who has no waist at all"—in Tamil it is conventional to describe a woman's beauty in terms of her large breasts, hips, and tiny waist. Sometimes, as here, this is taken to the extent of saying a beautiful woman has no waist at all.

143. 2971

"I will bring him"—i.e., Khara, the Rākṣasa general who is guarding Śūrpaṇakhā. "Your Death" is *kūṟṟuvaṉai*, the Tamil personification of death. "Hatred that had no calming" is G.'s gloss for *calam*.

## Paṭalam Six

2. 2973

Pariahs beating large drums would serve to announce the king's decrees to the people in Tamilnad. It is a Tamil poetic convention that cobras are attacked and killed by thunder.

3. 2974

"Anger at her words" is a literal translation. Crit. says it means anger at the words she would say, while G. says it means anger fiercer than words. For "his eyes stared fixed on the blood streaming from her nose," G. has "[and] she whose eyes were bathed in the blood from her nose [said the following]."

8. 2979

This is Crit.'s version. G. reads, "He heard her speak, he who [had not] seen [her nose until then], and saying, 'Show me your nose that has a hole like a dug-out palmyra fruit,' he rose . . ."

11. 2982

"Iron bars"—*tōmarams.* According to Crit., these are "pestles," i.e., iron bars shaped like pestles and used as a weapon. "Nooses of the God of Death" are, according to Crit., nooses that Yama holds in his hand and uses to kill creatures.

12. 2983

"What good is it to serve you unless we can do our work?" is literally, "What a good thing is our work as your servants!" This is said ironically: the troops are upset that Khara appears to be going into battle without them; hence our translation. The last part of the stanza is a bit hard to construe. Crit. takes it as meaning "If you go against the gods, that would be proper. [But] you are not going against them; you are going against men. And because you are going without ordering us [to go with you], though we stay here, we die."

15. 2986

According to G., the deity that Rāma keeps in his thoughts is Śrīraṅganātha, the Viṣṇu at the temple in Śrīraṅga; Crit. says it is his family god.

16. 2987

"Our king" refers to Khara; in South India, anyone in authority is considered a king under some circumstances. "As if they were encircling a mountain" is, according to G., "as if they were surrounding mountains."

18. 2989

By *cālai*, "hut," the text means *parṇaśālā*, "hut of leaves."

19. 2990

"Twenty-eight columns": Rāma is fighting fourteen Rākṣasas.

23. 2994

In Caṅkam literature, the drum mentioned here, the *muracu*, is the king's special drum, which was thought to give title to the kingdom. A different drum, the *taṇṇumai*, is beaten atop the elephant to tell of impending battle. Here, however, the word *muracu* is qualified by *mā*, "great"—perhaps meaning "the great *muracu* [as opposed to the normal, smaller one]." In any event, this same drum is called *pēri* (from Sanskrit *bheri*) in the next stanza. It would appear that the drums have changed somewhat from Caṅkam times. G. has several different readings and a different interpretation of this stanza: "As he ordered, 'Summon the strong Rākṣasa army,' his servants ran and in a moment raised the drum that [roared] like a cloud big atop the elephant, and they roared so even lions were afraid in their caves."

25. 2996

G. has different readings and construes: "The great drum of war [like] the roaring 'pom' [of the ocean], the long, great chariots [like] the waves of the water, [the army] arose roaring like the black ocean [sounding] like a thundering black cloud, whipped by the wind (*kāl*) at the end [of the yuga]. "

26. 2997

"Like a forest that had surged up so . . . it was hiding the sky" is G.'s interpretation. Crit. construes, "The great flags that spread everywhere, high, pressing on the forest and hiding the sky . . ."

27. 2998

In Indian languages, the normal word for an elephant's trunk is "hand." Thus the natural comparison of the trunk with the arms of the soldiers.

28. 2999

The "eye" of the drum is a spot rubbed on its skin. Presumably, the *muruṭu* drum has an eye on each of its two heads. G. points out the aptness of the simile in this stanza: Rāma is in the line of the sun, while the Rākṣasas are as black as darkness.

29. 3000

For the snake that supports the world, see "Śeṣa" in the Glossary. G. makes this plural: snakes, i.e., Ādiśeṣa etc., who carry the world.

31. 3002

"Mighty elephants" is *miḷikaḷ*. According to G., some construe this as "strong men," while Crit. says it means "demons." In G., "twisted demons" is *kūḷikaḷ*, which, according to the *Tamil Lexicon*, can mean just demon or may refer to a "dwarfish, malformed race of goblins constituting the army of Śiva." Crit. has *pūtaṅkaḷ*, "demons" or "ghosts," here.

32. 3003

"Monsters that ride the winds" is interpretative for *kāṟṟu iṉam*—literally, "wind hordes." G. says this means demons who assume the form of winds, while Crit. takes it with "donkeys" and says "yoked to donkeys that were like tying up the gathering of the winds." For "vultures who encircled the world as they appeared in all the directions," Crit. construes, "yoked to birds who [could] encircle the world the moment they were born."

34. 3005

"Staffs" translates *eḻu*, "pike-staffs" or "curving sticks." "War hammers" is *mucuṇṭi*, which according to G. is a small sword but according to the *Tamil Lexicon* is a sledgelike weapon of war. For "entire boulders, war hammers," G. reads "war hammers [*macuṇṭis*] that take [men's] whole [bodies]." See the notes on stanza 11 for iron bars and nooses of Death.

35. 3006

"Missiles" is Crit.'s meaning for *pālam*; G. says it means "twisted club." "Balls of fire" is what Crit. says *pantam* means; G. says it is a chainlike weapon that binds.

41. 3012

"Ferocious fires"—Crit. says this means underwater fire. See "Underwater Fire" in the Glossary.

44. 3015

"Casually"—Crit. points out that it would make sense to be afraid of the Rākṣasas when one is fighting them; but here Indra is frightened at even an ordinary time. "For lack of battles where all the three worlds come unhinged . . ." is literally "not having a battle in the three worlds that experience destruction, not keeping their form." According to G., this has two interpretations: 1. it is the shoulders that lose their form and are destroyed because they cannot have a battle; or 2. the worlds lose their form because they cannot support the Rākṣasas.

Our translation gives yet a different possibility. Crit. has a different reading and construes the stanza differently: "If they whose mountain shoulders itch, not getting a battle that consumes flesh, glance that way with anxious faces, even the king of gods on his rutting elephant whose tusks do not break would show his back [and flee]; the worlds, not bearing their [i.e., the Rākṣasas'] forms [i.e., their weight], would be destroyed."

46. 3017

"Proud" is *uvakaiyar*; it could also mean "happy."

49. 3020

See "World" in the Glossary.

50. 3021

"Scimitars" is *vāḷ*, whose usual meaning is just "sword." As this same word occurs in the previous stanza, G. says it means "scimitar" here.

51. 3022

"Conches" is Crit.'s interpretation of *kōṭu*. G. says this just means "sound" and goes with "drums."

53. 3024

"Chariots hanging golden ornaments" is literally "chariots possessing gold *tacumpu* ornaments." This is a decoration used at the top of an arch or roof that looks like an upside-down pot. "Deepest, finest gold" translates *paim poṉ*—literally, "yellow gold." This is an exceptionally fine kind of gold that is greenish yellow. G. interprets, "Even the chariot of yellow gold of the sun, [yoked to] yellow horses, became white."

56. 3027

The disease here is, according to the commentators, part of the perfected yogi's *prārabdhakarma*, the karma whose seeds are left over from before he was perfected and that must bear fruit before he can attain release from transmigration. Obviously, one facet of the *prārabdhakarma* is the disease that will kill the yogi when he dies.

59. 3030

For "uproar," G. reads "distress," i.e., "seeing the distress [of the lions and yāḷis fleeing]."

60. 3031

"Where light hovered" could also mean "that had light like lightning." According to G., "edged with gold" (*poṉ niṉṟa viṭimpiṉ*) means "with lovely tips"; Crit. says it means "with rims that have gold decorations."

61. 3032

"Of their liberation" is added at G.'s suggestion. "Whose hair has the smell of flowers" is *veṟik koḷ pūṅkuḻaliṉāḷai.* Crit. says "whose hair has flowers with fragrance," while G. construes, "whose hair has [natural] fragrance and flowers." It is an ancient debate in Tamil whether a woman's hair has natural fragrance. The poet Nakkīrar is said to have bettered Śiva himself by challenging the god when he said a woman's hair has natural fragrance. In Tamil, the sentences of this stanza are intertwined, giving a sense of urgency.

62. 3033

"The dark being with eyes like lotuses" is G.'s interpretation; Crit. says it means "he whose eyes were [like] black-colored lotuses." In the stanza, the order of the actions is: he put on his quiver, took up his bow, and put on his armor. Both commentaries change this order to that given by the translation.

63. 3034

According to Crit., Rāma is telling Lakṣmaṇa to leave the fighting to him. G. reverses this, and says Lakṣmaṇa is speaking to Rāma. The first of these seems better to us.

64. 3035

For "consented," G. has a negative (see the note on the preceding stanza): "As soon as the younger hero said this, Rāma did not agree." "In the hut" is added at Crit.'s suggestion.

65. 3036

Sītā's face is like the moon flowering on the vine of her body. A king going to battle is often compared to a tiger setting out from its cave in Caṅkam literature (for example, *Puṟanāṉūṟu* 52). Here, the tiger has been changed to a lion.

66. 3037

The sticks of bamboo rub against one another, kindling a fire.

67. 3038

"I will wear the vākai garland of victories"—literally, "I will gain [the] vākai." G. takes *vākai* as "victory," but its primary sense is the flower worn as a victory garland, which is how Crit. takes it.

68. 3039

"The life of this being who is meat for us"—literally, "the life of this one who has meat."

71. 3042

For "the horses that have such strength," G. reads, "the horses of those [generals] who have such strength."

72. 3043

Only bull elephants produce musth; that females do so here is against nature, and hence an evil omen.

74. 3045

For "enemies," G. reads "the gods."

75. 3046

For "screaming out, 'Grab him! Throw him down!'" G. reads "making noise like thunder [with] their throwing weapons [by crashing them together]."

76. 3047

"In war paint" is literally "with spotted faces." Spots were painted on the faces of elephants for special occasions and for war.

77. 3048

The *Tamil Lexicon* is no help for what kind of arrow the *pallam* was—it just says it means "arrow."

78. 3049

"Bracelets were cut off, axes were cut off together with the arms that held them" is G.'s interpretation. Crit. construes, "Arms were cut off with their bracelets; axes were cut . . ."

80. 3051

"Mountains . . . with arrows through their summits" is G.'s reading. Crit. reads, "like a mountain summit, or like mountains gathered together."

81. 3052

G. interprets "blackened dead trees" (*kār ulavaikaḷ*) as "great tree branches."

82. 3053

Rākṣasas have red hair and black skin. Crit. interprets "red-haired, black-skinned heads" as "great red heads."

83. 3054

It was common in Caṅkam literature to compare war to agriculture. In the stock imagery, the arrows raining down are likened to rain; the bodies with broken necks, to paddy bent over with the weight of its grain; the haystacks, to the piles of corpses; and the buffaloes threshing the grain, to elephants trampling the corpses. "They had altered the old wild state of the forest" means that they had made the wild forest into agricultural land. G. takes this stanza somewhat differently: "Great shores of the huge bodies of mountainlike Rākṣasas appearing in every place made tanks and made rivers. The sharp arrows that made showers made blood so [all those places] were full; and they changed the old state of the forest."

84. 3055

"Mountains"—i.e., elephants, which are often compared to mountains.

87. 3058

"Mountainous elephants"—literally, "mountains with trunks."

88. 3059

For "is it easy . . . ," G. reads "destruction comes easily to those whose bodies are like darkness." "The Order of the World" is *aṟaṉ*, the Tamil word for *dharma*. In Tamil, *aṟaṉ* (or *aṟam*) is often contrasted with *maṟam*, the ethic of killing and war associated with the endemic warfare that prevailed on and off in South India through the centuries. The Hindu "Order of the World," which involved rule by the upper-caste landholders in alliance with the Brahmins, stood in stark contrast with such endemic warfare; hence "whose nature is to give love [or grace—*aruḷ*]." See also the notes on 3245 and 3343.

91. 3062

"Out to the edge of the ocean ring around the world" means, according to G., to Cakrabāla mountain. Apte defines: "a mythical range of mountains supposed to encircle the orb of the earth like a wall and to be the limit of light and darkness." We have not put the mountain in the translation as the text does not refer to it specifically. For "dressed in their earrings," *miḷir kuṇṭala vataṉattaṉa*, Crit. reads *miḷir kuṇṭala mituṉattaṉa*, which he interprets as "[into] the [sign of the zodiac] called Mituṉam [Gemini] that is in the bright ether [*kuṇṭalam*]"; however, his reading could also be construed as "[heads] with pairs [*mituṉattaṉa*] of shining earrings [*kuṇṭalam*]."

92. 3063

"Who had disdained massive Mount Meru"—i.e., who were so huge they put the mountain to shame. G. has a different reading for the phrase about the wounds: "rivers . . . of blood coming from the wounds . . ."

93. 3064

G. interprets "garlands of gold" as "beautiful garlands." "Their bodies in the ocean of blood" is interpretative: "of blood" has been added to fit the context of the next stanza. Crit. says this means their bodies were carried by the rivers of blood and reached the ocean. The point of the stanza is that when the Rākṣasas die, they become gods and then change loyalties. G. has a different reading and interpretation for the end of the stanza: "By the rain of arrows, they gave up the fight; painfully they lost their bodies, and the gods gave voice and cried, 'They have attained undying bodies [in paradise]!'"

94. 3065

In "dense green lotus leaves," "lotus" has been added at G.'s suggestion. Crit. says it means "vines with green leaves," but there is no word in the text meaning "vine."

95. 3066

"Some bathed in the waves of the ocean of blood and fat" is literally "some bathed in the ocean of blood with waves, deep and mixed up." Crit. clarifies: "with fat etc. mixed up in it."

96. 3067

See "Churning of the Ocean" in the Glossary.

97. 3068

"Cloudlike bowman," i.e., black as a storm cloud. See "Śiva" in the Glossary for the story of the three cities.

98. 3069

"Attacked" is *poytār*. The *Tamil Lexicon* says this means "made fall down," while G., unsupported by the *Lexicon*, says "made a game of war." "Iron rods" is according to Crit.; G. says it means "curved sticks." "Of their anger" is added at the suggestion of both commentaries.

99. 3070

G. has "In the arrows that arose from his bow . . ." G. says "halo" is plural.

100. 3071

The beginning is literally, "The red milk [*cem pāl*—this can also mean simply 'blood'] [that came] as copious as rain from the bodies of the cruel ones full of delusion covered the bright earth like a flooding river [or like flooding rivers]." "Seized the lives" is G.'s interpretation. Crit. says "Death's messengers, who go fast and seize lives, with cruel swiftness caught hold of their [own] legs [until the pain from running so fast went away]."

102. 3073

For "as they came," G. reads "with saddles." G. construes, "The arrows that radiated . . ." differently: "the arrows that flew from [Rāma's] bow that was like a cloud [showering down rain] ran and ran into the directions." That the bodies emitted sparks as they died is evidently a sign of their ferocity.

105. 3076

G. interprets, "the wheels, horses, and drivers, cut [in pieces] seemed mountains . . ."

109. 3080

"Knowledges" is *kalai*, "arts and sciences," of which there are said to be sixty-six *kalais*. The Dravidian word, from the root *kal*, "to learn," is the source of the Sanskrit and modern Indian *kalā*, "art."

110. 3081

G. says "below him and above him" means on the earth and in the sky.

113. 3084

"Three-headed warrior": Triśaras—literally, "he who has three heads."

115. 3086

G. says that "dealt with" means that for every weapon shot or thrown at him by the huge army, Rāma shot an arrow and neutralized the weapon.

116. 3087

"Of royalty" is added for clarification.

117. 3088

"Handrests shaped like lotuses"—*koṭiñcu*. The *Lexicon* defines: "an ornamental staff in the form of a lotus, fixed in front of the seat in a chariot and held by the hand as a support." G. has a different reading for this: "the yokes of their horses of cruel anger cut along with their banners."

118. 3089

"Like a rain cloud filling the sky"—Crit. interprets, "like a rain cloud staying in the sky."

119. 3090

"Tossed and quivered" is G.'s suggestion for *āṭuva*, which can also mean "dance." "Sounding anklet" is *pāṭakam*, a kind of leg ornament.

120. 3091

This is a difficult stanza. We have chosen G.'s version, which makes more sense of the text (Crit. leaves "fields" unexplained—see below). "Made new," i.e., made red. "Sharks' fins"—literally, "sharks with high spines." "Saddles looming like ships" is *cilēṭai* (Skt. *śleṣa*), where one word (here, *paṇṇaiya*) has two meanings ("saddles" and "ships"). Crit.'s version is as follows: "Rivers of blood made new [i.e., made red] the ocean, [rivers that had] chowries and white umbrellas as their foam, elephants as dams, whirlpools where headless corpses sank, fields and cool *tuṟais* [watering places] where dense gems of many sorts were heaped."

121. 3092

"Around whose ornamented hair bees circle" is G.'s reading. Crit. reads, "who had curly hair where bees circled."

123. 3094

"The great battle past" is G.'s interpretation of *iru viṉai kaṭantu*. Crit. construes, "having crossed beyond the two actions [i.e., both good and bad karma]."

124. 3095

The idea is that words of false witness destroy the person who utters them—and, according to G., his family as well.

125. 3096

G. and Crit. say the transformation of the worms is effected by the wasps' stinging them. G. remarks, "a kind of bee called a wasp takes worms and keeps stinging them on the head. They, thinking themselves wasps, change into that form, grow wings, and fly away." He speculates that this stanza concerns the development of larvae into wasps. As the Rākṣasas die, they are metamorphosed into gods.

126. 3097

"Pitched" is G.'s interpretation for *calam koḷ*. Crit. takes in its more natural meaning, "very angry," "filled with malevolence."

128. 3099

"That father" is, of course, Daśaratha.

129. 3100

"Engraved with flowers" is Crit.'s interpretation of *pū iyal*. G. says this just means "beautiful" or "shining."

131. 3102

"Streaming" translates *aḻintāl*, which, in addition to its usual meaning of "be destroyed," can mean "to swell," "to increase." G. reads *iḻintāl*, "descending," instead.

133. 3104

"A kite": the toy, not the bird.

134. 3105

"Putting into practice all his great skills of illusion"—literally, "[battle] that had great deception (*māyā*) that was well-developed."

135. 3106

"He came grasping after Rāma"—literally, "he entered," "he went."

137. 3108

"Ran so fast that under their feet . . ." translates G.'s *kāl koṭu paṟappār*—literally, "they flew [i.e., went very fast] using their feet." Crit. reads *kāl koṭu pataippār*, "they trembled [as they] walked."

138. 3109

"Garlanded" is *vēynta*. Crit. remarks that warriors customarily garlanded their weapons. G. glosses this simply as "which they held [in their hands]." "Sank into it" is Crit.'s interpretation of *nilaiyār*—literally, "were without a [steady] state."

140. 3111

G. remarks that these men are looking for a mountain cave to hide in and think the hole in the elephant is such a cave.

141. 3112

"Panicking"—literally, "like that," i.e., in such a state of demoralization. "Men whose hearts" is literally "those whose hearts . . ."; "men" is added at Crit.'s suggestion. G. says this does not refer to all men, just to Rāma and Lakṣmaṇa.

142. 3113

For "will not take you to them" (*kūṭār*), G. reads "are not afraid [of you]" (*kūcār*). "You live like children with fear in your hearts" is literally "they are young and fear is in their hearts." G. has a different reading: "fear, which is cause for blame, is in their hearts."

143. 3114

The highest three gods are Brahmā, Viṣṇu, and Śiva.

144. 3115

For the last part of the stanza, G. reads, "O you who hide [i.e., are in the process of hiding] yourselves in your cities, going and falling [over each other] with swords in your hands! Will you enjoy pleasures as you embrace your women with luscious eyes as their breasts sink into your chests to make you happy?"

145. 3116

The reddish-bronze color that the Rākṣasas' eyes showed before was a sign of anger; their milk-white color now is an indication of fear. To have a back wound is an ignominious mark of cowardice.

147. 3118

"Who live by trade" is G.'s interpretation. Crit. says "of full wealth," but this is farfetched. That the Rākṣasas should have turned their weapons into plow blades means that they have lowered themselves from the Kṣatriya *varṇa*—the second varṇa—to the fourth and lowest varṇa, which in Tamil is the Vēḷāḷaṉ, or cultivator of land, instead of the Śūdra, or servant in the Sanskrit system. In a hierarchical culture like that of South India, this is a strong insult (even though the Tamils do not really have varṇa—see "Varṇa" in the Glossary).

148. 3119

Each major Rākṣasa has his own army that fights with him.

149. 3120

See the notes on 117 above for the arm support of a Tamil chariot. This stanza describes the fourfold army (*caturaṅgasenā*—"army that has four limbs") that consists of infantry, elephants, chariots, and cavalry. G., implausibly, does not accept this and construes *paṭai* in the first line as "weapon" instead of "infantry": "strong weapons with hands [still holding them] were cut [i.e., hands were cut off along with the weapons in them]."

151. 3122

"Chests" is *āvi*, which Crit. takes in its more normal sense of "life."

152. 3123

"As if at play" is G.'s interpretation of *āṭal koṇṭaṉaṉ*; Crit. says it means "he who had victory."

153. 3124

"Their thinking blurred by burning rage"—literally, according to Crit., "of hot anger that obscured [their knowledge]." G. interprets (taking this with the next phrase), "who hid the [very] directions they were in by their numbers."

155. 3126

See stanza 23 of the previous Paṭalam for another reference to the tufts worn by soldiers in ancient Tamilnad. "Generals of his own clan" is G.'s suggestion for "Rākṣasas from his own race [or clan]."

157. 3128

G. has "the moon that makes the darkness of the world go away"; he says the moon is compared to Rāma on account of its coolness. Crit. comments that usually Death seeks out life, while here the process is reversed. The chariot has difficulty moving because of the piled corpses it must go over.

158. 3129

G. reads "The pure one who looked at Dūṣaṇa . . . with grace favored him a little bit . . ."

159. 3130

The problems with this difficult stanza are two. First, what does *vaṭṭam* (here translated as "circling") mean? Most probably it means that if you go around from one direction to the other you travel in a circle. More difficult is "one of the two who are along with the eight . . ." Both commentators give as their first choice the following: the two are Ādikūrma and Ādiśeṣa, the primeval tortoise and snake who support the world. The one of the two means Ādiśeṣa, the snake, one of whose *aṃśas*—partial manifestations—is the *pāduka*, or sandal of Rāma. G. clarifies: "When Rāma went to live in the forest and was staying at Citrakūṭa [mountain], Bharata came from Ayodhyā and begged him to come back and rule the kingdom. That lord did not agree, but to make him happy gave him his sandal and sent him back. Bharata took the sandal to Ayodhyā, installed it on the throne, put a crown on it, and, treating it as a king and himself as subordinate to it, looked after the affairs of the kingdom until Rāma should return." Alternatively, G. suggests that the two might be Viṣṇu's two implements, the conch and the wheel, and that the "one" means "Bharata, who was an *aṃśa* of one of these and was left to rule the kingdom by Rāma." In that case, the elephants have to be construed as follows: "The two (weapons) [which support, i.e., protect] the earth just as the elephants support [i.e., hold up] it." See "Elephants of Space" in the Glossary.

162. 3133

Crit. interprets "nor army" as "nor weapon." For "murderous elephant," G. reads "elephant of good lineage."

164. 3135

"The snake" is literally "that endless one." See "Śeṣa" in the Glossary.

165. 3036

"And the horses and chariots"—Crit. takes this as "horses [yoked to] chariots," while G. says, "chariots with horses [yoked to them]." "Crowned heads"—or "heads with tufts." "Right" is added at Crit.'s suggestion—evidently, warriors did not wear bracelets on their left arms.

168. 3139

"In secret" is *maṉṟiṭai*, which Crit. takes as "court of justice"—presumably, the court where the king dispenses justice. We have followed G., who says this means "a place outside."

169. 3140

See "Churning of the Ocean" in the Glossary.

171. 3142

See "Śiva" in the Glossary for "the god whose neck is like a dark jewel" and how Rāma broke his bow.

173. 3144

See "World" in the Glossary for the Seven Worlds.

174. 3145

"Bit his lower lip with his white teeth" is G.'s interpretation of "his white teeth moving [over] his [lower] lip."

177. 3148

Crit. comments on "as was proper": "When a warrior who is fighting is without his weapon, he stretches his hand out to the servant who is standing behind him and giving him the weapons he needs, and he gets the weapon that he requires." G. construes, "agreement previously made." He comments, "After Rāma vanquished Paraśurāma, he gave to Varuṇa the Viṣṇudhanus [the bow of Viṣṇu] he had gotten from Paraśurāma, and he ordered him to keep it carefully and give it back at the proper time." See the story in the next stanza; obviously this interpretation is preferable to Crit.'s.

178. 3149

The story of the bow, as told by G., is as follows: Once Viśvakarmā made two bows. One was taken by Śiva, the other by Viṣṇu. The gods wished to see which was best, and so Brahmā started a fight between Śiva and Viṣṇu. As they were fighting, Śiva's bow was a little broken. Śiva gave the bow to a king named Devarādha of the line of Janaka. That ultimately was handed down all the way to Janakamahārāja (the father of Sītā), who made bending it the test to be passed for a man to marry Sītā. It was broken by Rāma. Now the bow of Viṣṇu, which wasn't broken, was given by Viṣṇu to Rucikamuni. It passed on to his son Jamadagni, and to his son Paraśurāma. Paraśurāma, who wanted to end the race of Kṣatriyas, heard that Rāma had broken Śiva's bow, grew angry, came, and said, "It's no big thing to bend a bow that's already broken. Try bending this bow." And he gave Rāma Viṣṇu's bow, which was in his hand. Rāma easily bent the bow, strung it, fitted an arrow to it, and asked, "What is the proper target for this?" Then, he destroyed the strength of Paraśurāma's tapas with the arrow and so vanquished him. Then Rāma gave that bow to Varuṇa, who was among the gods who had come and were praising him, and told him to keep it safely. He (Varuṇa) gave it to Rāma when he was in Agastya's ashram in the Daṇḍaka forest, but Rāma gave it back to him and told him to keep it safely and give it at a time when it was needed. Thus Varuṇa now brought it and gave it to him.

179. 3150

"The right path" is literally "the way." It is a bad omen for the left arm or eye to twitch.

180. 3151

Death is dancing in joy at the prospect of taking so many lives. G. omits "deadly."

183. 3154

"Iron bar" is *ulakkai*, a pestle. See the notes to 11 above.

185. 3156

In this elaborate conceit, the death of Khara is said to be as bad for Rāvaṇa as if one of his ten heads were cut off.

186. 3157

Crit. says that the white flowers are from the heavenly kalpaka tree.

187. 3158

Sītā without Rāma is compared to a lifeless body lying on a battlefield.

188. 3159

"Who had been freed for heaven"—literally, "who had gone to the sky."

189. 3160

"To the great ocean"—so G.; Crit. has "to the distant directions." G. construes "the voice of united oceans" as "the ocean whose waves come in a row."

192. 3163

"She, the means" is *kuṟittāḷ*—literally, "she who had the intention [or aim]." "A great wind building to a cyclone" is literally "the strong, great whirling wind that attacks."

## Paṭalam Seven

1. 3164

The word translated "that now has vanished" in this and following stanzas, *maṉ*, is a particle implying, among other things, change, transformation, what is past and gone.

2. 3165

According to G., Takṣan's ability to make whatever he thinks of is compared to the power of a righteous action to grant a wished-for result.

3. 3166

It is conventionally said that great kings, who never bow their heads to enemies, at least submit to their wives in lovers' quarrels. Rāvaṇa is portrayed as being so proud that he has never even bowed to his women.

4. 3167

The sun is supposed to rise from behind *udaya* ("sunrise") mountain. See "Elephants of Space" and "Kalpa" in the Glossary.

5. 3168

In Indian folklore, cobras are thought to carry light-emitting jewels on top of their hoods. The snake here is Śeṣa (see Glossary), who is supposed to support the earth.

11. 3174

The land of the dead is traditionally supposed to be in the south. Its king is Yama (see Glossary).

12. 3175

See "Kailāsa," "Elephants of Space," and "Indra" in the Glossary.

13. 3176

"Vedas as sweet music"—Crit. takes this as meaning "Veda of music." See "Nārada" in the Glossary. The tāla is the rhythmical beat of a song, while the rāga is its musical mode.

14. 3177

"Trees of the gods"—see "Kalpaka" in the Glossary.

16. 3179

Bṛhaspati, the preceptor of the gods, is identified with the planet Jupiter (called simply "gold" in the text). The evening star, Śukra (Tamil Veḷḷi, "silver"), is the preceptor of the demons.

17. 3180

Yama covers his mouth so that his saliva will not unwittingly spray out and contaminate anyone. Even today, in some Tamil parts of Ceylon, some lower castes cover their mouths when they talk to people of much higher status.

19. 3182

All of these objects are known for giving in abundance whatever one desires. See "Kalpaka," "Cintāmaṇi," "Kāmadhenu," and "Kubera" in the Glossary.

24. 3187

Śūrpaṇakhā has no earrings because, of course, her ears have been cut off.

31. 3194

Viṣṇu is thought to rest on a snake in the primeval ocean; Śiva lives on his mountain, Kailāsa.

34. 3197

For "new world era," see "Kalpa" in the Glossary.

38. 3201

"Plowing with the sword"—i.e., fighting in battle.

46. 3209

See "Śeṣa" and "Elephants of Space" in the Glossary.

54. 3217

As a condition of going to the forest, Rāma and Lakṣmaṇa have to dress as ascetics; hence the bark garments. Yet they still have the anklets of warriors. The sacred thread is a mark of the twice-born *varṇas*, of which the kingly (or Kṣatriya) varṇa is one—see "Varṇa" in the Glossary.

58. 3221

"As if unused"—so G. for *viruntu*. Crit. takes the other meaning of this word and construes, "that [is honored] like a guest."

59. 3222

"Can you say it will return to me . . ." is G.'s interpretation. Crit. suggests, "Can you say it [i.e., Śūrpaṇakhā's nose] will return [to her face] . . ."

60. 3223

The god who drank the ocean's poison is Śiva. See that entry in the Glossary for the stories referred to here.

64. 3227

The sun's rays cause the lotus to open in the morning.

66. 3229

The point of the first image is that ghee, when poured into a fire, goes into it and is part of it while it feeds it; just so, his grief was part of his anger, even as it fed it. See "Underwater Fire" in the Glossary.

67. 3230

The goddess Śrī sits on a lotus. Here Sītā is obliquely compared to her.

69. 3232

"Who sing the rāgas melodiously"—literally, "who have singing melodious with the *kāmara* rāga."

71. 3234

For the story of Śiva and Kāma, see "Kāma" in the Glossary. G. suggests that the smell of Sītā's hair here is natural, thus raising a controversy that is quite ancient in Tamil literature. See the note on stanza 61 of Paṭalam 6.

72. 3235

"Our enemies"—the gods. The three worlds are heaven, earth, and the underworld (where the Nāgas live).

74. 3237

In addition to "grass," *pul* can mean "baseness, lowness, meanness."

75. 3238

See the note on the next stanza. The god with six faces is Skanda, also known as Murukaṉ in Tamil.

76. 3239

Umā, the wife of Śiva, is sometimes considered a part of that god, whom he may manifest at will. One of his forms is Ardhanārīśvara, "the half-man, half-woman," which may be seen in many sculptures. Viṣṇu is supposed to hold his wife Śrī against his chest, while Brahmā sustains Sarasvatī on his tongue.

77. 3240

"You will not go wrong"—both commentaries construe this as meaning, "you will not act contrary to Sītā's desires; you will give her whatever she wants." "Plunder" is G.'s plausible suggestion for *koḷḷai*. Crit. says this means "wealth that is taken [from your other wives]."

78. 3241

See "Churning of the Ocean" in the Glossary. Of Sītā, Apte writes, "She was so called [her name means furrow] because she was supposed to have sprung from a furrow made by king Janaka while plowing the ground to prepare it for a sacrifice which he had instituted to obtain progeny."

82. 3245

"Courage" is *maṟaṉ*, whose connotations include valor, cruelty, and an unreasoning warlike mentality—the word can be used in either a positive or negative way. It is often contrasted with *aṟam*, which is the Tamil word for *dharma*, and stands for a way of life regulated through the Vedas and the institutions of Hinduism rather than by the naked questing after power by military means suggested by maṟaṉ. "Righteous act"—*taṉmam*—is G.'s reading; Crit. reads "an act of tapas" for this. (See also the notes on 3059 and 3343.)

83. 3246

Kāma, the god of love, shot one of his flower arrows at Śiva and made him love Pārvatī. For this sin he was reduced to ashes by the fire from the third eye of Śiva. "Curse" is *varaṉ*, which Crit. says means exalted position. G. says it means those good boons he got by his tapas but remarks that some have construed it as "curse": that Rāvaṇa was cursed by Vedavatī and Rambhā that "If you begin to take a woman by force, you will die."

84. 3247

Crit. notes that Rāvaṇa had learned a thousand Vedas.

85. 3248

The image in this stanza is apparently taken from *Kuṟuntokai* 58, where a woman compares her suffering in love to butter melting on a hot ledge while a man with no hands or feet tries to keep it from melting.

86. 3249

G. remarks, "Just as when a foolish man without learning does evil deeds in secret and they are revealed afterward by fate, so Rāvaṇa's lust first became established in the mind, then spread outward to his five senses."

89. 3252

"Glittering" is *poṅku*, which could also mean "high." "Coverlet of flowers"—Crit. remarks that the bed was decorated with a covering and hanging ornaments made of flowers, pearls, etc.

90. 3253

The meter changes here to a rhythm that is sharply marked and insistent to suggest the anguish of Rāvaṇa. See the Glossary for the "Elephants of Space."

91. 3254

"Not thinking himself evil"—or "not thinking [his desire for another man's wife] evil." The eyes of a beautiful woman are compared to a cut unripe mango because of the curving shape of that fruit. Both of the flowers used as similes for Sītā's eyes—the *kāṉal* and the *kāvi*—mean blue nelumbo, according to the *Tamil Lexicon*.

93. 3256

See "Elephants of Space" in the Glossary.

95. 3258

"Gold-skinned Sarasvatī"—*poṉ*, literally, "gold." Sarasvatī, the goddess of learning, is supposed to be light-skinned, a fact that inspired Vijjakā a Sanskrit poetess, to write a famous verse about the writer on aesthetics, Daṇḍin: "Not knowing that I, Vijjakā, am as dark as the petals of the blue water lily, Daṇḍin said falsely that Sarasvatī is all white." The *yāḻ* is a Tamil lute, used by low-caste bards in Sangam literature.

96. 3259

*Vēṅkai* is *Pterocarpus marsupium*, a tree with small yellowish flowers that is often said to look like a tiger. Trumpet-flower trees are Tamil *pāṭalam*, or *pātiri*. According to the *Tamil Lexicon*, these can be yellow, purple, or white.

99. 3262

The six Tamil seasons are (in Tamil, Sanskrit, and English): *kār*, *varṣa*, rainy season; *kūtir*, *śarad*, autumn; *muṉpaṉi*, *hemanta*, early cold season; *piṉpaṉi*, *śiśira*, late cold season; *vēṉil*, *vasanta*, spring; and *mutuvēṉil*, *grīṣma*, summer. Cold season here is *śiśira*.

100. 3263

"Burning" is *tīya*, and it could also be considered the action of the cold, which turns things black: "the gentle dew [whose coldness] turns trees with strong branches black and enters mountains so they grow cold." In his subcommentary, G. asserts that the poet has skillfully suggested both meanings. The meaning of the statement at the end of the stanza is, evidently, that those with good minds experience happiness, while those with evil minds experience suffering.

103. 3266

"Everything alive" is Crit.'s interpretation. G. says "all the seasons, leaving, did not do [things that were proper] for their various times." The state of Freedom is beautifully described above in the second Paṭalam, stanza 2697: "that place which is imperishable / even when every being is swept away in the great wind, / a place that is utter purity, no growth, no lessening, / the unchanging state beyond the smallness of time."

104. 3267

"The force of self-control" is *cīlattāl* (Skt. *śīla*), literally, "good character."

105. 3268

The cloud, the lotuses, the sandalwood paste, and the pearls are all things that are cooling.

107. 3270

G. and Crit. have different readings and interpretations for this stanza; this translation combines both. Crit. does not have "like a wheel" and construes the simile as "just as those who have been enemies and been defeated go against the strong one [who defeated them] when, because he has ruled in a way that incurs fault, having left the wheel [of law—departing from the proper way], vulnerability comes to him." G. construes, " . . .go against the strong one, harming him so he is destroyed."

108. 3271

The lord who sleeps on the serpent bed is Viṣṇu, whose chief weapon is Sudarśana, his discus.

109. 3272

The moon is said to be a reservoir of amṛta, the drink that confers deathlessness (Greek ambrosia).

110. 3273

In Indian literature, fame is said to be white.

111. 3274

Anklets are worn by warriors; thus, the heroic and warlike nature of Death is suggested here.

113. 3276

G. suggests that Rāvaṇa has never known frustrated desire because he always got any women he wanted easily. The moon is the enemy of the lotus because the lotus closes at night when it comes out.

114. 3277

The moon is marked with a blemish—the sign of a hare—and hence is black inside. This could also mean the moon is angry in its heart. In verse 2.1.6 of Nammāḻvār's *Tiruvāymoḻi*, an almost identical poetic convention is used. There, a woman speaks to the moon, imagining it is also suffering from being in love. Ramanujan translates:

One-day moon:
are you languishing too
like us

with no strength
to drive away the dark today,

faint
and shrinking,

jilted by the true-seeming words
of our lord
fast asleep
on the five-headed serpent,

our lord of the mighty wheel,

have you also lost
the natural light of your body? (A. K. Ramanujan, *Hymns for the Drowning*, page 45.)

115. 3278

G. has a long, involuted note on the flower simile here. He says that, according to some, the simile hinges on the fact that the moon is supposed to close the lotus flower and open the water lily flower. Since the water lilies are inside the lotus, here the moon cannot close the lotus without also closing the water lilies. Nor can it make the water lilies bloom without letting the lotus remain open. Hence its defeat.

117. 3280

One of the central parts of any Vedic sacrifice is pouring the oblation of ghee into the sacred fire.

119. 3282

The next few stanzas describe what has happened because the sun has suddenly appeared at the wrong time.

120. 3283

The men leave for work because the sun has come up and they think it is daytime. For the wives, however, it is still the middle of the night and they are distressed that their husbands have left them alone at such a time.

124. 3287

Certain flowers, such as the lotus, are supposed to close at night and bloom during the day.

126. 3288

For "the length of day become their refuge," Crit. construes, "coming to their nests as places of refuge." Cakravāka birds are supposed to be separated from their mates at night and united with them during the day. They live on the sun's rays.

127. 3290

Some flowers, like the water lily, are supposed to open only at night, and to close in the day.

129. 3292

This is G.'s interpretation. Crit says, "The astrologers . . . did not realize the strength of [his] command [i.e., didn't know he could make the sun rise at the wrong time and so didn't know what was going on]. The cocks that crow were [still] sleeping."

132. 3295

"A dark blue mountain with all his peaks"—Rāvaṇa is black and has ten heads, which have red hair.

133. 3296

What else is as worthwhile as tapas, which gave Rāvaṇa even power to change the phase of the moon?

134. 3297

See "Śeṣa" and "Underwater Fire" in the Glossary.

135. 3298

At the churning of the ocean, Śiva drank the vicious Hālāhala poison, which otherwise would have killed all living creatures, and this turned his throat blue-black. He wears in his hair the Ganges and the crescent moon.

136. 3299

"Black-marked throat"—literally, "with a heart with a black mark." Crit. remarks that a snake's heart is on its neck below its head and that very poisonous snakes have a black mark there.

139. 3302

"The faultless Vedas"—*kēḷvi*, the translation of Sanskrit *śruti*. This could also mean "sacred books."

140. 3303

See "Hālāhala Poison" in the Glossary.

143. 3306

It is common to compare the face of a beautiful woman to the moon.

144. 3307
The poetic conceit is that Sītā's waist is so thin that it is invisible. This is common in Tamil literature.

147. 3310
"Whose energies are so powerful" is construed by Crit. to mean "who have strong legs." *Tāḷ* can mean both effort and leg.

149. 3312
Kings and great heroes are supposed have long arms so that their hands hang down to their knees. G. remarks that connoisseurs should appreciate this section, where Kampaṉ describes the love of Rāvaṇa and Śūrpaṇakhā for Sītā and Rāma in dramatic form. Some, he says, call it "Kampaṉ's play."

150. 3313
"Those whose lot is the earth"—men.

151. 3314
Śūrpaṇakhā means that since everyone knows that Rāvaṇa has a weakness for beautiful women, it is natural that he should mistakenly see Sītā everywhere.

155. 3318
The moonstone is the *candrakānta*, which is supposed to ooze with water under the influence of the moon.

156. 3319
"The carpenter who lives in the great sky" is Viśvakarman, the carpenter of the gods. G. points out that Viśvakarman is able to make anything by thought alone. That he engages in actual exhausting physical labor is a sign of how much he fears Rāvaṇa. The text says only "jewels," but the commentators say that moonstones are meant.

161. 3324
Both commentators point out that at the time of death, the senses withdraw and one becomes unaware of them.

162. 3325
"The realm of Freedom"—*mokṣa*, release from the cycle of transmigration. Amṛta—the ambrosia that gives the gods deathlessness—was the final result of the churning of the ocean. See "Churning of the Ocean" in the Glossary.

163. 3326

"Smoky fragrance"—from incense. See "Churning of the Ocean" for the genesis of amṛta.

164. 3327

"With eyes flowing fire" is G.'s reading for Crit.'s "He whose nature [was such that his eyes would] flow fire."

165. 3328

The god is Vāyu, the wind god.

166. 3329

"Since there is this opening here" is G.'s suggestion. This might also mean, "When [you are] here, there is no obstacle to his entering," in which case the servants are referring to a previous order of Rāvaṇa's to let the south wind in.

169. 3332

The gods and holy men were distressed because, seeing Rāvaṇa's ministers going to Rāvaṇa's palace, they feared something terrible was about to happen.

171. 3334

"Full of fear as soon as Rāvaṇa arrived" is G.'s interpretation. Crit. says this means, "Mārīca who was [there], as soon as that Rāvaṇa arrived full of fear . . ."

172. 3335

Yama is the king of the dead. The king of the gods is Indra, and he lives in paradise, where kalpaka trees give everything one asks.

173. 3336

"Before even the gods"—Crit. points out the force of this: even before the gods, who cower afraid of us.

179. 3342

G. gives the story of Rāvaṇa's tapas: Rāvaṇa went to Gokarṇāśrama to do tapas and fasted a thousand years. Then he cut off one head and two arms and put them in the sacrificial fire. He did this nine times, and sacrificed nine heads and eighteen arms, spending nine thousand years. As he was about to sacrifice his last head, Brahmā appeared to him, gave him his heads (and arms) back and also whatever boons he wanted.

180. 3343

The beginning of the stanza is translated according to G.; it means literally, "Did you gain your wealth by doing tapas in the proper ways, or by *maṟam*? Tell!" Crit. reads, "You gained your wealth by doing tapas in all the proper ways; [yet now] you speak out of *maṟam*." The word *maṟam* is often used to refer to the opposite of *dharma* (translated "the Order of the World.") Its literal meaning is "valor, bravery." As it stands for a militaristic and violent approach to the world, it receives its extended meaning. The translation "from outside, hostile to it" is an attempt to capture this extended meaning of *maṟam*. (See also the notes on 3059 and 3245.)

182. 3345

"Enjoy your handsome self" is G.'s suggestion. Crit. interprets, "How many women as beautiful as Śrī enjoy your wealth." See the Glossary for the story of Ahalyā.

183. 3346

The god who brought the world into being is Brahmā.

187. 3350

Mārīca's mother was Tāḍakā; his brother was Subāhu. See "Mārīca" in the Glossary.

189. 3352

"He who caught the Ganges in his matted hair" is Śiva. See "Kailāsa" in the Glossary for this story.

192. 3355

G. says of this rather strange stanza, "When Śiva was destroying the three cities, it is well known that Meru mountain was his bow. Because Rāma broke Śiva's bow, he refers to it as 'the broken mountain.' Because it was Śiva's bow, (the poet) expresses the similarity between Meru and Śiva's bow that served as the test (for marrying Sītā). The comparison is between the two mountains: Meru is even greater than Kailāsa."

194. 3357

"Herald's drum"—the *paṟai* was beaten by untouchables (pariahs, who got their name from the drum they beat) as they announced edicts of the king and other news.

195. 3358

G. remarks, "When Rāma killed Tāḍakā, at the command of the gods who came rejoicing, the great muni Viśvāmitra gave many divine weapons to that lord (Rāma). They all came happily to Rāma and stood ready to do what he ordered."

196. 3359

Note that Kārtavīryārjuna once defeated Rāvaṇa. The story of Paraśurāma defeating Kārtavīryārjuna is as follows: once when Kārtavīryārjuna stole Jamadagni's oblation cow (*homadhenu*) at his father's behest, Jamadagni's son Paraśurāma killed Kārtavīryārjuna with his axe. Subsequently, Rāma defeated Paraśurāma. The story is that when Rāma was returning from Mithilā after breaking Śiva's bow and winning Sītā, Paraśurāma came up, gave him Viṣṇu's bow, and said, "Bend this if you can." Rāma cocked it and with one arrow destroyed all of Paraśurāma's tapas. (See also the notes on 3479.)

197. 3360

"Your mother's brother" is *mātulaṉ*. In his *Purāṇic Encyclopedia* (in the article on Mārīca), Vettam Mani says that Mārīca is Rāvaṇa's uncle, but he does not explain how or why. None of the genealogies of the two figures appear to intersect.

198. 3361

The beginning of this is translated according to G. Crit. construes, "The king of Rākṣasas, who scorned him [Mārīca] who had spoken after thinking [deeply] of all these things he said . . ." Similarly, the last sentence is translated according to G. Crit. reads, "Is it proper [even] to think that you are someone [who might be of use] to someone else?"

199. 3362

"Aren't these positive, persuasive words" is G.'s interpretation. Crit. says that this is a sarcastic reference to Mārīca's speech: "[Yes, indeed,] those were positive, persuasive things [you said], weren't they!"

202. 3365

"As if he were someone . . ." is literally "like water poured over molten bronze, he began to speak." Both commentators say the point of the simile is that, like the water, Mārīca changed his nature and became humbled. But G. suggests it may also mean that he began to conciliate Rāvaṇa, just as water cools off molten bronze, which is the meaning we have taken.

203. 3366

Rāvaṇa's destruction is at hand, and hence he sees the good advice of Mārīca as bad. G. cites the Sanskrit saying, *vināśakāle viparītabuddhiḥ*—when it is time for one's destruction, his judgment becomes perverse.

205. 3368

See "Mārīca" in the Glossary for the story given here.

212. 3375

G. says that the point of this image is the lack of any recourse: the fish will die whether it stays in its pond or leaves it.

213. 3376

See "Mārīca" in the Glossary for the two stories referred to here.

216. 3379

It is conventional to say that a woman's waist is so thin it seems not to exist. For the first part, we have used G.'s interpretation; Crit. says it means, "Walking so that her waist (*iṭai*), which already hurt because of the words people said [words behind one's back] that 'it [i.e., her waist] is false [i.e., doesn't exist]' hurt [still more]."

221. 3384

Rāma is an avatar of Viṣṇu, who is higher even than Brahmā, the god who sits on a lotus and who created the world.

225. 3388

The story is as follows: The seven sons of Bharadvājamuni practiced yoga, but because of faults in their practice, died without attaining results. In the next birth they were born as sons of Kauśikamuni in Kurukṣetra. After their father died, they became students of Gārgamuni. Once, suffering from hunger, they killed his oblation cow (*homadhenu*), offered some of it as *śrāddha* (offering) to ancestors, and ate the rest. For this they underwent several bad and several good births, the killing being a sin, the offering of śrāddha an act of merit. For their next to last birth, they were born as seven golden geese in Lake Mānasa.

228. 3391

Viṣṇu left the serpent bed, in which he rested on the ocean of milk, in order to be incarnated as Rāma.

234. 3397

"Something fierce and raging"—literally, "those who are fierce and raging," which the commentaries take to refer to Rākṣasas.

235. 3398

G. remarks that Daśaratha got into trouble because he was cursed when an elephant he shot turned out to be a muni in disguise. Crit. adds that kings have a duty to kill dangerous animals and so protect their subjects, but should not kill innocent animals like deer for recreation. "You in whose strong arms the goddess Śrī rests"—the goddess here is *poṉ*, which is usually a name of Śrī. Crit. says that by this the poet means Śrī or Lakṣmī as goddess of heroism; in any case, the sense is to emphasize the heroic nature of Rāma's arms.

236. 3399

Rāma is an incarnation of Viṣṇu, the father of Brahmā.

237. 3400

"If not . . ." Both commentators take this as "If [this] is not [a magic deer] . . ."

240. 3403

See "Mārīca" in the Glossary for this story. At Viśvāmitra's sacrifice, Tāḍakā died when it started, Subāhu as it was happening. Only Mārīca escaped.

243. 3406

See "Vāmana" in the Glossary for the story of the dwarf incarnation of Viṣṇu who measured the three worlds with his foot.

245. 3408

According to Crit., its body indicates that it is a good creature, its actions, that it is bad.

247. 3410

"Lord" is *aiya* (probably from Sanskrit *ārya*). Crit. understands this as from the word for "doubt" or "amazement" (*ai*) and says it means "he whose qualities are amazing."

248. 3411

The dying Rākṣasa called out, "Ah Sītā, Ah Lakṣmaṇa," imitating Rāma's voice. See stanza 3414.

249. 3412

It is uncommon for an older brother to call his younger brother "lord." Here, by doing so, Rāma stresses his appreciation of Lakṣmaṇa.

250. 3413

See "Mārīca" in the Glossary for the story of Viśvāmitra's sacrifice.

## Paṭalam Eight

2. 3418

"Gritted his teeth": according to Crit., this is to disguise his voice.

3. 3419

"My source of life" is *mutal vāḻvu*—or "my foremost life," according to G., who remarks that the best life for a woman is living with her husband. "Fallen in thick fire": G. reads *moy kuḻal* for *moy aḻal:* "(Sītā), whose hair was thick, rolled (on the earth) like a vine that falls (without support)." There is an old Tamil belief that thunder kills cobras, and hence that when thunder comes, cobras hide inside caves and crevices to escape its effects.

6. 3422

"Anywhere near them" is what both commentators say for the literal "the places that surround [all those things]."

7. 3423

For earth etc. see the Glossary under "Great Elements."

8. 3424

"That swarm above and below us" is the interpretation of Crit. G. says it means "would turn upside down and be broken."

14. 3430

Though this sudden forest fire strains the credulity of the reader, both commentators agree on this interpretation. Crit. mentions *Puṟanāṉūṟu* 246, where a queen about to enter the fire of her husband's funeral pyre says that for her, fire and a cool pond spread with flame-red lotuses are the same.

19. 3435

If the gods had not done tapas and if Lakṣmaṇa had not gone, Sītā would not have been taken away and Rāvaṇa would not have been killed.

20. 3436

"Three joined sticks of bamboo"—this is a *tridaṇḍaka*, one of the signs of an ascetic. Crit. says the three sticks imply mindfulness of Brahmā, Viṣṇu, and Śiva, or that they indicate he strives to vanquish the three attachments, which are desire, anger, and delusion.

21. 3437

Rāvaṇa is supposed to know music well and to be a great connoisseur of the arts.

27. 3443

Crit. remarks that the kokila calls without getting tired and it calls when other creatures are asleep at night.

28. 3444

The point of this is that no conventional simile is adequate to describe the intoxication of his eyes; you can only describe the intensity of that intoxication by saying it is like that of his mind. This is like the Sanskrit figure exemplified by the quotation *rāmarāvaṇayor yuddham rāmarāvaṇayor iva*—the fight of Rāma and Rāvaṇa was like the fight of Rāma and Rāvaṇa.

29. 3445

One of the characteristics of the gods is that their eyes never blink. The god Indra has a thousand eyes.

37. 3453

A Hindu woman is not supposed to utter her husband's name. This custom is found in the Tamil Caṅkam literature as well as in classical Sanskrit (Kālidāsa) but is absent in the *Rāmāyaṇa* of Vālmīki.

38. 3454

According to Crit., Rāvaṇa was in Kosala when, in the course of conquering the world, he arrived there and defeated its king Anaraṇya.

39. 3455

Kākutstha means, "he who is descended from Kakutstha." Crit. points out that Sītā avoids saying Rāma, her husband's name, but instead uses this patronymic (see the notes to 37 above).

41. 3457

Rāvaṇa is a Brahmin and is great-grandson of Brahmā. Crit. says that Rāvaṇa first describes his wealth and handsomeness because those are the things that would appeal to a woman.

42. 3458

For the story of Rāvaṇa's seizing Śiva's mountain, see "Kailāsa" in the Glossary. For the story of his subduing the elephants of space, see "Elephants of Space."

46. 3462

See "Three Worlds" in the Glossary.

47. 3463

The god who sits on a lotus is Brahmā. Crit. says Brahmā's boon was that he could not be killed by anyone except a man. He suggests that the constellations are cruel because they determine people's happiness and sorrow, and that if Rāvaṇa had power over them, he must be really strong.

48. 3464

See "Three Gods" in the Glossary.

50. 3466

G. reads, "Then, my heart inclined to leave, I returned here."

53. 3469

G. has a different reading: "When she who was without fault said, 'Cruel-eyed Rākṣasas with swords' and was afraid, he who had no boundary, having heard her, observed her truthfulness and said . . ."

58. 3474

Crit. remarks that if Sītā cries for what happened to the Rākṣasas, their fate must have been terrible indeed. G. reads, "what happened to him . . ." and construes this as meaning Rāma: Sītā wept thinking of the difficulty Rāma suffered in battle.

61. 3477

Crit. remarks that the red silk-cotton flower is light as cotton; when the wind blows, it falls from its tree.

62. 3478

See "Underwater Fire" in the Glossary.

63. 3479

Crit. clarifies: While Rāvaṇa was conquering the world, he went to do battle with Kārtavīryārjuna. Learning he was bathing in the Narmadā, he also bathed there, made a linga on the shore with sand and did ***puja*** (worship). Kārtavīryārjuna, who was relaxing in the water on the opposite side, felt there wasn't enough water for him, and with his five hundred hands made the water come to his side. When the water rolled back, it destroyed Rāvaṇa's Śivaliṅga. Rāvaṇa fought with Kārtavīryārjuna but was imprisoned by him. Subsequently Pulastya went to Kārtavīryārjuna, gave him the title of Rāvaṇajit ("Conqueror of Rāvaṇa"), and gained Rāvaṇa's release. Paraśurāma killed Kārtavīryārjuna when he was stealing Jamadagni's ***homadhenu*** (cow that gives milk for an oblation) from his ashram. (See also the notes on 3359.)

65. 3481

"This person" is ***ivaṉ***, the impolite form of the third person pronoun. It contrasts with the respectful form that she used to refer to him before (e.g., in stanza 25).

67. 3483

Rāvaṇa means he would have lost his life because he loves Sītā so much.

71. 3487

See "Elephants of Space" in the Glossary.

72. 3488

Literally, "a goddess for the goddess." Śrī is added at the suggestion of the commentators. According to Crit., the mountains that support the earth are the eight ***kulamalais***. These are evidently the Sanskrit ***kulācalas***, which Apte says are seven. They are defined as "principal mountains" and are supposed to exist one each in each division of the continent (of India).

74. 3490

G. gives the story as follows: While Rāvaṇa was conquering the world, he set out to go to the world of the gods and went to Kubera's Alakāpurī. He saw Rambhā, the mistress of Kubera's son Nalakūbara, felt desire for her, took her by force, and raped her. She grew angry and said to Rāvaṇa, "If you forcibly touch any woman against her wish, you will be burned by the fire of her chastity and die." Nalakūbara, who learned of that, said, "If Rāvaṇa touches by force anyone else's woman, his head will explode and he will die." Crit. reads "not touching her . . .

because he thought of the curse of Brahmā on him." See "Brahmā" in the Glossary for this story. We have followed G., as the story of Nalakūbara is given in the Vālmīki *Rāmāyaṇa* in the *Uttarakāṇḍa*, while the story followed by Crit. seems less well known.

85. 3501
See "Kailāsa" in the Glossary for the story mentioned here.

86. 3502
"Carved image" is *pāvai*, a word that often means "doll." Another meaning is "pupil of the eye," and G. says that this meaning is also suggested in order to evoke the preciousness of Sītā.

88. 3504
"The sea, swelling . . ." is G.'s interpretation. Crit. takes these verbs with "wind": "which [wind] rises, swelling so the sea and the earth become one and are destroyed."

89. 3505
Garuḍa (see Glossary) is the traditional enemy of cobras.

92. 3508
Literally, "Because he had the strength to block the chariot, he was like . . ." Crit. suggests this stanza refers to an incident where Kailāsa blocked Rāvaṇa's chariot. Jaṭāyus's red body looks like the sunset reflected by the silver mountain Kailāsa.

97. 3513
I.e., you are like someone who tries to stop an elephant charging him by throwing a handful of mud at it.

99. 3515
The savage action is desiring another man's wife.

101. 3517
The god on the bull is Śiva. See "Śiva" in the Glossary.

102. 3518
"The one who lives well in heaven" is Daśaratha, Rāma's father and Jaṭāyus's close friend. This is literally *āḷpavaṉ*, "he who rules."

103. 3519
"Don't spit . . ." is G's interpretation. Crit. says, "Don't drive me off."

104. 3520

The figure of water "eaten" by molten iron appears also in *Puṟanāṉūṟu* 21: "That fortress [of Kāṉappēr] is gone like water vaporized [lit., eaten] by iron heated in a glowing fire by a black-handed smith." The Tamil notion seems to be that the water is absorbed by the molten metal.

107. 3523

Crit. remarks that it is fitting for Rāvaṇa, a fancier of music, to have a veena for his banner. It suggests that he was able to play that instrument so beautifully that he could make an enemy who had come to destroy him give him a boon by his playing.

112. 3528

It is a common conceit in Indian poetry that clouds drink water from the ocean, move to the land, and then rain down the water they have drunk.

116. 3532

See "Indra" and "Śiva" in the Glossary for the stories mentioned here.

117. 3533

"Bow which matched . . ." is G.'s interpretation. Crit. interprets, "his good bow, that was equal to the strength of [Death], who destroys the world . . ."

126. 3542

For G.'s reading, "lost his breath," Crit. has "fainted."

128. 3544

See "Indra" in the Glossary for the story of the mountains losing their wings.

133. 3549

This is reminiscent of the speech of Kaṇṇaki (*Kaṇṇaki Vaḻakkurai*) when her husband has been killed unjustly in the *Cilappatikāram.*

136. 3552

The commentators say this means, "even though I am doing my duty by remaining chaste, the bow of Rāma and my clan incur shame because Rāma doesn't come to rescue me."

137. 3553

“All alone” translates G.’s reading *tanimai.*

140. 3556

Jaṭāyus considers Rāma and Lakṣmaṇa his sons; hence, Sītā is his daughter-in-law.

142. 3558

Viṣṇu is black and lies on a snake in the ocean of milk when the world ends.

143. 3559

See “Brahmā” in the Glossary.

148. 3564

When Rāma left Ayodhyā to go into exile, he left his younger brother Bharata to rule in his stead (as was demanded by his stepmother and Bharata’s mother, Kaikeyī). Bharata did not consent but followed Rāma to the forest to ask him to return and rule, and only consented to be king in Rāma’s stead when asked to do so by Rāma.

149. 3569

Rāma’s skin is the dark cloud; his red eyes, his lips, his hands, and his feet are the lotuses.

154. 3570

Crit. remarks, “While it is *dharma* for a woman to enter the fire with [the corpse of her] dead husband, it is the sin of suicide and against dharma for her to enter the forest fire while her husband is alive.”

159. 3575

“For his old age” is added for clarification by Crit.

160. 3576

Crit. says that everything whirled because the mind of Rāma, who is everything, whirled. G. remarks that Rāma is *sarvāntaryāmin*, the indweller of all (creatures).

162. 3578

See “Kalpa” in the Glossary for a description of beliefs regarding the end of the world. “Together with its creating god [i.e., Brahmā]” is Crit.’s interpretation. G. interprets, “the world ends, [being absorbed] in [Viṣṇu], its root cause.”

168. 3583

The word translated "bamboo" could also mean "mountain," which is how G. takes it.

172. 3588

See "Churning of the Ocean" in the Glossary. The moon is supposed to have sixteen digits. G. has a different reading and construes, "He [whose body is so white it looks like] a digit of the moon must have bitten and broken it."

175. 3591

G. has a different reading: "Bright blood lay with the flesh (of Rāvaṇa); and they came to where he (i.e., Jaṭāyus) lay, as if the sky lay upon the earth." Given the events, Crit.'s reading seems better.

176. 3592

There are twelve suns at the end of the earth—see "Kalpa" in the Glossary. The point of this is the unnatural number of earrings, as Rāvaṇa has ten heads.

178. 3594

"Śrī": Sītā, who is imagined to be either as lovely as Śrī or an avatar of her. Lakṣmaṇa is the son of Sumitrā. "No more than one being . . ."—G. says that Lakṣmaṇa's logic is based on the fact that evidently the being had only one pair of legs and hence could only be one person; Crit. says it is based on his having heard about Rāvaṇa previously.

179. 3595

Crit. interprets a bit differently and says, "like Mount Mandara on the milky ocean in the other world."

180. 3596

Śiva's silver mountain is Kailāsa.

182. 3598

First, Rāma's real father, Daśaratha, died when Rāma went into exile in the forest; now, Jaṭāyus, who was like a father, has died.

183. 3599

"While I, a fool . . ." is G.'s interpretation. Crit. says, "I, foolish, not knowing what will happen in the future, unable to fulfill my duty as a relative—for what purpose do I suffer, my father?"

188. 3604

"Now all my shame is gone"—according to the commentators, Jaṭāyus feels that he can tell Rāma and Lakṣmaṇa what happened to Sītā and that they will surely conquer Rāvaṇa and bring her back, thus removing the shame of his failure.

189. 3605

Smelling a person's head is a sign of affection.

193. 3609

G. remarks, "If something new happens, is that by us? [No, it is by fate.] Pleasure and suffering are from fate. If we accept that, then we can overcome fate by the power of our knowledge; otherwise, we cannot. Thus you should not think it your fault that Sītā was taken."

194. 3610

The story is that one of Brahmā's five heads said, "I am Brahmā, and Śiva is my son." In anger, Śiva cut off that head, leaving Brahmā with only four.

195. 3611

The story is that, as penance for killing one of Brahmā's heads, Śiva had to spend a long period begging, using Brahmā's skull as his begging bowl. An ascetic—someone who performs tapas—often begs. Here Jaṭāyus says that that action was forced on Śiva by fate; it was not part of the god's ascetic practice.

196. 3612

See "Rāhu" (the snake planet) in the Glossary.

197. 3613

The point of the stanza, Crit. says, is that even though Indra did what Bṛhaspati said, it didn't help, as one's fate is determined by karma. G. has a different interpretation, which he supports with a story: "because of the true words (i.e., curse) of Bṛhaspati . . ." He says that once, when Indra was sitting in state, Bṛhaspati arrived, but Indra ignored him. The Asuras heard that Indra was weakened by this slight to Bṛhaspati, attacked him, and defeated him.

198. 3614

G. gives the story of Śambara: An Asura named Śambara, who was skilled in magic, opposed Indra and the other gods, fought them, and won. He took away Indra's kingdom, and Indra went and complained to Daśaratha. That king went, fought, and began to subdue the Asura, who, using his magic power, disappeared and ran away. Daśaratha followed him to all the places he ran to, fought him, destroyed him, took his kingdom, and gave it back to Indra.

199. 3615

Dharma (the Order of the World) has been set aside by the Rākṣasas, who now rule the world.

207. 3623

The sun is supposed to rise from behind Mount Meru, the great mountain around which the heavens turn, in the morning, and to disappear behind that mountain in the evening. The young prince is Lakṣmaṇa.

209. 3625

"The lord who sits on the blossomed lotus" is Brahmā. "Maintain the Order of the World"—literally, "do *dharma.*"

210. 3626

For the story of the churning of the ocean, see "Churning" in the Glossary.

215. 3631

See "Great Elements" in the Glossary.

216. 3632

According to Crit., "those who live in the highest world" are the Nityasūris, immortals residing permanently in Viṣṇu's heaven.

219. 3635).

Lakṣmaṇa says that if Rāma cannot kill Rāvaṇa and thereby remove his shame, he might as well become a true ascetic and renounce all violence—obviously, something that would be demeaning under the circumstances.

223. 3639

Rāma must bathe after the ritually polluting act of cremating the dead body of Jaṭāyus. The water from the river is offered as *tarpaṇa*, an offering given to the spirits of deceased ancestors—in this case, to Jaṭāyus. The shoots are dark like Rāma's skin; the flowers are red like his eyes.

224. 3640

This is a problematic stanza. Since Viṣṇu is the source of all beings, the water he drinks is also drunk by them; hence the first simile. The problem is that Jaṭāyus drinks the water, not Rāma. Crit. says that since Jaṭāyus has bowed to Rāma's feet, he has become identical with him, and that the feeder and eater are ultimately the same, in any event. G. remarks, "as soon as our lord drank a little water, it was as if all beings drank it, since they shared in his being." But he does not explain why Rāma should be drinking the offering he is making to Jaṭāyus.

## Paṭalam Nine

1. 3642

"The summit of which was turning red"—in the evening twilight. G. construes this as "the summit of which was reddish [with the mineral *sindūra* —red lead]." Rākṣasas have black bodies and red hair, and so are compared to the black mountain with a red summit. It is a convention in Tamil to emphasize the suffering of a separated lover at night.

2. 3643

"Their father"—Jaṭāyus.

4. 3645

Lotuses are supposed to close in the night and open when the sun appears at dawn. "Woman, divine and lovely"—literally, "Śrī."

5. 3646

Lakṣmaṇa's eyes did not close because he was guarding Rāma. G. mentions that Lakṣmaṇa stood guard every night through the fourteen years of exile. "Never closed for an instant"—literally, "did not blink."

8. 3649

"He kept thinking of her alone" is G.'s interpretation. Crit. says this means, "He lost consciousness," but this does not fit with the rest of the stanza.

10. 3651

It is a convention for a woman separated from her lover to look in all directions for her beloved to come.

12. 3653

For the snake that eclipses the moon, see "Rāhu" in the Glossary.

20. 3661

The most difficult time for lovers is conventionally said to be the evening. One must suppose that in the previous stanzas, it was still evening verging on night. In a famous poem (*Kuṟuntokai* 234), a woman, separated from her lover, says,

The sun goes down and the sky reddens, pain grows sharp,
light dwindles. Then it is evening
when jasmine flowers open, the deluded say.
But evening is the great brightening dawn
when crested cocks crow all through the tall city
and evening is the whole day
for those without their lovers.

21. 3662

The royal line of Rāma is supposed to go back to the sun.

22. 3663

Aruṇa, the charioteer of the sun, has no thighs and hence is lame.

23. 3664

The *tuṭi* is a small drum shaped like an hourglass.

24. 3665

"They who live with violent courage" is *maṟattiṉārkaḷ*—literally, "those who possess *maṟam*," a word that connotes prowess and valor in war as well as brutishness and violence. It is often contrasted with *dharma* (Tamil *aṟam*—"the Order of the World"), as here. (See the notes on 3059, 3245, and 3343 for more on *maṟam*.) For G.'s interpretation "inflicting torments through their strength," Crit. says, "inflicting all sorts of torments."

25. 3666

Crit. suggests that Kāma, afraid he might be hurt as before by Śiva, does not try to shoot straight but rises up in the sky to shoot from a less vulnerable position. See "Kāma" in the Glossary.

26. 3667

For the story of how Kāma's body was vaporized by Śiva's third eye, see "Kāma" in the Glossary.

27. 3668

See "Kalpa" in the Glossary.

28. 3669

Viṣṇu, whose incarnation Rāma is, sleeps on an ocean of milk. The end of this stanza is translated according to G.'s reading, which seems superior to Crit.'s "[yet] if the few arrows that reminded one of the accoutrements of battle did not sound, was there any way his life could remain?"

30. 3671

"Its summit looked as if a crown had been set down upon it" is G.'s interpretation. Crit. says, "whose summit was set on the crest of the mountains." Sītā is supposed to be an incarnation of the goddess Śrī, who sits upon a lotus. Lotuses close in the evening and open in the morning.

37. 3678

"The dominant in a rāga" is *iḷi*, defined by the *Lexicon* as "the fifth note of the gamut." Indians see a hare in the moon and say that the moon is flawed by the marks in it.

44. 3685

See "Kalpa" in the Glossary for the notion of the end of the universe. A woman's face is usually compared to the cool moon, not the burning sun.

47. 3688

For G.'s "'These eyes are like the burning eyes of Śiva,'" Crit. has "'These eyes are like the fire at the end of the world.'"

48. 3689

The *Lexicon* defines *tāli* as "the central piece of a neck ornament solemnly tied by the bridegroom around the bride's neck as a marriage-badge." Here, it appears to mean just "necklace." A yāḷi has the head of an elephant and the body of a lion. Her necklace consisted, according to Crit., of yāḷis connected together by their trunks and legs.

59. 3700

The black Rākṣasī moving along with the light-colored Lakṣmaṇa resembles a cloud carrying the moon.

60. 3701

Ayomukhī is black like the ocean and cloud; Lakṣmaṇa, white like the mountain and Indra. G. suggests that Ayomukhī is compared to the peacock, the vehicle of Murugan, while Lakṣmaṇa is compared to that god to show the different status of the Rākṣasī and of Rāma's brother. See "Murukaṉ" in the Glossary for the story of his fight with the demon Cūr.

61. 3702

Śiva killed the elephant that appeared at the sacrifice of the munis at Dāru forest, killed it, and wore its skin.

69. 3710

"Hero to whom enemies bow!"—Crit. points out the effect of this: even your enemies bow to you and like you, yet you leave me, who am your older brother and not an enemy, like this.

87. 3728

"Mysterious ocean"—literally, "ocean that is fit for investigation." Crit. says this refers to the riches hidden in the ocean, while G. says the ocean is fit for investigation to determine whether it is in truly endless.

90. 3731

"Even in your anger at what the base woman had said" is G.'s interpretation. Crit. interprets, "even though you saw the acts occasioned by the anger she indulged in with desire," but this is forced.

92. 3733

Crit. suggests Lakṣmaṇa acts with grace by following the rules of his lineage, which forbid killing a woman.

93. 3734

"Varuṇa mantra" is Crit.'s interpretation; G. says they loosed the Varuṇa weapon so rain would come.

97. 3738

It is a common conceit that the waist of a beautiful woman is so thin that it is invisible.

99. 3740

See "Great Elements" in the Glossary. The eyes of beautiful women are conventionally said to be long, reaching almost to their ears.

100. 3741

The blisters in the sky are the stars. "Fire of universal conflagration"—at the end of the world.

## Paṭalam Ten

4. 3746

Ruling with clearly established distinctions means, according to the commentaries, making each *jāti* (caste) do its proper function and act in the proper way.

7. 3749

Rāma and Lakṣmaṇa think that Sītā's chastity is powerful enough to destroy the Rākṣasas who have abducted her by making them attack Rāma, an act that will surely lead to their destruction. See the Glossary under "Nemi."

10. 3752

See "Churning of the Ocean" in the Glossary for the snake Vāsuki that was pulled as the churning rope by the gods and demons.

12. 3754

G. suggests the sharks are compared to his teeth. Since his shape is that of a headless corpse, his mouth is on his stomach. A *kātam* is about ten miles.

13. 3755

See "Churning of the Ocean" in the Glossary.

14. 3756

See "Underwater Fire" in the Glossary.

15. 3757

The Indian notion is that the moon is swallowed by the snake planet: see "Rāhu" in the Glossary.

16. 3758

See "Great Elements" in the Glossary. The five sins are lying, killing, stealing, drinking, desiring another man's wife.

17. 3759

"The fierce serpents"—Rāhu and Ketu. See "Rāhu" in the Glossary. "In idleness" because, according to G., Kabandha had swallowed even the sun and moon.

19. 3761

Kālanemi aided the demons and enabled them to defeat the gods when they were being overcome in battle. The gods all worshiped him, and he became proud and went against Viṣṇu, who had killed his father Hiraṇya. Viṣṇu cut off his hundred heads and hundred arms with his discus, and when Kālanemi still fought on as a headless corpse, Viṣṇu's vehicle Garuḍa felled him with his chest.

20. 3762

The headless Rākṣasa is like the summitless mountain. The story is that once an argument occurred between the wind god and Śeṣa, the snake who supports the world, about their respective strengths. To test this, they had Śeṣa protect the summits of Meru while the wind god tried to blow them off. As Śeṣa surrounded and protected Meru's thousand summits with his thousand hoods, the wind god managed to blow down three of them.

23. 3765

For the boar incarnation of Viṣṇu, see "Varāha" in the Glossary.

26. 3768

The king of Mithilā is Sītā's father.

27. 3769

"That I need to be shielded by my younger brother" is G.'s interpretation. Crit. says this means "I could not protect her; my desire is rather for protecting [i.e., ruling] the earth . . ."

29. 3771

Crit. comments on "Those . . .are heroes who conquer suffering": "Conquering suffering means not grieving when pain happens but conquering the cause of that pain."

37. 3779

Kabandha means that Rāma and Lakṣmaṇa must have bad karma to come to their certain death by confronting him. "In fury" is G.'s interpretation for *uruttaṉar.* Crit. takes the more usual meaning of "were afraid," but this does not suit the context.

40. 3782

The text has only "who rules"; "all beings" is added at Crit.'s suggestion.

41. 3783

G. says that "he who stands there before the eyes of Brahmā and all the other gods" means that he is perceived directly as they meditate on him.

42. 3784

"Witness" is G.'s interpretation of *cāṉṟu*, which Crit. takes as "epitome," a meaning not supported by the *Tamil Lexicon*. G. suggests this means that Rāma is the one who witnesses the good karma people do and ensures that they get the proper good fruit of *dharma*. The highest three are Brahmā, Viṣṇu, and Śiva.

43. 3785

G. says that at the time of Pralaya (the end of the universe—see "Kalpa" in the Glossary), a banyan tree appears in the middle of the ocean and Viṣṇu appears as a child sleeping on one of the leaves of that tree, having swallowed the world into his stomach.

44. 3786

This evidently refers to the eye in its passive and active sense as that through which one perceives and that by which things are perceived.

45. 3787

This is G.'s interpretation. Crit. takes everything in the stanza up to the mass of light as utterances of the Vedas: "Since the Vedas say, 'You are Brahmā . . .'"

46. 3788

This is G.'s interpretation. He remarks that the eight directions are the walls of the great temple [or palace—*kōyil* has both meanings] that is the universe; the fourteen worlds (consisting of seven lower worlds and seven upper worlds) are its stories; the three *maṇḍalas* [the regions of the sun, of Mercury (Budha) and Venus (Śukra)] are its lamps. He further says, "In the highest place, above all worlds in the Tirumāmaṇi Maṇṭapam [the hall of the great jewel], on a *dharmādipīṭha* [the first throne of dharma] that [rests] on Ādiśeṣa [the snake who supports the world], [there is] a twelve-petaled lotus. In the pericarp of its flower, our lord [Viṣṇu] rests." He suggests that the bud is unchanging, not unfolding and then contracting again like a normal lotus.

Crit.'s reading and interpretation are as follows: "The place for the entire great temple [*kōviṟku*—or palace] that is the universe arranged in seven plus seven stories, whose thick wall is the eight directions, [was] the seed of the [still] opened bud of the lotus, standing [before the creation of the universe] above the three beautiful spheres (*maṇṭalaṅkaḷ*) [the sphere of the moon, the sun, and the constellations]."

47. 3789

Viṣṇu is both the gods, who eat the Vedic sacrifice, and the sacrificer [*yajamāna*], who feeds the sacrifice to the gods.

49. 3791

"Were the vast Vedas conceived after witnessing your acts?" is G.'s interpretation. Crit. construes, "Did they intend (to describe your actions to the world), having seen your acts?"

50. 3792

"The enmity I showed you in my ignorance" is G.'s suggestion for the literal "opposition that is my ignorance." Crit. says this means the opposition between ignorance and knowledge.

53. 3795

G. gives the story of Danu. He was the son of Śrī and used to change his shape at will from a lovely to a terrible form and afflict people. Once, he took some roots and tubers that a muni named Sthūlaśiras had put aside for food. The muni got angry and cursed him to keep his terrible form. When Danu begged him to lighten his curse, he said he would lose the form when Rāma cut off his arms. Danu performed tapas and got the boon of long life. He grew proud and fought Indra. With his thunderbolt, that god put his arms in his stomach and his head in his chest. When Danu pleaded with Indra, saying he could not have long life without consciousness, Indra gave him arms that were one *yojana* long (so he could live more normally).

55. 3797

The beginning of this is translated according to G. Crit. says, "[After all, having help in fighting] is something that is blameless, and it is manliness. What use of saying [more]? Even Lord Śiva . . ." See "Bhūta" in the Glossary.

57. 3799

"Him who is the bright color of gold"—Sugrīva, the king of the monkeys, who are the main subject of the next book of the *Rāmāyaṇam*, the *Kiṣkindhākāṇḍa*.

Paṭalam Eleven

5. 3805

Both commentators indicate that Rāma means the pain and exhaustion of travel.

6. 3806

Sugrīva, the monkey king, is the son of the sun-god. See the notes to 3799.

# Glossary

(In the Glossary and the Notes, Crit. stands for the critical edition, G. stands for the Gōpālakiruṣṇamācāriyar edition. See Editions Used.)

Ādiśeṣa: see "Śeṣa."

Agastya: The third Paṭalam is about this sage. Agastya lived in a hermitage on Mount Kuñjara to the south of the Vindhyas and was the chief of the hermits of the south. Various stories about him are told in the notes: how he killed Vātāpi (2759), how he went south to balance the earth and made the Vindhya mountain bow down (2760), how he drank the ocean (2758), and how he gave Tamil to the world (2762).

Ahalyā: The story of Ahalyā has different forms. In the Vālmīki *Rāmāyaṇa,* it is told as follows: Indra fell in love with the beautiful Ahalyā, and while the sage was out for bathing, Indra entered the ashram in the disguise of the sage and took her to bed. Before Indra could leave, Gautama returned, became enraged at seeing his wife and Indra, and cursed Indra to lose his testicles and Ahalyā to become a stone. Taking pity on her, he said that she would return to her original form the moment Rāma came to that place and touched the stone with his foot. (See 3345.)

Airāvata: the white elephant that is the vehicle of the god Indra. He was produced at the Churning of the Ocean, q.v.

Amṛta: ambrosia, the drink that gives immortality. It was produced at the Churning of the Ocean, q.v.

Arundhatī: The wife of the sage Vasiṣṭha, Arundhatī is the epitome of the chaste and modest wife. She is supposed to have acted as guardian angel to Sītā after she had been abandoned by Rāma. (2878, 3439, 3628.)

Asura: The Asuras are demons. They are sons of Kaśyapa. Those mothered by Danu are called Dānavas, while those mothered by Diti are called Daityas. See stanza 2805 (also 2706, 2818, 3018).

Avatāra: incarnation of a god, usually Viṣṇu. He had innumerable incarnations, but only ten are considered to be full. These are: the fish, the tortoise, the pig (or boar), the man-lion, the dwarf, Paraśurāma (Rāma with the axe), Rāma (the character in the *Rāmāyaṇa),* Balarāma (the brother of Krishna), Krishna, and Kalki. Sometimes Buddha is given instead of Balarāma.

Balarāma: the brother of Krishna, q.v. (2642).

Bhūta: dwarfish beings with huge pot bellies and tiny legs. They are supposed to have helped Śiva in his war with the Asura Andhaka (3797).

Brahmā: One of the three highest gods (who include also Viṣṇu the maintainer and Śiva the destroyer), Brahmā is supposed to have created the universe. He is considered the grandfather of every living creature (cf. 3399).

His creation of the universe. Many versions of this story are given. In Kampaṉ, he is said to be sitting on the lotus flower that grew from Viṣṇu's navel as that god lay sleeping on the ocean of milk. Brahmā went up and down the tube of the lotus to see the model of the universe, which was inside the god, and then created the universe outside the god. He is sometimes compared to a bee as he circles the lotus in his act of creation. (See 2650, 2657, 2706, 3668.)

Vettam Mani enumerates eighteen curses that Rāvaṇa is supposed to have incurred. One of these is the curse of Brahmā: "Rāvaṇa tried to humiliate Puñjikādevī, daughter of Brahmā, and the latter uttered a curse that Rāvaṇa should die with all his ten heads broken if he touched unwilling women." See stanza 3490 and the notes on it.

It is Brahmā who gave Rāvaṇa the boon that no living creature except man would kill him (3010, 3463, 3625).

The story of Brahmā's losing one of his heads, and of Śiva having to use that head as a begging bowl, is given in the notes to 3610 and 3611.

His wife, Sarasvatī, is supposed to rest on his tongue (3239).

Brahmin: the first of the four *varṇas,* traditional priests (see "Varṇa" and the notes to 2735).

Bṛhaspati: the teacher of the gods (3179, 3613).

Cakravāka: the ruddy goose. In Indian literature, the pair of cakravāka birds are supposed to be extremely devoted to each other and to grieve when they must spend the night separated (2832, 3289).

Candrakānta: the moonstone. This stone is supposed to shed water when exposed to the rays of the moon (2908).

Churning of the Ocean: Once, Indra is supposed to have slighted the sage Durvāsas, who thereupon cursed the gods to lose the prosperity and glory of their world. They began to grow old and wither. They went to Viṣṇu, who told them to join with the Asuras, bring all kinds of herbs, deposit them in the ocean of milk, and then obtain amṛta, the drink of eternal youth (3626), by churning that ocean using the mountain Mandara as the churning staff (3140) and the snake Vāsuki (3752, 3755) as the rope. This they did, with the gods on one end of the snake and the Asuras on the other, while Viṣṇu assumed the form of a tortoise as the support for the mountain (in 3755, it is the moon instead that serves as this support). As they churned, many things came up: the Kāmadhenu (q.v.), the moon, Indra's elephant Airāvata, Dhanvantari dressed in pure white robes and carrying a pot filled with amṛta, and then Śrī (also called Lakṣmī) (3241). Another of the things that arose was the deadly Hālāhala poison which Śiva swallowed, lest it destroy the universe—the source of the dark mark on that god's neck (3067, 3298). The Asuras snatched the amṛta away from Dhanvantari and refused to give it to the gods. Then, Viṣṇu transformed himself into a beautiful woman called Mohinī and went to the Asuras. Overcome by her beauty, they said that she should distribute the amṛta to them. Mohinī agreed, and said they should close their eyes and that the last Asura to open his eyes would marry her. As soon as she got the pot, Mohinī left and took it to the gods (2706). Subsequently, the Asuras fought the gods and were defeated. See "Rāhu" for the story of how that Asura was able to drink a little of the amṛta.

Cintāmaṇi: a gem that is supposed to give its possessor whatever he desires.

Dhoti: a garment worn by men even today in many parts of India. It consists of a cloth, usually white, that is wrapped around the waist and hangs down to the ankles.

Elephants of Space: literally, the elephants of the (eight) directions. These are the elephants that stand at each of the four cardinal points and each of the four intermediate points and support the world. When Rāvaṇa conquered the world, he is supposed to have opposed the Elephants of Space, to have broken their tusks, and quelled their power (2933, 2938, 3167, 3175, 3458, 3487). During the war between the gods and the Asuras (in which the Asuras tried to get the amṛta back from the gods), the Elephants of Space fought on the side of the gods—see stanza 2685.

Gandharva: "a celestial musician, a class of demi-gods regarded as the singers or musicians of gods, and said to give good and agreeable voice to girls." Apte. (2806, 3018.)

Gaṅgā: the Ganges river (3184).

Garuḍa: the king of the birds, the son of Kaśyapa by his wife Vinatā. He is an implacable enemy of the snakes, and hence is feared by cobras and the like (3505, 3526). He is supposed to be the vehicle of Viṣṇu and to have a white face, an aquiline nose, red wings, and a golden body. See the notes to 2642 for the story of him and Aniruddha.

Gods: the Devas. In Hindu mythology, the gods are generally benevolent, but they are always coming under the power of some Asura or other unfavorable creature (like Rāvaṇa). The gods have four notable characteristics: they do not blink, they do not sweat, their garlands do not fade or wither, and their feet do not touch the ground (2765).

Great Elements: the five so-called *bhūtas*—earth, water, fire, air, and space. From the earliest Tamil poetry, where it was conventional to compare a king to the great elements, the five bhūtas have symbolized the power and inalterability of nature. (See 3423, 3631, 3740, and 3758.)

Guṇa: strand. Sāṃkhya, an early Indian philosophical system immortalized in the *Bhagavad Gītā*, was based on the notion that all things can be seen as composed of three *guṇas*, or strands. The three are *sattva*, the purest, which is characterized by calmness and control, *rajas*, which is marked by passion and emotion, and *tamas*, characterized by sloth, indolence, and heaviness. (See 2697.)

Hālāhala: the poison that arose at the churning of the ocean and threatened to destroy all life until Śiva drank it, leaving a black mark on his throat. It is a symbol of blackness, virulence, and danger (2982, 3013, 3067, 3303, 3760). See "Churning of the Ocean" above.

Indra: the king of the gods. He has a thousand eyes (2701, 2840) and is married to Śaṣi (3238).

For the story of Indra and Bṛhaspati, see the notes on 3613.

For the story of Indra and Śambara, see the notes on 3614.

Vettam Mani gives the story of Indra cutting off the wings of the mountains: "In Kṛtayuga [the first age of the world], all the mountains in the world had wings. They used to fly about here and there like Garuḍa with the speed of wind. The sages and Devas feared that they might fall on their heads. The Devas held a conference and elected Indra to find a remedy for this. Indra cut off the wings of the mountains with his Vajra [thunderbolt]." (See 3544.)

When Indra was conquering the world, he came to Uśīravīra mountain, where a king called Marutta was performing a great sacrifice. Indra and the other gods came to receive their part of the sacrifice. But when Rāvaṇa arrived, they ran away in terror, Indra assuming the form of a peacock. (See 3335.)

During Rāvaṇa's conquest of the world, he fought Indra, making him run away in the sky (3532; see also 2931 and 3175).

Indrajit: G. gives the following account about Indrajit (in his commentary on 2931): While Rāvaṇa was conquering the world and had begun to subjugate all people of the earth, and as he was going here and there, fighting and winning, he reached the world of paradise *(svarga)* and opposed Indra. That god came with his army of gods, mounted on his great elephant Airāvata, and began to fight savagely in such a way that Rāvaṇa was amazed. Rāvaṇa's son Meghanātha disappeared magically, rained down a shower of weapons, and put Indra in a bad position, so that the god became afraid and ran away. Meghanātha caught the god in a magic noose so he could not go away, defeated him, returned with Rāvaṇa and his army back to Laṅkā, and put Indra in jail. Brahmā learned what had happened, came and saw Rāvaṇa, gave Meghanātha the name Indrajit (conqueror of Indra), gave Indrajit a boon, and so got Indra out of jail. (See 2939.)

Jaṭāyus: The son of Aruṇa and Śyenī, Jaṭāyus is a great vulture who is the subject of Paṭalam 4 and again of Paṭalam 9. As he had been a close friend of Daśaratha, Rāma and Lakṣmaṇa consider him a father. When Rāvaṇa abducts Sītā, Jaṭāyus attempts to stop him but is wounded by the demon. Subsequently, Rāma and Lakṣmaṇa come upon the dying Jaṭāyus, discover what happened, and then cremate the great bird after he dies.

Kailāsa: the silver mountain in the Himālāyas on which Śiva lives. While returning from his conquests in the heavenly chariot that he had taken from Kubera, Rāvaṇa found his path blocked by Kailāsa. Informed by Śiva's gatekeeper, Nandi, that Śiva's mountain would not let people pass over it, Rāvaṇa used his twenty hands to uproot and move the mountain. (2867, 2933, 3175, 3206, 3352, 3355, 3458, 3531.)

Kākutstha: an epithet of the kings of the solar dynasty. In the text, it is sometimes used for Rāma.

Kalpa: the end of the world, when everything is destroyed. Kalpa may also mean a day of Brahmā or a thousand *yugas* (see the notes to 2618), or 432 million years. It is described by Mani Vettam as follows (under *Pralaya):* "At the end of a thousand yugas the world will look famished. Then there will be excessive drought for a hundred years together and everything in this world will be destroyed then. Then Mahāviṣṇu [i.e., Viṣṇu], lord of everything in this universe, will present himself in the seven big rays of the sun and drink to emptiness all the waters of all the three worlds, earth, ocean, and Pātāla. Then by the divine power of Mahāviṣṇu the seven rays of the sun, which have grown fat by drinking this water, will become seven separate suns. These suns will burn all the three worlds including Pātāla . . . Kālāgnirudra [Śiva] will burn the earth and the heavens. Because of this, all the worlds will look like globes of fire . . . Then from the face of Viṣṇu will originate clouds and lightning in different forms. Those clouds will rain incessantly for a hundred years and destroy the fire prevailing everywhere. When the rains become unbearable, Vāyu [the wind god] will encroach upon the seats of the Saptarṣis [the Seven Sages] in the ocean and by that breath of Viṣṇu destroy all the clouds. At that time Viṣṇu, lord of all, will lie on the back of Ādiśeṣa for a period of a kalpa in yogic slumber . . . After that he will take on the form of Brahmā and start creation." In Kampaṉ, there are twelve rather than seven suns (3167; 3592). Kampaṉ also mentions the idea that Viṣṇu swallows the world at the end of the kalpa (3785, 3786). In 3785 there is the beautiful notion that Viṣṇu appears as a boy sleeping in a banyan tree arising from the ocean after the end of the universe. The kalpa is one of the most common motifs in Kampaṉ, appearing again and again as an image of destruction, confusion, fury, and distress.

Kalpaka: a tree in the world of the gods that has the power of giving anything that one wishes to have. There are supposed to be five of these trees. (2801, 2861, 2988, 3177, 3182, 3320, 3335, 3801.)

Kāma: the god of love. Apte has the following information about this god: "His wife is Rati. When the gods wanted a commander for their forces in their war with Tāraka, they sought the aid of Kāma in drawing the mind of Śiva toward Pārvatī, whose issue alone could vanquish the demon. Kāma undertook the mission; but Śiva, being offended at the disturbance of his penance, burnt him down with the fire of his third eye . . . He is armed with a bow and arrows—the bowstring being a line of bees, and arrows of flowers of five different plants." Kāma's bow is usually said to be made of sugarcane, though in 3666 it is made of flowers (Manmathatantra flowers, according to G.), in accord with the Tamil tradition. (See also 2973, 2840-41, 2873, 2901, 2907, 2916, 2933, 2960, 3234, 3648, 3666-67.)

Kāmadhenu: the heavenly cow that yields everything one desires (3182).

Karma: the actions that one has done, which, in Hinduism, are thought to entail reward or punishment, that is, to bear fruit. Since not all actions bear fruit in this life, one's karma necessitates rebirth.

Kārtavīryārjuna: the king of the Haihayas, who ruled at the same time as Rāvaṇa. See the notes to 3359 and 3479 for stories about him.

Kātam: a Tamil unit of distance—about ten miles.

Ketu: See "Rāhu."

Kinnara: a mythical being with a human figure and the head of a horse (3173).

Kubera: The god of wealth, Kubera lives on Mount Kailāsa and is a friend of Śiva. He is the half brother of Rāvaṇa and Śūrpaṇakhā. He is supposed to be deformed, having three legs, only eight teeth, and a yellow mark in place of one eye. See the notes to 2670 for the story of Kubera and Tumburu. (See also the notes to 3490.)

Kumbhakarṇa: See the notes to 2941 for the story of this brother of Rāvaṇa's.

Lakṣmī: See "Śrī."

Mandara: the mountain used to churn the ocean. See "Churning of the Ocean."

Mārīca: Rāvaṇa's brother, who turned himself into a golden deer to draw Rāma from Sītā and who was then killed by Rāma (this forms the subject matter of Paṭalam 7).

Vettam Mani gives the story of the death of Tāḍakā, Mārīca's mother, and Subāhu, his brother: "Once [the sage] Viśvāmitra decided to conduct a *yajña* [sacrifice] for the happiness and contentment of all people. At the very commencement of the yajña, Rākṣasas, in batches, tried to spoil it, and Mārīca and Subāhu, sons of Tāḍakā, were the leaders of the obstructionists. Viśvāmitra knew that Rāma was the most effective weapon against the Rākṣasas and requested Daśaratha to lend him Rāma's help . . . Accordingly Daśaratha sent Rāma to the forest in the company of Viśvāmitra . . ." As they went to the forest, Viśvāmitra told Rāma and his brother many stories. In the middle of the story of Tāḍakā, that very Rākṣasī appeared and attacked them. Rāma killed her, and then, when they got to the site of the sacrifice, Subāhu. Mārīca ran off in fright and hid himself in the sea. (See 3350, 3368, 3376, 3403, 3413.)

In his commentary on 3368, G. gives the story of Mārīca's second encounter with Rāma: "Mārīca, who became an enemy of Rāma because he had killed his mother and younger brother and shot an arrow at him, afterward when Rāma was staying at Daṇḍaka forest in Pañcavaṭi Āśrama, took on the form of a deer with two Rākṣasas, came to Daṇḍaka forest, approached the places where the munis were bathing and doing *homa* offerings, and was hurting them, killing them, and eating them. Seeing Rāma dressed as an ascetic with Sītā and Lakṣmaṇa, thinking, 'This [Rāma] won't kill us because he is dressed as an ascetic,' he came running up near him and tried to kill him by striking him with his antlers. That great one grew angry, shot arrows at him, and the two Rākṣasas who had come with him, hit by arrows, were beheaded; only he escaped, ran and hid, and disguised himself as an ascetic." (See 3368, 3376.)

Māyā: Apte defines this as "unreality, the illusion by virtue of which one considers the unreal universe as really existent and as distinct from the Supreme Spirit." (2664, 2708.)

Meru: the mountain around which the planets and sun are said to revolve (3167, 3676) and which forms the center of the Dvīpas, or continents, that make up the earth. It is called Śiva's mountain (3355), is gold-colored (2843), and is strewn with jewels. See the notes on 2760 for the story of how the Vindhya mountain tried to grow even taller than Meru and the notes on 3762 for the story of how Meru lost its summits under the assault of the wind. In his note on 3355, G. says that Meru was the bow that Śiva used when he destroyed the three cities (see Śiva).

Moonstone: See "Candrakānta."

Mountains: See the notes on 3488 for the seven (or eight) mountains that support the earth.

Muni: a sage, holy man, or ascetic.

Musth: a state of murderous frenzy that male elephants sometimes experience during the rutting season. Here, *musth* is also used in its Indian sense to mean ichor, a dark brown odorous exudation from tiny holes above the eyes that occurs when a male elephant is in rut.

Murukaṉ (often Murugan in English): the son of Śiva and Pārvatī, called also Subrahmaṇya, Skanda, and Kumāra, who killed the demon Cūr (Skt. Śūrapadma). G. gives the story in the notes to 3488. Three Asuras named Śūrapadma, Siṃhamukha, and Tāraka together did tapas and sacrifice to Śiva, received from that god limitless boons, became proud, fought the gods and defeated them, and afflicted the earth. The gods went to Śiva and asked him to engender a son who was like himself and who could oppose the Asuras. Śiva engendered Murukaṉ, who defeated them. When Murukaṉ split into two parts the body of Śūrapadma with his spear, one half became a peacock and the other a cock, which subsequently became the vehicle and the flag of Murukaṉ.

Nāga: Apte gives the following definition: "a fabulous serpent-demon or semidivine being, having the face of a man and the tail of a serpent, and said to inhabit the Pātāla [the lowest of the three worlds—see "Worlds"]." (See 2818, 2864, 2994-95, 3174.)

Nemi: In the notes on 3749, G. writes, "[This is also called] Cakravāḷa Mountain; it is a great mountain [range?] that is arranged as a circle around the ocean which [in turn] surrounds the land." (See also 3763.)

Order of the World: this translates the Sanskrit word *dharma* (Tamil *aṟam*). (See the notes on 3095, 3245 and 3343.)

Paraśurāma: For the story of Paraśurāma and Viṣṇu's bow, see the notes to 3149. For the story of Kārtavīryārjuna and Paraśurāma, see the notes to 3359 and 3479.

Rāhu: Apte writes as follows: "When the nectar, that was churned out of the ocean [see "Churning of the Ocean"], was being served to the gods, Rāhu disguised himself and attempted to drink it along with them. But he was detected by the sun and the moon who informed Viṣṇu of the fraud. Viṣṇu, thereupon, severed his head from the body; but as he had tasted a little quantity of nectar, the head became immortal and is supposed to wreak its vengeance on the sun and the moon at the time of conjunction and opposition." See 2837, 2647, 2905, 3612, 3643, 3747. Rāhu is one of the nine planets, as is Ketu, which, according to Apte, is the body of Rāhu. (See 3759.)

Rākṣasa: a particular group of Asuras, to which Rāvaṇa and his family belong. Rākṣasas have red hair and black skin.

Rambhā: See the notes on 3490 for the story of this Apsaras.

Rāvaṇa: For the story of his tapas, see the notes to 3342. For the story of how he was cursed never to touch a woman, see above under Brahmā and the notes to 3490.

Ṣadhu: a holy man.

Śeṣa (or Ādiśeṣa): a snake said to have a thousand heads. Sometimes he is said to form the couch of Viṣṇu, sometimes to carry the world on his heads (3168, 3297; see also 2662, 2678, 3209).

Siddha: Apte defines as "a semidivine being supposed to be of great purity and holiness, and said to be particularly characterized by eight supernatural faculties called *siddhis.*" See 3018, 3172. The siddhis include such abilities as making oneself as small as an atom and becoming as light as one wishes; they are said to be attained through the practice of yoga.

Sītā: the wife of Rāma. See the notes to 3241 for the story of her birth.

Śiva: One of the three highest gods (who include also Brahmā the creator and Viṣṇu the maintainer), Śiva is supposed to destroy the universe. He rides a bull named Nandi; his consort is Umā, who is sometimes said to be half of him (making him half-man half-woman—see 3239). His sons are Gaṇeśa and Murukan̠. He lives on Mount Kailāsa (q.v.), and he is often associated with the burning ground and with the ashes with which he smears himself. In his hair, he has the Ganges river (3352) and the crescent moon (3298). His throat is stained black from drinking the deadly Hālāhala poison when the ocean was churned (see "Hālāhala" and "Churning of the Ocean"). He has a third eye on his forehead, which he used to emit fire and destroy Kāma (2840). He is an ally of Kubera (2867). Kampan̠ mentions him often, usually in association with one of the following stories:

See the notes to 3149 for the story of Śiva's bow.

See above under "Kailāsa" for the story of how Rāvaṇa moved that mountain.

See under "Kāma" for the story of how Śiva burned up that god with his third eye.

See the notes to 3610 and 3611 for how Śiva cut off one of Brahmā's heads and was forced to use that skull as a begging bowl.

One of the most famous stories about Śiva is his destruction of the three cities. Vettam Mani's account, which is taken from the Purāṇas, is as follows: Three Asuras did severe tapas and received a boon from Brahmā: that they would live in three cities that could move freely through the three worlds, that every thousand years the three of them should join together along with their three cities, and that they could die only if they were killed by one arrow when all together. Then the three Asuras proceeded to give trouble to the gods, their ancient enemies. The gods went to Śiva for help, and he agreed to destroy the three Asuras. Using the mountain Mandara as his bow (in his commentary on 3355, G. says that Meru mountain was the bow), Vāsuki the snake as the string, and Viṣṇu as his arrow, Śiva destroyed the three cities and the Asuras who ruled them. (2777, 3068, 3611.)

Rāvaṇa received his sword from Śiva. The story, given by G. in his note on 2932, is that when Rāvaṇa moved Kailāsa, Śiva, who was on it, pushed it down with his big toe so that it crushed Rāvaṇa's hands. Rāvaṇa, suffering and unable to move the mountain, screamed out and, at the advice of his ministers, sang songs from the Sāmaveda and so praised Śiva for a long time.

Finally, propitiated, Śiva relented, released Rāvaṇa, gave him the name Rāvaṇa ("the screamer"), and gave him long life and a sword named Candrahāsa ("Laughter of the Moon"). (See 2932, 3223, 3616.)

Śrī: another name of Lakṣmī, Viṣṇu's wife. She is said to live on a lotus (2794, 2680, 2947, 3230, 3445, 3672). She is also said to rest on the chest of Viṣṇu (2661, 2686). As she is the wife of Viṣṇu and Sītā is the wife of Rāma, the avatar of Viṣṇu, Sītā is sometimes considered to be the avatar of Śrī (see G.'s note on 3594). Her loveliness is often used as a simile for beauty in women.

Tāḍakā: the mother of the Rākṣasa Mārīca, q.v.

Tapas: This word is generally translated as "austerities," a rendering that is neither accurate nor felicitous. *Tapas* comes from the Sanskrit root *tap,* "to burn," "to be hot," "to suffer." It and its nominal derivative, *tapas,* subsequently came to refer also to the generation of magic heat or power by ascetic practices, and hence to the performance of any ascetic practice, usually with the aim of forcing some divine agency to do what one wishes. That is how it is used in this text.

Three Cities: see "Śiva."

Tridaṇḍaka: the three staffs of an ascetic, tied together to form a single staff. (See 3436.)

Underwater Fire: This fire is supposed to exist under the sea. According to the *Tamil Lexicon,* the submarine fire is "in the form of a mare's head, believed to consume the world at the end of a *yuga.*" (2630, 3012, 3229, 3297, 3478.)

Vāmana: the dwarf incarnation of Viṣṇu. He was a Brahmin student. At his initiation ceremony, the king Bali, who was a demon known for his generosity, wished to know what he would like. The dwarf asked for as much ground as he could cover in three steps. When granted that gift, Vāmana grew enormous, covered the earth with one stride, the heavens with the second, and with the third pushed Bali down into hell. (2662, 2757, 3406.)

Varāha: the boar incarnation of Viṣṇu. An Asura named Hiraṇyākṣa quarreled with the gods and, angry, picked up the earth in his hands as a ball and went under water. Viṣṇu appeared from Brahmā's nostrils in the form of a boar, went down into the waters, found the earth, defeated Hiraṇyākṣa, and brought the earth back up on his tusk. (2662, 2664, 3764.)

Varṇa: the system (often erroneously called the caste system) which divides society into four categories: the Brahmins, who are priests; the Kṣatriyas, who are kings and warriors; the Vaiśyas, who are merchants and agriculturalists; and the Śūdras, who are servants. Sometimes a fifth class, the Pañcamas or untouchables, is added. This system has probably never had much real social validity (except for the category of the Brahmin); rather, Indian society is to this day characterized by the Jāti, or caste, system, which divides society into hundreds of groups determined mainly by occupation. In the Tamil country, two percent of the population is Brahmin; the rest (technically at least) are Śūdras and untouchables. From the most ancient times, the fourth class was called not Śūdras but Vēḷāḷar (the name given the most prominent landowning caste) in Tamil literature. It is this class of non-Brahmin landholders and not the Brahmins who have traditionally been the most powerful group in Tamilnad and other parts of South India.

Veda: strictly, there were originally three Vedas—the *Ṛgveda,* the *Sāmaveda,* and the *Yajurveda.* To this was added a fourth, the *Atharvaveda.* (But see the notes to 2762.) The Vedas may also encompass much of the Hindu sacred lore in Sanskrit. For Kampaṉ, the term "Vedas" is also used to encompass a world order of gentleness and enlightenment. It is contrasted with the cruel reign of Rāvaṇa.

Vidyādhara: a group of demigods. They wear garlands and live in the sky. (2880, 3171, 3177.)

Viṣṇu: One of the three highest gods (who include also Brahmā the creator and Śiva the destroyer), Viṣṇu is supposed to maintain the universe. His wife, Śrī, is supposed to rest on his chest. Rāma is an avatar of this god. For Kampaṉ, Viṣṇu is the ultimate deity, of whom all the gods and everything else are merely emanations. For more on Viṣṇu's role in the creation and destruction of the universe, see Brahmā and Kalpa.

World: Apte writes (under *loka*), ". . .roughly speaking, there are three *lokas* [worlds] . . . , but according to fuller classification the *lokas* are fourteen, seven higher regions rising from the earth one above the other . . . , and seven lower regions, descending from the earth one below the other." (See 3020, 3484, 3622, 3788.) Often, there are said to be seven worlds, referring to the seven higher regions. They are said to be one above the other, like umbrellas stacked up (3144, 3156, 3183, 3215). The three worlds are heaven, earth, and the underworld (3192, 3462). In general, the gods live in heaven, and the Nāgas live in the underworld.

Yakṣa: Apte writes, "name of a class of demigods who are described as attendants of Kubera, the god of riches, and employed in guarding his gardens and treasures." (See 2964 and 3018.)

Yāḻ: a stringed instrument that resembles the lute.

Yāḷi: The *Tamil Lexicon* defines this animal as "a mythological lion-faced animal with elephantine proboscis and tusks." In Kampaṉ it is an extremely powerful and formidable animal. (See 2610, 3002, 3016, 3030, 3034, 3593, 3685, 3689.)

Yama: the god of death. Mani Vettam writes (under Kāla I): "When the life span of each living being allotted by Brahmā is at an end, Yama sends his agents and takes the soul to Yamapurī (the city of Yama). From there, the holy souls are sent to Vaikuṇṭha (Heaven, the abode of Viṣṇu) and the sinful souls to Hell." (See 2612, 2982, 3174, 3180, 3211, 3335.)

Yojana: a measure of distance equal to eight or nine miles.

Yoni: the loins of a woman.

Yuga: an age of the world. (See the notes to 2618.)

# Editions and Reference Works Used

There are three major annotated editions of the *Kamparāmāyaṇam.* All are modern, written in the past thirty or forty years. The oldest, and the edition that in many ways has the finest commentary, is that of Gōpālakiruṣṇamācāriyar (abbreviated as G. in this work). For his meanings, Gōpālakiruṣṇamācāriyar relied heavily on the published works of U. V. V. M. Caṭakōparāmānujācāryasvāmi (who, unfortunately, died before he was able to comment on the entire work). As both Gōpālakiruṣṇamācāriyar and Caṭakōparāmānujācāryasvāmi were deeply grounded in Srivaiṣṇava lore, of which the *Rāmāyaṇa* is a significant part, one can suppose that many of G.'s interpretations are quite old. G. attempted to get the best readings for each of his stanzas, but he did not make a thorough study of the manuscripts available.

Subsequently, Annamalai University published a critical edition of the *Kamparāmāyaṇam* with a new commentary composed by many different scholars. This edition has been abbreviated as Crit. in this work. The Annamalai scholars carefully went through all of the manuscripts they could obtain and produced a critical edition, giving all recorded readings for each stanza. Their version of Kampa<u>n</u>'s text is surely the closest to the original that we have, and for that reason we have followed the reading of Crit. wherever possible. Where G.'s readings seem better than Crit., or where his gloss on the text seems superior to that of the commentator for Crit., we have followed him, remarking on Crit.'s reading and/or interpretation in the notes. The numbering of the stanzas given in this book follows those of Crit. and has two parts: the number of the stanza in its Paṭalam followed by its number in the entire *Kamparāmāyaṇam.*

The other major annotated edition, that of the U. V. S. Swaminathaier Library, appeared after Crit. but was based on work of Swaminathaier himself and others. We have not used this edition very extensively, as it does not often add anything to Crit. and G. In difficult spots where Crit. and G. seemed to be incorrect, however, we have sometimes followed the interpretation and reading of this edition, remarking on that fact in the notes.

A fourth edition, published by Kampa<u>n</u> Ka<u>l</u>akam recently, lacks notes and critical apparatus. In its introduction, that edition claims to have followed a method that gives superior readings to any preceding edition, including Crit. In the absence of a critical apparatus, however, we could not take this claim seriously, and we have not used this edition.

The editions and reference works are as follows:

Apte, Vaman Shivaram. *The Practical Sanskrit-English Dictionary.* 3 vols. Rev. ed. Poona: Prasad Prakashan, 1959.

*Kamparāmāyaṇam: Irāmāvatāram.* Madras: Kampaṉ Kaḻakam, 1976-.

*Kampar Iyaṟṟiya Irāmāyaṇam* [critical edition of the *Kamparāmāyaṇam*]. Annamalainagar: Annamalai University Press, 1956-.

*Kamparāmāyaṇam.* Madras: U. V. Swaminathaier Library, 1957-.

*Kamparāmāyaṇam Mūṉṟāvatu Āraṇiya Kāṇṭam.* Madras: Gōpālakiruṣṇamācāriyar Company, 1965.

Mani, Vettam. *Puranic Encyclopedia.* Delhi: Motilal Banarsidass, 1975.

*Tamil Lexicon.* 6 vols. Madras: University of Madras, 1936. *Supplement*, 1938.

The following are responsible for the commentaries to the critical edition:

Paṭalam 1, 6, 7: K. Irāmānujaiyaṅkār.
Paṭalam 2: P.S. Irāmānujācāriyār.
Paṭalam 3, 4, 5, 8, 10: C. Vēṅkaṭarāmac Ceṭṭiyār.
Paṭalam 9: K. Veḷḷai Vāraṇaṉ.
Paṭalam 11: K. Cuppiramaṇiya Piḷḷai.

Gōpālakiruṣṇamācāriyar is responsible for the commentary to his edition.

# Further Reading

Very little has been written on the *Kamparāmāyaṇam* in English or other Western languages. We here list sources in English that may be consulted to learn something more about the poet and his work, together with short comments to guide the reader.


Aiyar, V. V. S. *Kamba Ramayana: A Study.* Bombay: Bharatiya Vidya Bhavan, 1965. This is actually a reprint of Aiyar's important work. It contains many ideas and insights and is worth the attention of the general reader interested in Kampaṉ.

Dakshayani, K. V. *The Metres in Kamparāmāyaṇam.* Annamalainagar: Annamalai University, 1979. This exhaustive study is mainly for the specialist. This book is especially interesting because of Kampaṉ's extraordinary skill with rhythm.

Goldman, Robert, ed. *The "Rāmāyaṇa" of Vālmīki: An Epic of Ancient India.* Princeton: Princeton University Press, 1984, 1986. So far, the first two Kāṇḍas (Bāla and Ayodhyā) of this English translation of the critical edition of the Sanskrit *Rāmāyaṇa* have appeared. In addition to a scholarly and readable translation, these volumes contain a wealth of facts and insights about the Rāma story and its history.

Jesudasan, C., and H. Jesudasan. *A History of Tamil Literature.* Calcutta: Y.M.C.A. Publishing House, 1961. This general history helps place Kampaṉ in Tamil literature. It is a good general introduction to Tamil literature.

Naidu, S. Shankar Raju. *A Comparative Study of Kamba Ramayanam and Tulasi Ramayan.* Madras: University of Madras, 1973. This is mainly for those interested in how Indian *Rāmāyaṇas* differ from one another.

Narayan, R. K. *The Ramayana.* New York: Viking Press, 1972. This is a retelling of the whole of Kampaṉ's *Rāmāyaṇa.*

Rajagopalachari, C. R. *The Ayodhya Canto of the Ramayana as Told by Kamban.* London: George Allen and Unwin, 1961. This is actually an abridged translation. It gives some idea of how the *Ayodhyā Kāṇṭam* flows.

Sharma, C. R. *The Ramayana in Telugu and Tamil: A Comparative Study.* Madras: Lakshminarayana Granthamala, 1973. This is for the specialist who is interested in different versions of the *Rāmāyaṇa.*

Shulman, David. "The Cliché as Ritual and Instrument: Iconic Puns in Kampaṉ's Irāmāvatāram." *Numen* 25 (1978): 135-155. This and the next two articles by David Shulman are distinguished by their author's insight and scholarship.

———. "The Crossing of the Wilderness: Landscape and Myth in the Tamil Story of Rāma." *Acta Orientalia* 42 (1981): 21-54.

———. "Divine Evil in the Tamil Tale of Rama." *Journal of Asian Studies* 38 (1979): 651-669.

Zvelebil, Kamil Veith. *The Smile of Murugan: On Tamil Literature of South India.* Leiden: E. J. Brill, 1973. This work, which consists of observations on Tamil literature by one of the major Western scholars of Tamil literature, is good both for specialists and the general reader. His chapter on Kampaṉ (pp. 207-217) is informative and interesting.

———. Tamil Literature. A History of Indian Literature, vol. 10. Wiesbaden: Otto Harrassowitz, 1974. This is the best history of Tamil literature that we have in a Western language. It has an extensive section on Kampaṉ (pp. 147-159).

# Transliteration of Sanskrit and Tamil Words

Sanskrit and Tamil are unrelated languages, but in many ways their pronunciation is similar. Where possible, we have used Sanskrit in this text, as most familiar with India will know the many of the Sanskrit words (whereas few will know their Tamil equivalents). Below we give first the Sanskrit pronunciations, and then some of the salient principles of Tamil pronunciation (which is too complex to be treated in detail here).

The following pronunciation is for Sanskrit words.

*a* is like the *u* in but.

*ā* is like the *a* in father.

*i* is like the *i* in pill.

*ī* is like the *i* in machine.

*u* is like the *u* in put.

*ū* is like the *u* in rule.

*ṛ* is a short vocalic *r* as in some Slavic languages.

*e* is pronounced like the *ay* in *pay* but as a single continuous sound, not diphthongized.

*o* is pronounced like the *o* in no.

*ai* is like the *ai* in aisle.

*au* is like the *ow* in now.

All aspirate consonants (*kh*, *gh*, *ch*, *jh*, *ṭh*, *ḍh*, *th*, *dh*, *ph*, *bh*) should be pronounced with a strong explosion of breath after the initial consonant. For example, *ph* is to be pronounced like the *ph* in uphill (though as a single sound), never as an *f*, and, similarly, *th* should be pronounced like the *th* in anthill, never as English *th*.

*c* is pronounced like the *ch* in child.

*ṭ*, *ṭh*, *ḍ*, *ḍh*, the nasal *ṇ*, the sibilant *ṣ*, and *ḷ* are retroflex or cerebral sounds not occurring in English and pronounced with the tongue folded back against the roof of the mouth.

*ś* is like English *sh* but pronounced with the tongue closer to the teeth; *ṣ* may also, for convenience, be pronounced in this way.

*r* is trilled, as in Spanish or Italian.

*ḥ* is a brief echo, preceded by an aspiration, of its preceding vowel.

*jñ* is approximately *gny*.

In Tamil, these same general principles apply, though the letters are fewer. The stops (*k*, *c*, *ṭ*, *t*, *p*) are, however, pronounced differently in different places. In general, after nasals and when surrounded by vowels, they are voiced (e.g. *ṭ* is pronounced as *ḍ*). When doubled or initial, they are unvoiced. The most important word affected by this principle is *kampaṉ*, which is pronounced like "come bun."

*ṟ* and *ṉ* are pronounced the same as *r* and *n* for the most part.

*ḻ* is pronounced somewhat like *ir* in the American pronunciation of sir.